Gee Vaucher

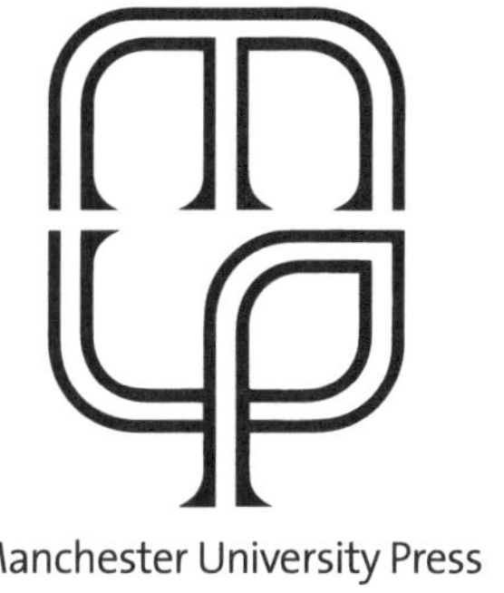

Manchester University Press

Gee Vaucher

Beyond punk, feminism and the avant-garde

REBECCA BINNS

Manchester University Press

Published by Manchester University Press
Oxford Road, Manchester M13 9PL
www.manchesteruniversitypress.co.uk

British Library Cataloguing-in-Publication Data
A catalogue record for this book is available from the British Library

ISBN   978 1 5261 4789 9   hardback

ISBN   978 1 5261 4791 2   paperback

First published 2022

The publisher has no responsibility for the persistence or accuracy of URLs for any external or third-party internet websites referred to in this book, and does not guarantee that any content on such websites is, or will remain, accurate or appropriate.

Typeset
by New Best-set Typesetters Ltd

Printed in Great Britain
by TJ Books Ltd, Padstow

Table of contents

List of figures

List of plates

Acknowledgements

There are many people I need to thank for supporting me to complete this monograph. Firstly, I would like to thank my editor, Emma Brennan at Manchester University Press, for her enthusiasm and flexibility, as well as the support she has shown throughout the writing process. I'm also grateful for the insightful and knowledgeable feedback that I received from reviewers at the proposal stage, who helped me to see that this book was not just a shot in the dark, and that it would make a significant contribution to art, cultural and political histories; or rather herstories. I'm also thankful for the support, advice and encouragement I've received from Dr Russ Bestley and Professor Matt Worley since I began this project, and for the input I've received from Tony Credland, Professor Lucy Robinson, Professor Roger Sabin and Dr Ian Horton.

I'm especially appreciative of Gee Vaucher's generosity in granting me access to an archive of her original work, and with her time. Throughout the eight-year period that this book has taken shape, aside from providing several in depth interviews, I've benefitted from the more informal opportunities I've had to experience her living and working environment, at Dial House and further afield. Despite her prolific output, hectic exhibition schedule and the intense demands of life at Dial House, she has never failed to make time, for which I'm hugely appreciative. I'm likewise thankful for Penny Rimbaud's encouragement since the project's inception and for his interviews and conversation. Thanks also goes to Steve Ignorant and a number of other people in Vaucher's circle for further shedding light on her approach and life. Banksy, Mike Diboll, Alistair Livingstone (sadly departed) and Dominic Thackray deserve a special mention in this respect; as does Brandon Taylor for his encouragement, Harvey Birrell for introducing me to Gee and Penny, and my old friend Charlotte (Pink) Brennan for sharing her mother's anecdotes about teaching Penny and Gee at art school. My peers in the Punk Scholars Network and the Subcultures, Popular Music and Social Change Forum have also been vital resources for information exchange and support.

I'm also grateful to archive holders Stevphen Shukaitis, Douglas Atfield, Matt Worley, Russ Bestley, Ana Raposo, Alistair Gordon, Chris Low and Tony Credland for granting me access to their collections. More generally, I'm appreciative to all the people mentioned here for their open and collaborative working ethos; something that fits with the approach of this artist and the networks and culture she has endeavoured to support throughout her life.

Above all I'm thankful for the immense support provided by my husband, Rob Curry, which has included proof reading and editing, as well as providing a listening ear throughout the writing process, which coincided with the joys (and mental health issues) of lockdown and home-schooling our children throughout the pandemic. His encouragement ensured I completed this publication in massively testing circumstances. Finally, I'm grateful for my children, Charlie, Arran and Francis, for providing such a welcome diversion, and to friends who have kept me grounded. Further appreciation goes to the punk scene of my youth and beyond that inspired me to follow the unorthodox path that has led me to this project.

Introduction

In more recent years, the artist and designer, Gee Vaucher (b. 1945), has been granted long overdue critical and media recognition for her idiosyncratic and powerful art and design work and the role it has played in shaping alternative culture over the last half century. Her work now features prominently in academia, in exhibitions and publications, and in the mainstream media. Yet, to date, despite her raised profile, she remains an elusive figure who prides herself on her political and creative autonomy; a position that doesn't always sit easily with art world appreciation.

Born into a working-class family in Barking in the aftermath of the Second World War, Gee Vaucher benefitted from an art school education during the 1960s, when social mobility meant a diverse range of voices were involved in the formation of new art movements and culture. She was one of the earliest occupants of the enduring Essex commune Dial House (later home to punk provocateurs Crass), was closely involved in the 1970s Free Festivals scene (in particular with the formation of the Stonehenge Free Festival) and participated in various avant-garde performance art groups, often with her lifelong collaborator Penny Rimbaud. During the 1970s, she produced an extensive body of illustrations for mainstream magazines such as *New York Times, Rolling Stone, New York Magazine* and *Ebony*. Her groundbreaking journal *International Anthem* (1977–84) gave her an outlet for more transgressive and controversial forms of expression that were highly attuned to the social and political changes of the time. She is most often associated with her designs for the anarchist punk band and collective, Crass (1977–84), that were crucial to establishing the band's identity and prominence. These went on to inspire a generation of artists working in music graphics and beyond. Her work at this time formed a sophisticated critique of structural inequality, an assault on war and militarism, and holds a unique place in the history of feminist art. Vaucher has steadfastly avoided being defined by feminism – or indeed any other isms – but her humanitarian critique of female subordination marks her out from her contemporaries, both in punk and in protest art. She is best known for her collage work, in which she adopted the raw cut 'n' paste style of early punk design and the underground press, and turned it into a sophisticated, painterly form of expression. Her photomontage works are often not collages at all, but intricately painted, photorealistic depictions of a skewed reality masquerading as collage.

The ideas of Crass (1977–84) and what has retrospectively been termed 'anarcho-punk'[1] were still highly influential within the punk social milieu that I was involved in during my teens, when I lived in communal squats in North-East London, despite the band having long since disbanded. Vaucher's designs for the band were well known in this scene and made a powerful impression on me. They offered an insightful take on the world at that time, and together with the music provided a vision that was exciting and emancipatory. 'It's your world too; you can do what you want.'[2]

While the artwork had a great impact in these ways, the artist herself remained anonymous. Crass had operated as a collective, subsuming their identities and individual contributions within the group as a whole. Indeed, there was a more or less widespread assumption that the graphics accompanying their record releases had been produced by a man.

This began to shift in the 1990s as Vaucher began exhibiting her Crass material alongside newer work, but when I decided to return to higher education to complete an MA in Art History (UCL, 2010), I found there had been very little written about her and the profound impact she'd had in these milieus. This was despite a historicisation process being well underway with regards to communal and radical political art, the counterculture and punk. Comparators of hers, such as the performance art and music collective, COUM Transmissions (1969–76), and political photomontage artists Peter Kennard and Martha Rosler, have all been more feted. Her work was omitted from publications concerned with radical art production in the 1970s, despite the fact it makes a major contribution in this area.[3] When its significance in this respect has been recognised, it has often mistakenly been subsumed into the prevailing leftist political narrative of that era. No doubt the fact her work existed outside the existing funding structures of the time, as well as the absence of an overtly leftist positioning, has contributed to its marginalisation in this context. Similarly, in the history of punk graphics, her work has received nothing like the attention afforded her contemporaries such as Jamie Reid and Linder Sterling.

It was at this point that I first approached Vaucher for an interview, through a mutual friend. She agreed, kindly collecting me from Epping tube station in her beat-up car. As I approached the enigmatic, ancient (seventeenth-century) cottage and extensive gardens of Dial House, I experienced a feeling of coming home that is apparently common to many visitors. For me personally, it firstly evoked memories of a bohemian childhood in Leamington Spa (Warwickshire), a place that was especially characterised by so much of the imagination, freedom and idealism of the era. It felt as though these qualities had not been eroded, but instead continued here; a place appealingly out of step, out of the march of time. I was also stirred to be visiting the birthplace of Crass, to be seeing for myself the 'anarchist', open house 'commune' that had sheltered numerous punks who turned up to see how Crass lived, passing through transitorily, or living there for a while, camping out in the garden. From its inception in 1967, Rimbaud intended the house to provide respite for weary travellers, a phenomenon he saw being reciprocated by numerous other open houses around the country. This practice has continued to this day, with 'hipsters' (2000–10s), replacing the hippies (1970s), punks (1980s), artists, ecologists and others seeking respite or inspiration.

While Vaucher's work during the Crass era provided a stimulus for both a social movement and a shift in the production of music graphics more generally, it is from the 1990s onward, after returning to art production after the burnout that resulted from the Crass years, that she truly blossomed as an artist. From that point on, her work has built on the collage aesthetic, but manifested in a host of mediums, from installations to oil paintings to street art. It has also taken on a more complex and subtle means of communication, although it continues to provide an idiosyncratic reflection of the times. In this it provides a stark contrast to the approach of the Young British Artists in the late 1990s, while both inspiring and contributing to the more politicised art movements of the twenty-first century.

While this book is the first monograph about this singular artist, over the last decade her work has received increased recognition. A series of prominent publications and exhibitions, on punk art and design in the 2010s, foregrounded her work for Crass and *International Anthem*. It now features prominently in exhibitions, publications and academic conferences, particularly those concerned with punk and post-punk graphics and the intersection of feminism with punk. Simultaneously, her wider body of art and design work has reached larger audiences, particularly in the context of the media coverage of her first major retrospective at Firstsite Gallery, Colchester in 2016, an event that coincided with her *Oh America!* painting being adopted as a motif for the election of Donald Trump.

This recognition of Vaucher's worth is part of the wider shift towards the acceptance of creators who had previously been situated outside the parameters of mainstream culture. Rather than being modelled along hierarchical lines, cultural institutions increasingly view their role as representing more diverse, oppositional and alternative positions and subject matter. This mirrors an interest among younger, more politically engaged audiences that have emerged in the wake of Occupy (2008), that express disillusionment with the overarching paradigm of corporate driven, globalised capitalism, and scepticism towards hierarchies and leaders. In a backlash against the 1990s, the twenty-first century has also witnessed a trend towards valuing visual culture for its 'authenticity', its engagement with the world and embodiment of discernible meaning. Vaucher in many ways embodies this new set of values, and it is her perceived authenticity that imbues her work with cultural value, as reflected in the considerable space provided for it in cultural magazines such as *The Wire, The Quietus* and *Vice*.

Despite this recognition, Vaucher's desire for a free and authentic form of expression continues to guide her approach. She continues to only work with institutions and organisations she has an ethical affinity with. She refuses to sell to private dealers, and while she is happy in principle for public institutions to collect her work, in practice, she has thus far backed down from parting with it. I had a personal taste of this when I was approached by the curator of the New Hall Art Collection at Cambridge University, who expressed an interest in acquiring an artwork. I passed the request on, but, characteristically, Vaucher has yet to follow it up. While on the face of it this may seem self-sabotaging, especially for an artist in their seventies, this book argues that it is precisely this reticence, this refusal to engage with the expectations of mainstream society, that gives her work its authority and enduring relevance.

Notes

1   Anarcho-punk has retrospectively become the term used to describe this subgenre and subculture. During the first wave of anarcho-punk (1978–84), anarchist or Crass punk and then peace punk were predominant (as evidenced by their widespread use in fanzines and the music press). The word 'anarcho' was in circulation from at least

1980 but used intermittently. See 'Breakin' thru in 82" tips' in *Sounds* (2 January 1982) p. 7; a fanzine review in *Acts of Defiance 4* (October 1982), p. 20; a letter to *Sounds* (26 June 1982), p. 46 by Ian Bone who founded Class War; and Tony D's review, 'Singles' in *Punk Lives*, No 8 (1983), p. 8.

2 Zounds, This Land, *The Curse of Zounds* LP, Rough Trade, 1981.

3 See, for instance, J. A. Walker, *Left Shift: Radical Art in 1970s Britain* (London: Taurus, 2002).

The changing face of British arts, politics and culture during Vaucher's art school years

Gee Vaucher (b. 1945) was born into a working-class family in Dagenham within weeks of the Second World War ending, the first and much longed for daughter in a family of three sons.[1] In the aftermath of the Blitz, when London suffered severe damage and heavy casualties, many East End communities migrated to the fringes of the city, including Dagenham. The joy that people felt at the war ending was counterbalanced with sadness at the loss of life, injury and hardship that many had endured. Vaucher's childhood was overshadowed by the horrors of that war, including the news that seeped out about the German death camps, the legacy of the atomic bombing of Hiroshima and Nagasaki in 1945 and a burgeoning fear of an atomic future.[2]

The post-war decades saw the growth of a movement against war and militarism, which was itself symptomatic of a wider social shift away from deference towards hierarchies. The rigid class structure that required subservience among the masses towards a privileged minority had already started to shift during the inter-war years, but the process accelerated after the Second World War. The sweeping socialist and egalitarian changes brought about by the post-war Labour government suggested that for the first time politics was directed from below, in the interests of working and lower middle-class people. However, both major political parties still relied on public faith in government and deference to the experts. A disconnect would emerge between this form of governance and the politics and culture of younger generations during the ensuing decades.

While Vaucher's life at Dial House (from 1969) was symptomatic of the countercultural trend to form communes, it was in the context of her childhood that her communal way of living and working was forged.[3] In interview she recalls, 'I've always lived communally. If anyone had a problem, they'd bring it to my mum and they'd know the door was open. The key was hanging on a bit of string.'[4] Reflecting the interconnectedness of life on her street, she further comments,

> It seemed that everyone just walked into one another's houses. I'm sure they didn't, but it felt like that to me as a kid. Being just after the war, people were short of everything, so everyone shared stuff. There was the odd house you didn't go near, but otherwise it all felt very friendly to me, and everybody kept an eye on each other's children especially. If my mother asked: have you seen my daughter? They'd reply 'yes, she's two streets over there playing about' or something to that effect. Then she'd know I was alright.[5]

She also recollects the humour that prevailed in the face of adversity. One well-worn family story told of the time a bomb had exploded near their house during the Blitz. Her dad's first reaction had been to run to save one of his beloved chickens, whose neck had been half-severed by the blast. When he called out for needle and thread to save it, the neighbour's response was, 'what colour would you like'.[6] Comedy and absurdity is shown to be present in both the ordinary and more troubling aspects of life throughout Vaucher's oeuvre, something that is often overlooked by viewers who can be unsettled by the darker subject matter of much of her better-known work.

While Vaucher had some involvement with the peace movement as a young woman, her pacifism, which is intertwined with her wider concern with injustice, also originated in the social context of her working-class youth.

> Of course the circumstance of my parents and of most of the people in Dagenham then was connected politically. You couldn't avoid it as everyone worked for Fords [the Ford Motor Company had opened its factory in Dagenham in 1931], and trade unions were very strong then. All of that awareness is formed when you're young. I could see the injustice on the streets of Dagenham. I think kids are aware when something is wrong. They might not be able to pinpoint what it is exactly, but they know when there is an injustice. I definitely felt there was an imbalance, not only on the streets where I grew up, but at home where a shortage of money was always felt and I didn't see dad much as he did shift work.[7]

Vaucher mentions the death of her eldest brother, who died aged just twelve when she was three. He had been evacuated, like hundreds of other children, in a healthy condition, but returned in rags, undernourished and having caught Scarlet Fever. She recalls, 'It's something a family never gets over. There's always a residue, a sense of guilt and sorrow, which my parents carried for the rest of their lives.'[8]

The devastation of the war and its aftermath fed into Vaucher's wider stance against war and militarism; in particular her concern with how it impacted on ordinary people, with its worst effects being felt by the most vulnerable. She later dedicated one of her self-published journals, *International Anthem – War* (1983) specifically to this subject, while her work with the anarcho-punk band and collective, Crass (1977–84) reiterated this stance, often in relation to the resurgence of Cold War politics and the ensuing arms race in the early 1980s.

One direct impact of the war was that three quarters of a million houses were destroyed or severely damaged. However, it was in this post-war landscape that Vaucher, like many of her contemporaries, experienced a sense of freedom as a child, playing in bombsites around Dagenham and also Whitechapel when visiting relatives.[9] Such sites came to be a recurrent feature in her work.

This preoccupation is most clearly represented in one of her most iconic works, the cover of the Crass album, *Feeding of the 5000* (1978). As with

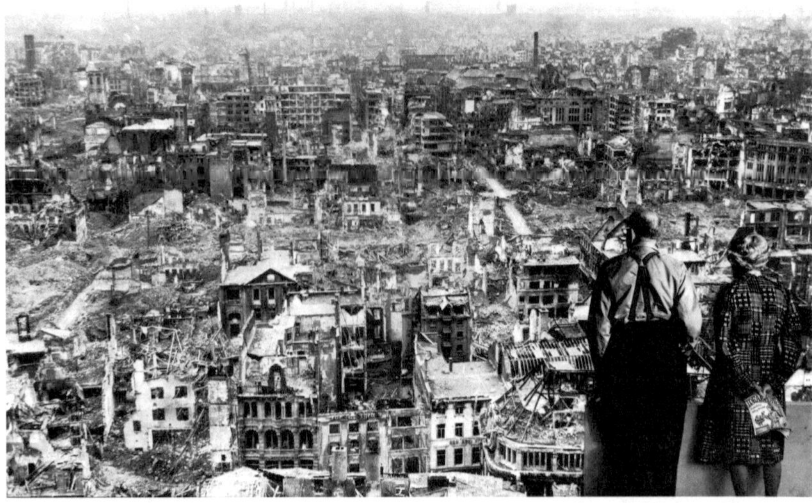

Figure 1.1 Gee Vaucher, Ideal Home, *International Anthem 5: War*, 1983, collage, 410mm × 310mm

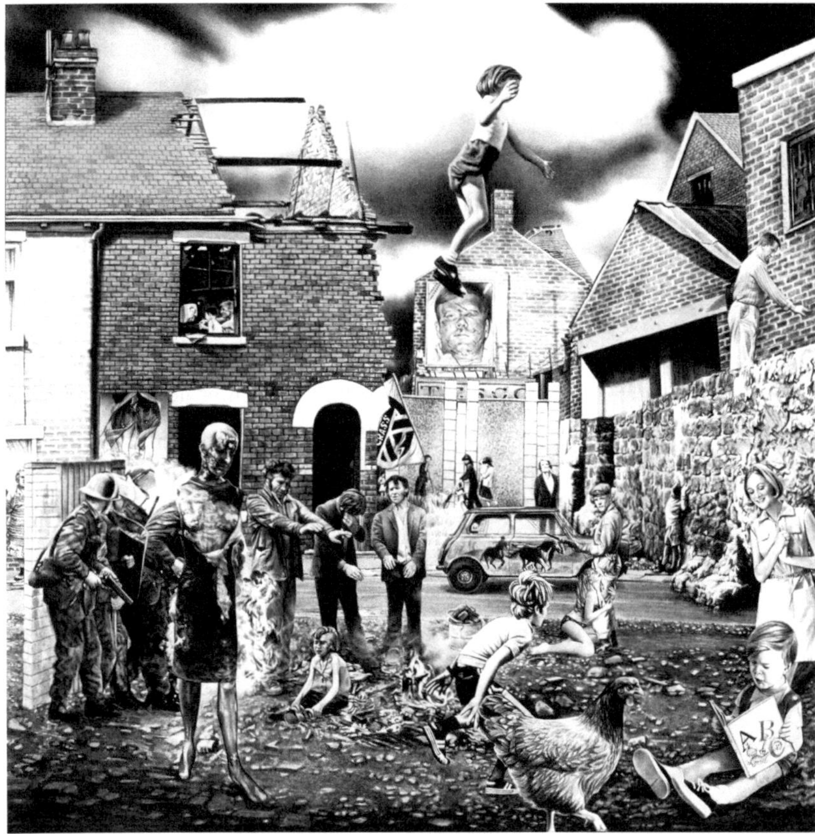

Figure 1.2 Gee Vaucher, Cover for the first Crass album, *Feeding of the Five Thousand* (1978), gouache, 260mm × 260mm

much of her work in the Crass era, this image utilises a gritty, monochrome and declinist aesthetic that was already evident in punk design at that time (see Chapter 4). Vaucher's illustrations from this time often juxtapose children playing in the rubble with newsreel imagery depicting contemporary political events. The soldier in the illustration references The Troubles in Northern Ireland, while the billboard image features a face from a bus advert warning drivers of the dangers if they didn't 'clunk click' (safety belts in cars had just been introduced).[10] The mannequin on fire in the foreground evokes the Pulitzer prize winning photograph by Malcolm Browne of the self-immolation by the Buddhist monk Thich Quang in Saigon (1963).[11] Vaucher, however, is characteristically more equivocal about it. 'Oh it's just a picture I had of a mannequin. The whole picture has reference to what was happening in the news. You can interpret it however you like. But, obviously it was of its time and about what was happening in the world. It would be pointless otherwise.'[12]

The depiction of new houses under construction stands in contrast with the bombed out Victorian terraces. As such they are seemingly symptomatic of the sterile conformity ushered in by the consumerism of the 1950s, which became an object of derision within punk. Similarly, the stifled, squeaky-clean boy, who obediently reads his book while his mother looks proudly on, contrasts with the freedom enjoyed by the scruffy children at play in the rubble. Reconnecting with the bomb-damaged landscape of her youth (replete with one of her father's beloved chickens) Vaucher depicted the setting as providing opportunities for liberation rather than just being symptomatic of economic and social deprivation. The image is dominated by a child figure suspended above the buildings. Vaucher notes 'the one that's in the air is the freest one. So, she's the figure of hope. She's in isolation. She's flying there. She's a modern day fairy if you like.'[13]

Vaucher's work frequently explores the negative impacts of social conditioning, instilled through the nuclear family and other social institutions, on children. While this perspective originated in the context of her youth, it also prevailed in anarchist and feminist milieus that she was exposed to in the 1970s. At this time feminists including Kate Millett voiced arguments against the notion of ownership within monogamous partnerships and families and advocated raising children communally.[14] Such initiatives link the largely socialist women's movement to anarchist ideas, including those developed by the writer and social historian Colin Ward, who advocated raising children communally, outside of patriarchal family structures.[15] On this issue, Vaucher commented,

> I value trying to undermine how society approaches and treats children. I'm interested in how we share with children. I don't have much faith in most schools *per se* and I don't believe in someone teaching the child and not understanding that the child has a lot to teach them. Children have a lot of the answers. They just don't have the experience to articulate it in adult ways, but if you listen with a different ear, different eyes, you will learn so much.[16]

Vaucher has also critiqued religion for coercing children into conformity, largely through guilt. A preoccupation with patriarchal oppression engendered through Western Christian culture also features strongly in her work. Perhaps surprisingly, though, Vaucher has positive memories of her Methodist upbringing. She remembers having fun attending church in a little local hall, adding, 'The kids were put into groups and told stories from the Bible, but they were very kind, gentle people and they kept you occupied and interested until playtime.'[17] Rather than religion playing an oppressive and instructional role, she recalls storytelling by both the church and her father as something more expansive. Reflecting the observational humour that runs through her work, she recalls, 'My dad was a great storyteller. Not religious ones even though we were Methodists, but just stories. All the neighbours used to come in to hear him tell funny stories. I just remember them, all big women with big tits and whenever they laughed everything used to bounce up and down.'[18]

The positive influence of her parents seems to have shielded her from any of the potentially insidious effects of religion. She comments,

> So religion is just a shared thing rather than 'thou shalt not'. We weren't sinners, even though there was a song I had to learn in the Brownie camp about coming as a sinner to Jesus. 'At Calvary's cross is where you begin, when you come as a sinner to Jesus'. I just remember it really well. I sung it to a friend of mine the other day. Can you believe these words that an innocent child is forced to learn? Isn't that barbaric? You're too young to think about the words as a kid. But I used to enjoy just singing and I loved my mum and dad singing, and being happy, especially to the hymn 'Jesus wants me for a sunbeam'![19]

Despite Vaucher's relatively unproblematic experience of religion as a child, she developed a hostile visual vocabulary in relation to it as an adult, particularly through her work for Crass and her self-published journal, *International Anthem* (1977–84), while her later print series *Much Ado About Something: A Play of Metaphors* (1996–) highlighted the twisted manifestations of the psyche that can be brought about by religious conditioning (see Chapter 7). However, this more critical stance provides less of a rupture in her sensibility than it may at first seem. Her attack on religion is part of a wider scepticism towards the artifice of idealised representations, which in fact indicates her underlying morality. As she notes, 'I'm an extremely moral person to the point of being ridiculous. But, my morals are mine.'[20]

As with her pacifism and sense of social injustice, what can be seen as a feminist perspective in Vaucher's work also originated in the context of her childhood. Her sense that being female was no bar to living autonomously arose from growing up in a family of boys, which meant that she had to fight to be accepted on her own terms.[21] She also appreciates her parents allowing her a reasonable amount of leeway for a girl at that time. It was this early independence that facilitated her sense of empowerment as a woman. This distinguishes her from many of her contemporaries, whose sense of empower-ment followed their articulating their own oppression within patriarchal society as adults, primarily through the women's movement. Asked how she felt as a young woman about the concept of the conventional family, given what the expectations were at that time, she responded, 'I didn't consider myself a *young woman*. I've never, ever felt separate from the other side of the race [sic]. It's got no presence in my life.'[22]

By her teens, Vaucher had already rejected many of the social expectations of her age. There was still huge social pressure, above all for working-class girls, to get married, which Vaucher resisted. She notes, 'I had said very early on, "I'm never getting married mum." Her response was, "You're not going to live in sin, are you?" I had to laugh. I said, "Mum, what do you mean, living in sin?" She said, "But who's going to look after you when you're older if you don't have children?" I said, "Mum, how many kids look after their parents when they're old? Can you tell me?"'[23] Ironically, Vaucher would later take meticulous care of her mother in her old age, giving up art for a period to nurse her through her final years (see Chapter 7).

Vaucher acknowledges how both her idiosyncrasy in relation to social norms and the acceptance shown by her mother enabled her to follow a different path.

> I think she accepted it in the end. I think she was saddened that she wasn't going to have grandchildren by her daughter. She had grandchildren by her sons but not by her daughter, but I said, 'Mum, I cannot have children just because you want them. I can't. That wouldn't be honest, sorry.' She was a dear soul. She had to accept all that. She knew I was crackers. I wasn't normal like other people, but she accepted it with grace and with great love. You couldn't have asked for any more, really. She would never, ever step in the way, only encourage.[24]

Vaucher continued to refute the societal constraints placed on women due to her personal quest for autonomy. This must not have always been easy within the male dominated countercultural and punk circles in which she later moved. On the one hand, she is acutely aware and critical of the oppression and exploitation women often faced. On the other, she did not identify with the 'sisterhood' that was so fundamental to the women's movement during the 1970s. It's worth noting that despite this, she appreciated its purpose. In response to a question about feminism she commented, 'I wasn't deeply involved in it until a call for arms, very specifically Greenham Common. First of all, I hesitated because it was a call just to women. I thought, why not men? I very soon realised, on the first mass action, why not men.'[25]

While Vaucher is often seen as feminist for carving her own path and refusing to conform to social expectations, this imperative arose from her resistance to all forms of external authority and was evident from a young

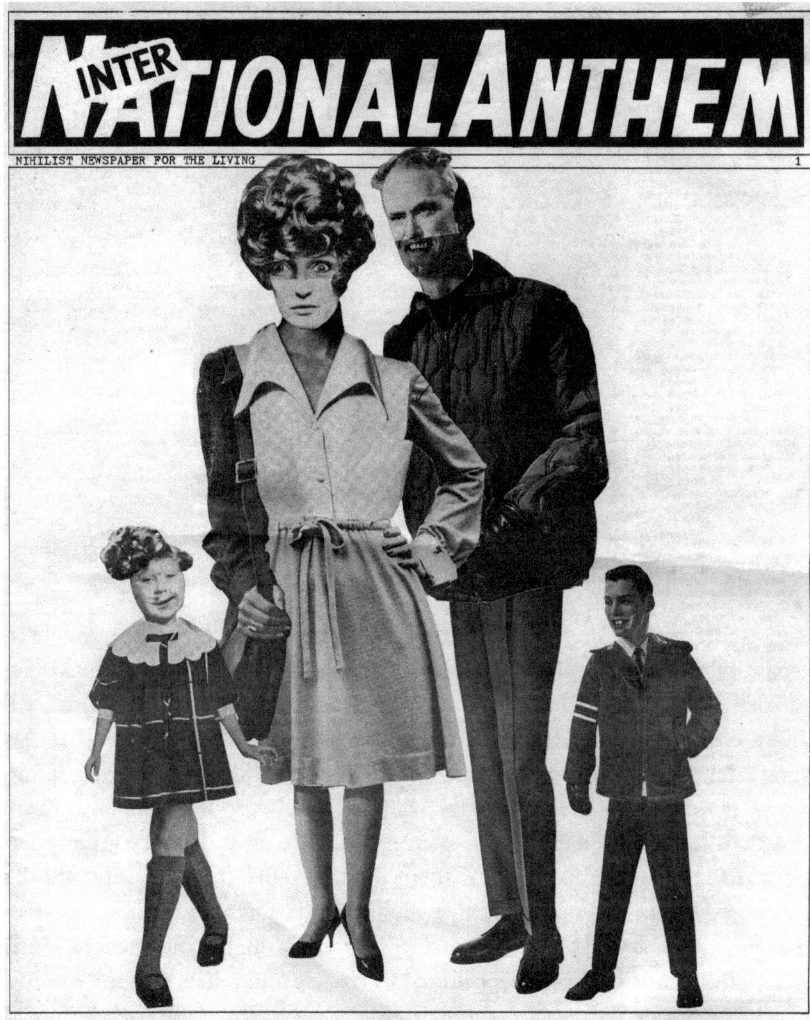

Figure 1.3   Gee Vaucher, Cover for *International Anthem 1: Education*, 1977, collage, 420mm × 300mm

age. Her work criticising the traditional family structure and the constriction of women within it developed from this position, despite the obvious overlap with ideas circulating within the women's movement.

Vaucher grew up in a time when magazines such as *Woman*, *Woman's Own* and *Good Housekeeping* promoted restrictive familial and gender roles, as a vital component of the burgeoning consumer society of the era.

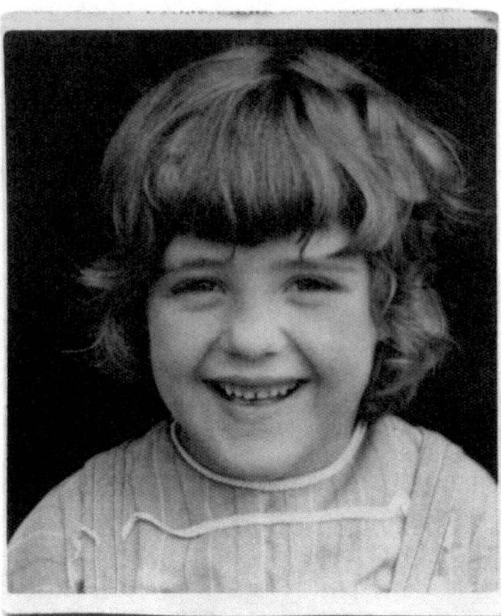

Figure 1.4   Anon, Gee Vaucher, wearing a pinstripe smock, age four, 1949, photo

Representations of the idealised family and home were centred on material aspiration. They advocated for the adoption of middle-class values, including smaller families, and an associated straightened sense of social conformity.[26] The more stringent codes of dress and behaviour within families that this entailed is something that recurs as an object of derision – or commiseration where the child is concerned – throughout Vaucher's work. She also more widely critiques the rise in the mass production, dissemination and consumption of culture that accompanied this societal shift. Vaucher has maintained the autonomous and DiY sensibility that she acquired from her childhood, despite the sterility and fast fashion associated with an increasingly consumerist society. Throughout her life she has continued to recycle and reuse, rather than buy, which is again something that she learned as a child. 'They [her parents] could make something from nothing because they had to. We never went without, and it was always exciting to see what toys dad made or which clothes mum made for us next. My favourite dress was a pinstripe smock she'd made from an old suit: I have a photo of me in that, definitely looking happy.'[27]

Stevphen Shukaitis, who co-curated Vaucher's major retrospective *Gee Vaucher: Introspective* (2016–17) at Firstsite (Colchester), has highlighted how Vaucher's tendency to make something from nothing is evident in her approach to gardening as well as art. With reference to Richard Hoggart's observations in *The Uses of Literacy* (1957) on the decline in working-class culture due to the mass media and consumerism of the 1950s, Shukaitis observes that Vaucher's refusal to assimilate is political. He notes, 'Vaucher would add to this by saying that although it is a strength within the community, adaptation plays very well into the hands of those in control.'[28] This inclination was further fostered through the counterculture that influenced her as an adult. She notes,

> Before the hippies in this country, there wasn't a lot of youth culture even though Elvis had opened up the music world. Youth didn't really have a voice at all, and it was only through what came from the west coast of America, and how that got translated in this country that things really did start to change. As we didn't have the space or the long summer skies which went with the idea of 'hippies', it had to be adjusted. Also a lot of the things that were happening in America, like building your own home and creating big scale projects yourself wasn't possible here. When it was tried, it was trodden on.[29]

This DiY ethic is woven into Vaucher's consistency in both situating her work outside and refusing to compromise her personal, creative or political integrity for the requirements of mainstream production. As the political photomontage artist Peter Kennard (b. 1949) has noted, 'Gee is a prime example of what Walter Benjamin called "the author as producer".'[30]

Vaucher attended art school at a time that many consider to have been its heyday. Authors including Fred Vermorel and the countercultural figure and anarchist Mick Farren (1943–2013) have recalled the licentiousness, marginality and bohemianism that prevailed.[31] British art schools had long fostered bohemianism, but during the 1950s and 1960s, unorthodox and radical teaching that reflected wider social change flourished. A sense of the experimental, permissive and unconventional permeated the work that students produced, and this was then dispersed into popular culture. This was aided by the fact that universities and art colleges were still free from the commercialised bureaucracy that came to govern their functioning from the 1980s onwards, due to underfunded expansion programmes imposed by successive Conservative governments.[32] Vaucher has criticised this change, also perceiving it to engender an empty rhetoric associated with postmodernism. On the present-day situation in art schools, Vaucher has commented,

> It seems a lot of the art is there to be sensationalist. And I'm not interested in sensationalism. You know, I try hard. I go into galleries and I try to understand, but I leave thinking 'where is the soul, the commitment, the love?' But I'll continue looking, I'm always hopeful. It's so sad because I feel a lot of young artists have been short changed, sold art as a commodity, a career. They seem to have lost the passion, but then, maybe there never was

one; only the idea of becoming a rich artist, a superstar in the art world at all costs.[33]

The vibrant art school scene of the 1960s nurtured a host of musicians and music graphic designers who became integral to reshaping culture in the ensuing years.[34] These included Vaucher's friend and fellow Essex resident Ian Dury (1942–2000), as well as punk protagonists Jamie Reid (b. 1947), Vivienne Westwood (b. 1941) and Malcolm McLaren (1946–2010).[35]

A sense of egalitarianism also pervaded these environments as high art and culture were democratised. Universities and art schools were well resourced and many enlarged their intake to include students from working- and lower middle-class homes for the first time. Therefore, the emerging cultural participants and protagonists were drawn from more varied social backgrounds, and their attitudes, experiences and ideas fed into the changing cultural environment. Higher education, particularly art schools, also provided the basis for the emerging counterculture in Britain.[36]

Vaucher was accepted to attend art school at the age of fifteen, on the strength of her portfolio. She comments, 'I went to the South-East Essex School of Art and Design from 1961–66. I thought it was fantastic. In those days, working class people didn't really go to college; we were seen as factory fodder. The school I went to didn't even have any exams. Why would you need exams when you were expected to go and work in the local factories, Yardleys for the girls and Fords for the boys?'[37]

It is worth noting that while higher education was being democratised during this time, traditional class structures prevailed.[38] She notes, 'There was only one other girl who was working class and I'd never met anybody who came from the middle and upper classes before. They spoke and dressed differently and I was too shy to join in with a lot of the things going on.'[39]

Vaucher's recollection of art school conveys the sense of freedom that she gained through learning and developing her innate talent. However, rather than the bohemianism and licentiousness recalled by commentators such as Vermorel and Farren, she remembers its rigorous training along more traditional lines.[40] Vaucher notes,

> Back in the early sixties, art schools were places where you learnt your craft; all sorts of subjects I didn't even know that were somehow related to what I wanted to do: heraldry, anatomy, colour theory, history, perspective and hand lettering. We used to spend hours and hours just drawing the figures in the life room. If it wasn't a live model, it was from the casts: Leonardo da Vinci's anatomy figures, Michelangelo's dying slave, Venus de Milo. It was five years of classical training during which I learnt to see beyond looking.[41]

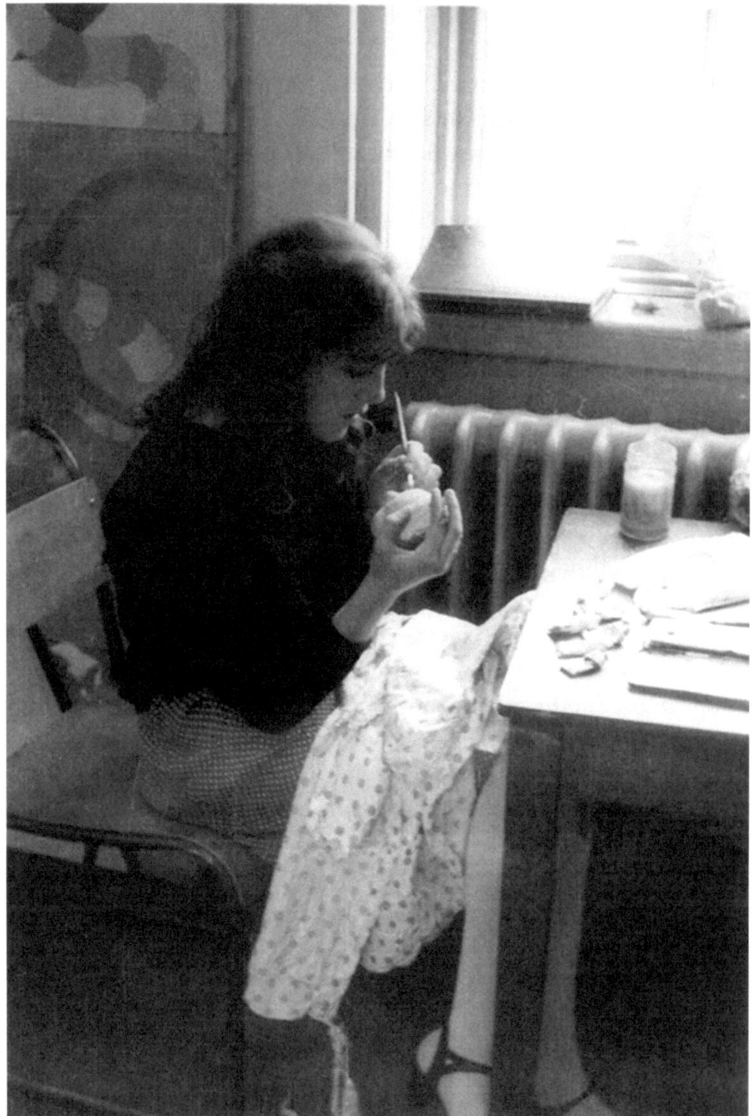

Figure 1.5 Anon, Gee Vaucher at art school, 1964, photo

This is something that is reiterated by Jamie Reid, despite both artists going on to become symptomatic of the wider changes afoot with the fine art/pop crossover and political radicalism of the late 1960s and 1970s.[42] Though Vaucher doesn't recall the radicalism of the art schools, similarly to Reid, her dedication to occupying an outsider space might well have been fostered by them.

While Vaucher made the most of the opportunities art school offered, it was also in this environment that she met her lifelong creative partner Penny Rimbaud. They were from very different backgrounds, and the attraction was certainly not instant. As Rimbaud recalls, 'She thought I was an upper-class prick and I thought she was a working class twat, you know, and that's how it started.' Rimbaud made the most of the libertarian art school environment, and by his own admission was a 'shocking womaniser', but it was Vaucher's difference to the majority of other students that eventually formed the basis of their attraction. 'She was much more interested in getting on with her work than going out drinking and having a screw. And that made her interesting. It was a model outside of the one that I knew, gung ho, yahoo twat that I was. Again, it was like – you're taking this seriously?'[43]

They bonded over their shared 'innate disobedience', which manifested in countless pranks. One of their art teachers, for example, recalls an incident where Rimbaud slipped some photos of himself naked into a slide carousel during a lecture.[44] One of their friends would later observe, 'They're always up to something. Although they always and still do probably argue like cat and dog, some of their arguments are amazing. But I think they've always sparked off each other.'[45] Rimbaud verifies this, recollecting, 'It was a sort of competitive element between us. She was a profoundly better draftsperson than I could ever hope to be. On the other hand, I was profoundly imaginative in coming up with cranky ideas and pulling at the edges; trying to break the rules.'[46]

This mix of sensibilities and backgrounds would be key to their collaborations together over the coming decades; first in performance art outfits in the 1970s and through their involvement in the Free Festivals movement, and then in Crass, the band Rimbaud formed with Steve Ignorant in 1977. It was also during this period, however, that Vaucher developed the pattern of working alone for extended periods of time. She recalls the supportiveness and flexibility she was shown by staff.

I'd be there early in the morning; finally getting them to keep it open until 10pm at night and the weekends. There were only a few of us who wanted to have access to everything all the time, but I fought hard and said, 'you don't switch your bloody art off at six o'clock, it's not a 9–5 job you know?' And because I got on with the head of the art school, he authorised the rooms to be left open. You didn't have to pay for much when I was at art school; just paper, pencils and paint. I did etching and they gave me sheets of copper plating. I did sculpture and they gave me clay and plaster and you actually got paid to go to art school. I got the biggest grant because my parents didn't have any savings.[47]

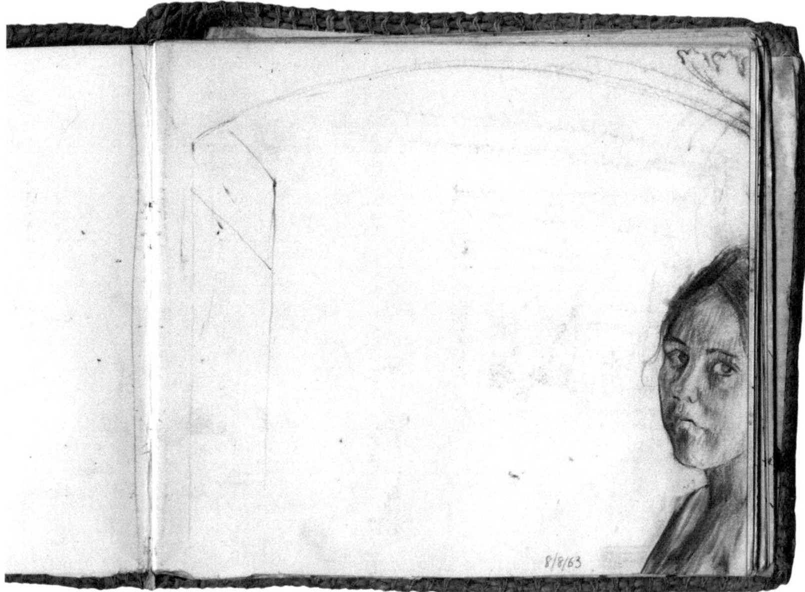

Figure 1.6   Gee Vaucher, *Self-portrait*, 1963, pencil

Vaucher completed a few self-portraits during this period, including a pencil drawing (see Figure 1.6) where she appears looking somewhat reticent in the lower right-hand corner of the page of a sketchbook. Her work in this period was mainly centred on life drawing.[48] She has commented, 'The most important room for me was the life room. As far as I'm concerned, that's where you learnt everything: colour, perspective, structure, time, space; how to express. There wasn't anywhere else I really wanted to be, unless I then wanted to translate a drawing into a print. Then I'd be in the print room where I did etching and silkscreen and stuff like that.'[49]

Vaucher's life drawings at this time capture the essence of a person, showing how human experience is manifest in the body. Her early studies of clothed figures also convey this sense of realism, embodied in Figure 1.8 through the heavily drawn face, the angularity of the body conveying a certain awkwardness, which together with the oversized hands gives them a Schiele-like quality. Meanwhile the slumped position of the sitter seems to indicate broodiness and/or introspection. There are correlations with the work of Käthe Kollwitz (1867–1945) through the empathy that Vaucher has for her subject and for how she captures the weight of human experience. However, unlike Kollwitz, Vaucher's figures are not politicised at this stage.

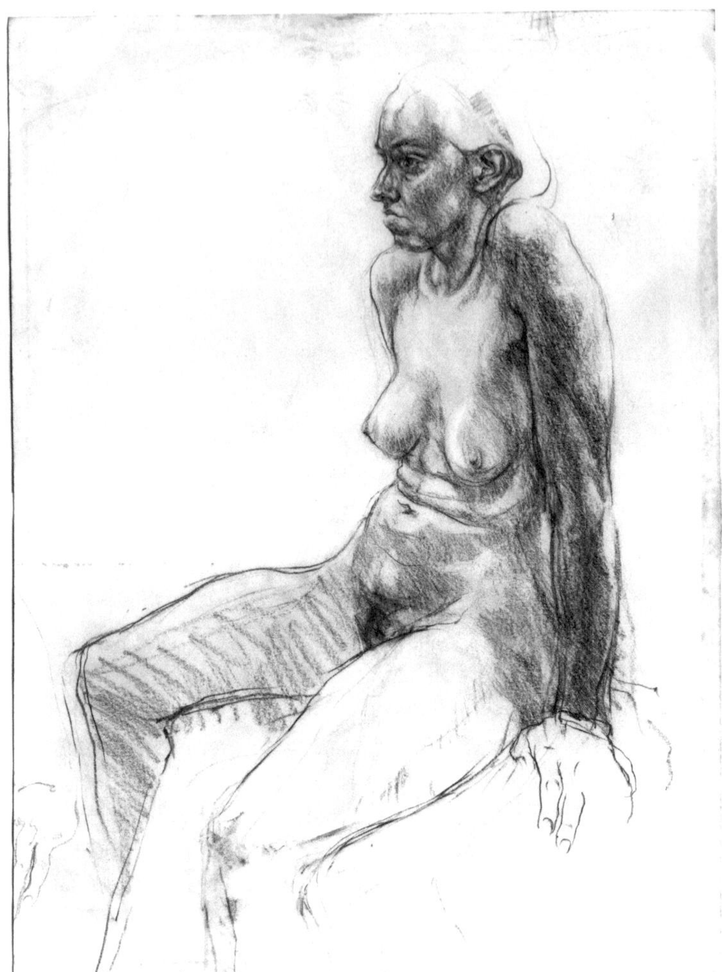

Figure 1.7   Gee Vaucher, Life drawing, 1964, pencil, 390mm × 300mm

During this time, Vaucher also created observational sketches of people she saw out and about in London. These studies reveal her close observation of habits and social mores, which became a distinguishing feature of her design language when she worked as a freelance illustrator in New York (1977–79). Her illustration of a woman on a bus (see colour insert, Plate 1), wearing a three-quarter length, black, Astrakhan coat, with short, styled hair observes the style consciousness of that period, while retaining a social-realist quality. As Rimbaud has observed, 'Quite apart from her work's technical brilliance and its often harrowing subject matter, there is a Lowryesque sense to it,

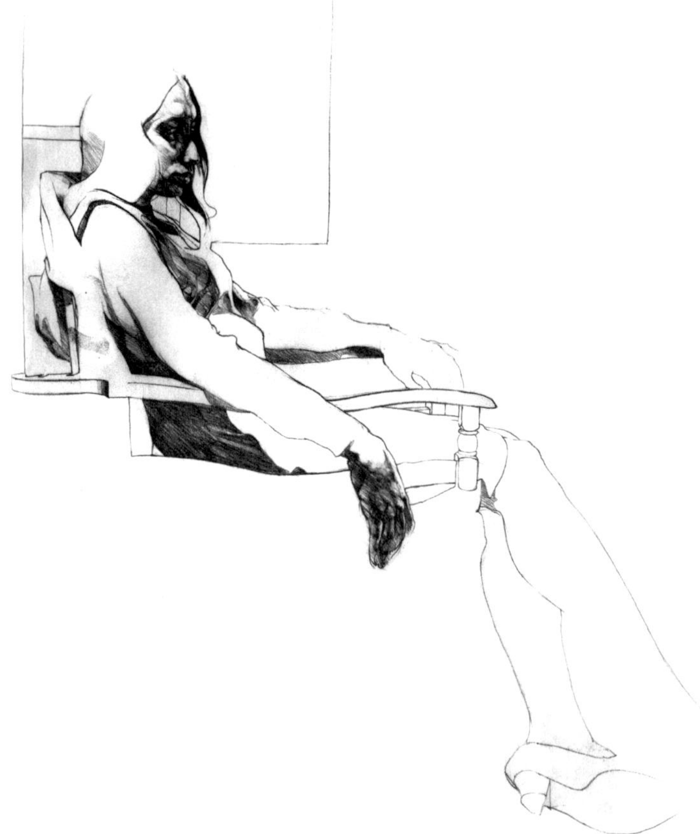

Figure 1.8   Gee Vaucher, Life drawing, 1965, pencil, 370mm × 260mm

one of everyday ordinariness and common kindness; it shines through the darkness. This is, I believe, a show of solidarity with the roots from which she has grown.'[50]

This observational quality, in this instance combined with an element of exaggeration and distortion, is also seen in her illustration of a crowd on a bus (Figure 1.9). This image captures something of the austerity that still pervaded Britain in the 1960s in the monochrome palette, the largely utilitarian clothing and the tight-lipped resilience of the people's expressions. However, it also shows their idiosyncrasy in, for instance, the defiant glamour of the woman wearing the sunglasses and fur-lined coat, and the man further along to the right wearing horn-rimmed spectacles and a bow tie. The male figure who's left the bus, wearing an ill-fitting coat and trousers, is in a hurry, pulling in one direction, while the girl whose hand he holds looks the opposite way.

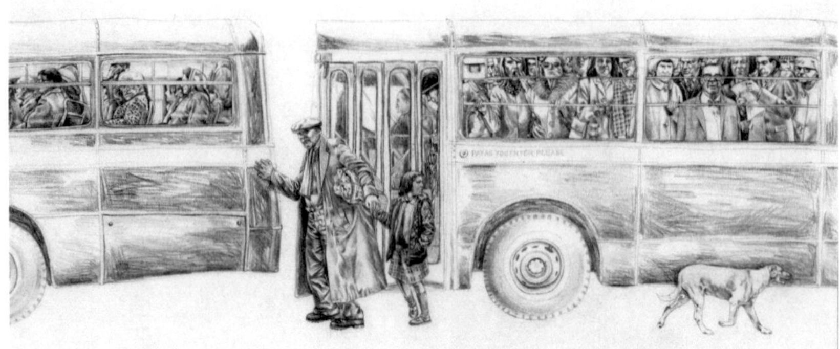

Figure 1.9   Gee Vaucher, *Bus*, 1964, drawing, 250mm × 455mm

All of these characters seem lost in thought; in a world of their own. Vaucher captures something quintessential about both everyday people en masse and the personalised experience of each individual.

While Vaucher's work at art school was often figurative, based on honing her observational technique, it was during this time that she became inspired by Pop Art. Despite the classical training that Vaucher so valued, the technical college in Essex she attended was more oriented to graphic design, and preparing its students for a career in advertising, by contrast with the classical 'painting' schools, which according to Rimbaud still largely followed the approach of Sir William Coldstream (1908–87).[51] Rimbaud has noted how this gave them an advantage in adapting to the changing times. 'Of course it was wonderful, because we were suddenly able to exploit the graphic design aspect into Pop Art. Suddenly we became the painting school in a way because we were right in what was happening.'[52]

It was in fact their mutual interest in Pop Art that drew Vaucher and Rimbaud together. During its heyday, Pop Art challenged the hierarchical distinctions within the art world by combining elements of highbrow and popular culture. Its definition of popular culture included underground or subversive output such as comic books, as well as advertising and lifestyle or aspirational magazines. The design language often used irony to expose, send up or undermine consumerism and the attendant mass media. Audiences who shared the cultural knowledge of the producers could understand and interpret the meaning conveyed through the iconography. As well as reflecting their use of 1950s consumerist iconography in her work, it was this aspect of Pop Art that became integral to Vaucher's approach with Crass. In particular, she has cited the influence of British artist, Richard Hamilton, whose output provided a particularly incisive critique of the mass media.[53] Hamilton played a key role in the British Pop Art Movement, The Independent Group, who had met at the Institute of the Contemporary Arts in London (1952–55).

In its American incarnation in the work of Andy Warhol and others, Pop Art commented on consumerism in a way that was often as celebratory as it was ironic. In this it can be seen to form the basis for postmodern art, which again lacked criticality. By contrast, Hamilton used methods such as collage and photomontage to subvert the meaning conveyed through the mass media, to provide social comment. Pop Artists also extended the range of subject matter in art and targeted audiences beyond the confines of the gallery. In this sense, Vaucher also has an affinity with their approach, although hers has been more idiosyncratic and her audience more niche.

Hamilton's collage, *Hugh Gaitskell as a Famous Monster of Filmland* (1963), satirised the leader of the Labour Party, by combining his facial features with those of a monster, giving him a deranged appearance. This was produced in response to Gaitskell siding with the Tories in supporting a nuclear deterrent.[54] Hamilton's use of exaggerated, partially abstracted facial features as a means of parodying the powerful provides an early instance of his later, more political work. This method, and the satirical intention behind it, features as a staple of Vaucher's design language through her work for Crass and *International Anthem* in particular. Created in the gloomier political climate of the late 1970s and 1980s, Vaucher's images formed a starker critical response.

One event that had a significant politicising effect on Vaucher was the Aberfan Disaster (1966), in which a junior school in South Wales was engulfed by a coal tip collapse killing 116 children. This heightened her anger at structural inequality, and the disregard for ordinary people's lives shown by powerful organisations. She comments, 'It brought it home, not only the injustice, but the hypocrisy and lies of those in control who did nothing to avoid the tragedy. That company knew the truth. They'd been told several times that there was a serious chance of that huge mountain of slag slipping onto the school. They'd been told so many times and they did nothing about it. Profit always comes first.'[55]

This tragedy also highlighted the divergent life experiences of Rimbaud and Vaucher. Aberfan occurred at a time when, unlike Rimbaud, Vaucher had not yet found her political voice. She recalls,

I was quite shy; I didn't feel I had the vocabulary to speak. I couldn't keep up with people's conversations, like debates because I'd never done it. So I was quite quiet and I was a good listener. But in my mind was always an image; even then the imagery was about the very things that people were talking about, but I couldn't vocalise it very well. So, I learnt through Pen and through listening and talking and my vocabulary has grown enormously. And I think I found a voice through Aberfan, because his reaction at the time seemed to be so callous and flippant. I think he laughed and I think he made some cutting remark. It was his way of trying to deal with this horrible thing that had happened to the children; to the whole village. And it wasn't just the children; it was the whole corruption of the system really, and especially being a coal mining community and dependent on each other. So I learned my voice there.[56]

Later, Vaucher realised Rimbaud had been as deeply affected and outraged by what happened as she was. She notes, 'I learnt very quickly after that that was his way of dealing with the pain. Maybe it was something to do with public school and being taught to keep a stiff upper lip.'[57]

In certain ways, Vaucher's experience of the 1960s differs from the predominant free and hedonistic narrative. The traditional class system prevailed in the circles in which she mixed. However, in common with a great number of her contemporaries, it was her exposure to the optimism of the 1960s that stoked her ability to re-imagine the world, which is something she has retained and stressed throughout her life's work. She notes, 'There was a huge rise in creativity in every field from David Hockney, Mary Quant, Vidal Sassoon, The Beatles, The Stones and so on; all different aspects of creativity coming to the fore from the art schools and they were feeding the imagination of people if you like. There was such a strong feeling of possibility; of change.'[58]

Reflecting this change, the 1970s would see Vaucher involved in forms of expression that diverged dramatically from the largely figurative work she'd produced during her traditional art school training/art school years. While she would earn an income as a freelance illustrator, in the first half of the decade her focus was on work with creative collectives, featuring Rimbaud and numerous others, that were avant-garde, experimental and symptomatic of the radicalism of that era.

Notes

1 G. Vaucher in interview with M. Groß, quoted in S. Shukaitis (ed.), *Gee Vaucher: Introspective* (Colchester: Firstsite, published in collaboration with Minor Compositions, 2016), p. 14.

2 G. Vaucher, *Crass Art and Other Pre Postmodernist Monsters* (Colchester: Firstsite, published in collaboration with Minor Compositions, 2nd edn, 2014), p. 2.

3 Vaucher in interview with Binns, 2013.

4 Vaucher in interview with Binns, 2013.
5 Vaucher in interview with Groß, 2015.
6 Vaucher, *Crass Art*, p. 2.
7 Vaucher in interview with Binns, 2017.
8 Vaucher in interview with Groß, quoted in Shukaitis, *Gee Vaucher: Introspective*, p. 14.
9 Vaucher in interview with Binns, 2021.
10 Vaucher in email correspondence, March 2021.
11 This observation is made by George McKay in G. McKay, 'Gee Vaucher's Punk Painting as Record Sleeves', in S. Shukaitis (ed.), *Gee Vaucher: Introspective* (Colchester: Firstsite, published in collaboration with Minor Compositions, 2016), p. 71.
12 Vaucher in interview with Binns, 2013.
13 Vaucher in interview with Binns, 2013.
14 K. Millet in interview with C. Braefield, 'Intellectual Eunuch', *Frendz*, 3:30 (4 June 1971), p. 18.
15 C. Ward, *Anarchy in Action* (London: George Allen & Unwin Ltd, 1973).
16 Vaucher in interview with Binns, 2013.
17 Vaucher in interview with Binns, 2013.
18 Vaucher in interview with Binns, 2013.
19 Vaucher in interview with Binns, 2013.
20 Vaucher in interview with Binns, 2013.
21 Vaucher in interview with Binns, 2017.
22 Vaucher in interview with Binns, 2017.
23 Vaucher in interview with Binns, 2017.
24 Vaucher in interview with Binns, 2017.
25 Vaucher in interview with Binns, 2017.
26 A Gallup poll in 1957 revealed that most people during this period aspired to have two children, in D. Kynaston, *Family Britain: 1951–57* (London: Bloomsbury Publishing Plc, 2009), p. 563.
27 Vaucher in interview with Groß, quoted in Shukaitis, *Gee Vaucher: Introspective*, p. 14.
28 S. Shukaitis 'The Door to the Garden: Gee Vaucher and the Cultivation of Artistic Counterculture' in S. Shukaitis (ed.), *Gee Vaucher: Introspective* (Colchester: Firstsite, published in collaboration with Minor Compositions, 2016), p. 14.
29 Vaucher in interview with Groß, 2002.
30 Peter Kennard quoted in Vaucher, *Crass Art*, Foreword, with reference to Walter Benjamin's famous essay, 'The Author as Producer', first published in 1936.
31 See, F. Vermorel, *Vivienne Westwood: Fashion, Perversity and the 1960s Laid Bare* (New York: Overlook Books, 1996) and M. Farren, *Give the Anarchist a Cigarette* (London: Pimlico, 2001). Also see Frith and Howard Horne's pamphlet, 'Welcome to Bohemia!' (University of Warwick, 1984), which argues that a Romantic notion of the artist as a free-thinking outsider pervaded art schools. In his sociological study, Frank Musgrove also uses the Romanticism of the late eighteenth–early nineteenth

centuries in Britain, as an analogy for the counterculture of the 1970s. F. Musgrove, *Ecstasy and Holiness: Counterculture and the Open Society* (Norfolk: Cox and Wyman Ltd, 1974), p. 13.

32 J. A. Walker, *Left Shift: Radical Art in 1970s Britain* (London: Taurus, 2002), p. 181.

33 Vaucher in interview with Binns, 2013.

34 The Walthamstow School of Art alone nurtured Pop Artists including Peter Blake and Derek Boshier, filmmakers Ken Russell and Peter Greenaway and fashion designers Celia Birtwell, Marion Foale and Sally Tuffin during the 1950s and 1960s (from the exhibition, Be Magnificent: Walthamstow School of Art 1957–67 at the William Morris Gallery 9 June–10 September 2017).

35 See J. Reid and J. Savage, *Up They Rise: The Incomplete Works of Jamie Reid* (London: Faber and Faber, 1987), p. 15.

36 Vermorel, *Fashion, Perversity and the 1960s*, p. 150. Also see Musgrove, *Ecstasy and Holiness*, pp. 5–6.

37 Vaucher in interview with Groß, quoted in Shukaitis, *Gee Vaucher: Introspective*, p. 31.

38 Vaucher in interview with Groß, quoted in Shukaitis, *Gee Vaucher: Introspective*, p. 30.

39 Vaucher in interview with Groß, quoted in Shukaitis, *Gee Vaucher: Introspective*, p. 32.

40 See L. Tickner, *Hornsey 1968: The Art School Revolution* (London: Frances Lincoln Ltd, 2008) for an account of the sweeping changes that would occur to art schools in the wake of the Coldstream Report, policies under the Labour government from 1964, and the student protests of the late 1960s.

41 Vaucher in interview with Groß, quoted in P. Rimbaud, 'A Very Private Person', in S. Shukaitis (ed), *Gee Vaucher: Introspective* (Colchester: Firstsite, published in collaboration with Minor Compositions, 2016), p. 36.

42 Reid and Savage, *Up They Rise*, p. 15.

43 Rimbaud in interview with Binns, 2021.

44 Charlotte Brennan (with reference to her mother, Jean Fraser) in conversation with Binns, March 2021.

45 Ignorant in interview with Binns, 2021.

46 Rimbaud in interview with Binns, 2021.

47 Vaucher in interview with Binns, 2013.

48 Vaucher in interview with Binns, 2017.

49 Vaucher in interview with Binns, 2013.

50 P. Rimbaud, 'A Very Private Person', in S. Shukaitis (ed), *Gee Vaucher: Introspective* (Colchester: Firstsite, published in collaboration with Minor Compositions, 2016), p. 36.

51 P. Rimbaud, 'Penny Rimbaud on Art Schools', 15 April 2014. Available at www.youtube. com/watch?v=UNXBq6–74Cs (accessed 27 May 2021).

52 Rimbaud, 'Penny Rimbaud on Art Schools'.

53 Vaucher in interview with Binns, 2013.

54 S. Sherwin, 'Richard Hamilton's portrait of Hugh Gaitskell: pop art goes agit-prop', The *Guardian* (4 November 2016).
55 Vaucher in interview with Binns, 2017.
56 Vaucher in interview with Groß, 2002.
57 Vaucher in interview with Binns, 2021.
58 Vaucher in interview with Binns, 2017.

Radical art collectives and the free festivals movement

Two key preoccupations that have recurred in Vaucher's work throughout her career are pacifism and autonomy. While these don't appear as coherent themes in her work until the late 1970s, their genesis can be seen in the cultural changes initiated by the growth of the counterculture in the 1960s. In place of the mass political movements that had thus far characterised the twentieth century, the 1960s saw a fragmentation of consensus, with numerous different positions adopted by groups coming from broadly speaking left or anarchist positions. Vaucher's interest in pacifism, however, reflected a common concern of the generation who instigated the counterculture. The countercultural protagonist and peace movement activist, Jeff Nuttall (1933–2001), for instance, described this complete change as a reaction to 'bomb culture', growing up in the aftermath of the Second World War, with the destruction caused by the atomic bomb still in living memory.[1]

The Campaign for Nuclear Disarmament (CND) had been founded in 1958 in response to Britain becoming the third nuclear power, and many people who became involved in the counterculture had previously participated in the peace movement.[2] Nuttall, who was a CND veteran, described the ineffectiveness of the peace movement in England during the 1950s as a decisive factor in how protest was to change course during the following decade. From an anarchist perspective, he cited dismay at how CND aligned the call for nuclear disarmament with its wider socialist intentions, observing 'They were squares, hardworking well-meaning squares, whose particular refuge was in the lie of socialist progress.'[3] Similarly, Vaucher talks about her lack of engagement with the peace movement. 'I went on a CND march, but that's about it.'[4] The anti-nuclear movement at this time was largely composed of middle-class, as opposed to working-class, radicals,[5] which lent it an air that some found patronising. CND's focus on reforming the Labour Party to wholeheartedly back unilateral disarmament not only proved futile but was also considered by those who turned to direct action and/or the counterculture to thwart creativity in political action. Nuttall, for instance, pointed to the gulf between the political standpoint of CND and what he termed the 'creative impulse'.[6]

While the political force of CND was on the wane by the late 1960s, it had sown the seeds from which newer, more direct forms of protest arose. The Direct Action Committee against Nuclear War (DAC) (1957–61) had been formed as a strand within CND, with the aim of carrying out nonviolent, direct action outside official channels. Anarchists within the peace movement had a decisive impact despite their small numbers, and this period saw direct action reconceptualised as nonviolent in line with the wider adoption of pacifism within their circles.[7]

In 1960, the Committee of 100 also emerged at the radical end of the peace movement, with a remit to use nonviolent resistance and direct action to achieve their aims. Formed by a hard core of one hundred activists, including the former President of CND Bertrand Russell, the decision-making structure of the C100 was based on direct democracy, offering an anarchistic alternative to CND's hierarchical structure. Within the anti-nuclear movement, the notion of direct action was appealing not just for its use as a propagandist tactic, but for its potential to interfere with the functioning of the state.[8] Direct action did not just refer to the action itself, but to its derivation from a concept of autonomy that entailed personal responsibility, as opposed to an individual simply towing the official line.

By the late 1960s, the focus of the peace movement shifted from the Cold War to the live war in Vietnam. Although Britain refused to commit troops, the government was still perceived to be complicit in the atrocities committed by the USA because of its refusal to publicly condemn them. The violent clashes between protestors and police at demonstrations against the war were seen to mark the beginning of an era of civil unrest.[9] As a result, anti-militarism became prominent among certain young demographics in the late 1960s, a development that was fostered by the New Left, which was staunchly anti-war in its outlook.[10]

The use of violence by more extreme political groups also contributed to a climate where political consensus was perceived to be breaking down.[11]

However, it's worth recognising that the actual threat such movements posed was often vastly overstated in the media.[12] It is also the case that, in reality, rather than abandoning mainstream politics, the British public largely retained their faith in the electoral process during this period.[13] The radical artistic, political and countercultural circles that Vaucher moved in were minority social milieus, at the cutting edge of social change. That said, Vaucher is immensely proud of their impact. 'It was over ground. This idea of the underground, I just don't understand it. It's as if we were rats squirrelling away underneath society. No, we weren't. We were right on the surface and that's what became dangerous for society I suppose, as far as governments were concerned, because the power of the people was rising up. It genuinely was.'[14]

At the time, anarchists situated their anti-nuclear stance within a wider opposition to state power, militarism and the associated social conformity and deference to elites. Echoing these sentiments, Vaucher's work expresses dismay at the extent of wartime atrocities, as well as the show of state technocratic power and violence that uses propaganda to coerce the population into compliance. These beliefs can be seen to fuel her autonomous life choices and provide the basis for the powerful political critique that characterised her work from the late 1970s.

Throughout her life, Vaucher has refused to participate in the political system, believing its parties and politicians to be opaque, unable to represent people and potentially corrupt. Instead, she believes in people sharing, participating and living as self-sufficiently as possible in small-scale communities, and the roots of this can be seen in the anarchist and anarcho-pacifist ideas that circulated in the counterculture of the 1960s. This period saw the nineteenth-century anarchist theorist Mikhail Bakunin's ideas being taken on by intellectuals and political movements. This included his belief in instinctive will, spontaneous action and workers' autonomy as prerequisites to freedom. His belief that the 'lumpenproletariat' (as well as the peasantry) rather than the proletariat would be the protagonist for social change, and that therefore this change would be subcultural in origin, was also widely adopted.[15] Bakuninist slogans, such as 'The urge to destroy is a creative urge' appeared around Paris during the events of 1968.[16]

The ideas of The Situationist International (SI), 1957–72, also permeated various libertarian movements during this period, and they were widely accredited with providing the spur for action during Paris '68. It is worth noting that their ideas were not well known in British society at the time, and were only translated into English during the 1970s.[17] However, their outlook permeated the counterculture in Britain to some extent via word of mouth and underground press publications such as *International Times* (1966), *Oz*

(1967) and other more politically orientated ones, *Friends* (1969) (which became *Frendz* in May 1971 and ceased publication in 1972), *Black Dwarf* (1968) and *Ink* (1971). *King Mob Echo*, the outlet for the English branch of the Situationist International, started life in 1968, and all these publications, along with some of the anarchist magazines such as *Black Flag* (1971–99),[18] *Freedom* (1866–present) and *Direct Action* (from 1970) that espoused anarcho-pacifist ideas,[19] were in circulation among Vaucher's associates.

On the influence of the SI at that time, Vaucher commented, 'There was a definite rise in energy, a rise in awareness of people and a rise of young people, which you can't have imagined before that. The young were seen but not heard. Suddenly Britain's youth was on the street, shouting loud.'[20]

In common with many utopians, the SI focused on the power of the imagination to create a perspective of the possible.[21] While they used Marxism as the theoretical underpinning for their ideas, their fusion of theory and practice through the transformation of everyday life, together with the prioritisation of desire, pleasure and expression, resonated with the strategies of earlier avant-garde art movements.[22] This sentiment also had a precedent in the ideas of early anarchists, including the feminist-anarchist and pacifist activist and writer Emma Goldman (1869–1940). In 1910 she wrote, 'Man is being robbed, not merely of the products of his labour, but of the power of free initiative, of originality and the interest in, or desire for, the things he is making.'[23]

Goldman's notion of de-conditioning as a prerequisite to freedom, which she set out in 1910, was revived for a new audience in the late 1960s.[24] This argued that freedom was achieved by liberating yourself from institutional, societal and familial conditioning, and manifested in Vaucher's milieu as the notion that freedom from external constraint was a prerequisite to realising personal desire and/or living more authentically.[25] This notion of de-conditioning also featured strongly within the avant-garde art movements of the early twentieth century. Surrealist artists, for instance, followed Freud in subscribing to de-conditioning as the means for uncovering repressed desire. However, during the 1960 and 1970s, revolutionary orthodoxies, such as those of Freud and Marx, were also criticised for being as flawed and hierarchical as the conventions they aimed to supersede.[26] One example is the radical movement against established psychiatric conventions that saw psychiatrists and psychologists, including R. D. Laing, argue for a de-conditioning process to heal individuals of familial trauma.[27] Laing analysed the breakdowns of people who were labelled schizophrenic by the psychiatric establishment, seeing the potential for breakthrough in this process. This was not to deny the very real instances of inherent psychosis, but to see if there was something we could learn from this process of ego-loss. His relation of the individual's condition to their wider familial and societal situation also de-individualised their condition. In this context, while psychiatry was radical in its inception, it was criticised for having become a powerful institution, which had potentially harmful and oppressive outcomes for its patients. Vaucher has specifically acknowledged Laing as an influence for her work on the family, and critiques such as his formed part of the wider backlash against the conformity that had been engendered through the war effort, the post-war political consensus and the stifling social mores of the 1950s.[28]

Such beliefs also characterised the counterculture itself, through which individuals tried to create sustainable lives on the basis of values that diverged from those of their parents' generation. The rejection of professionalism and the pressure to conform to a stratified, atomised existence was all part of this.[29] This attempt at living authentically through creating alternatives to mainstream politics and the consumer society was also articulated in the ideas of the North American anarchist author and activist, Murray Bookchin.[30] His vision strongly evoked that expressed contemporarily by the SI, in particular Vaneigem's thesis, *The Revolution of Everyday Life* (1967). Bookchin argued that much of what constituted work and purpose in centralised, capitalist societies was unnecessary, as technology had developed to the point where material scarcity no longer underpinned human existence. As people were no longer driven by their need to struggle for essential resources, they were less easily controlled and manipulated by overarching structures, such as the Church, State, marketplace or patriarchal family. Bookchin therefore advocated anarchism as realisable for the first time due to this 'post-scarcity' situation. As such, the protagonists of the counterculture were heir to freedoms unrealisable for all but the wealthy elite among previous generations. They were driven, not by any substantial material hardship, but by a sense of disillusionment with the world combined with their ability to do something about it.[31] Vaucher's working-class background distinguished her from many of her contemporaries, who often made a conscious choice to rebuff the path to material comfort enabled by rising affluence and welfare provision. However, she was likewise symptomatic of the times in receiving a higher, art school education and in rejecting the expectations of her background, instead forging an independent path and contributing to the shifting political and cultural terrain.

It is worth noting that Vaucher has not cited any anarchist theorist as a direct influence. In fact, she has consistently refused to be defined by any 'isms', not least the anarchism and feminism that are commonly ascribed to her.[32] There is, however, another clear parallel between Vaucher and Bookchin in his fusing of ecological principles with anarchism. This appears to be his greatest, original contribution to knowledge. His concept of 'social ecology' predicted the impending environmental crisis and advocated for living in a way that was more in sync with nature.[33] He argued, 'owing to its inherently competitive nature, bourgeois society not only pits humans against each other, but it also pits the mass of humanity against the natural world.'[34] His solution was to reverse the trend for industrialised farming and urban development, and he saw decentralised communities as a precondition to reversing environmental degradation. This imperative is clearly reflected in Vaucher's approach to life, most visibly through her gardening and ecological projects at Dial House, her primary home since the late 1960s, as well as her lifelong vegetarianism and commitment to animal as well as people's rights.[35]

From 1969, Vaucher lived with Rimbaud and various other people at Dial House. Rimbaud had moved into the abandoned farmhouse in Ongar Great Park in Essex in 1967, living there for free with a couple of friends while renovating it from the dilapidated state in which they found it. Rimbaud envisioned it as an open house where anyone could stop by and there would be a constant turnover of people.[36] It hosted a network of artists, musicians and other like-minded people during this period. Vaucher has drawn a comparison between the ethos at Dial House and the culture of openness she experienced during her childhood in working-class Dagenham.[37] However, the open and collaborative spirit of Dial House was symptomatic of the wider trend towards autonomous forms of social organisation that characterised the time. The most obvious parallel is with the Commune Movement, which aimed to create a federation of free communities that would largely render central government irrelevant.

Similarly to the communes, Dial House created an alternative to the patriarchal structures prevalent in society, in particular the nuclear family. Yet despite the prevailing communal ethos, Vaucher maintained a distance from the social hubbub. Like her time at art school, when she often worked alone for long stretches of time, Vaucher was often locked in her own world at Dial House.[38] That said, Dial House gave birth to a series of collaborative art projects, many of which she participated in. Before moving there, she had lived in Stanford Rivers Hall, a large house in the nearby Essex village of Stanford Rivers, and was part of the Stanford Rivers Quartet, which she described as:

> totally abstract. We wrote the musical scores ourselves, but with imagery,
> with colours, so anyone could read the music, because it was done in colour
> and the colour was expressed by you and the length and shape of the colour
> would dictate how you played it. Anyone could play it. It was great. I loved it.
> And of course it was imagery. It was imagery that translated into music.'[39]

While the group's name alludes to a classical music ensemble, the way it functioned was far removed from the elitism and fixity associated with the genre. It was open and accessible to all participants, regardless of their level of formal training. Vaucher notes, 'We were all creative in some way. We weren't all musicians. We weren't all artists. We wanted to have a laugh with it and see what worked out.'[40]

The approach of the Stanford Rivers Quartet is symptomatic of a wider trend towards open, experimental and self-governing creative collectives at this time. Such groups intended their creativity to be part of a social process, rather than orientated towards individual acclaim. In their openness towards participants regardless of their level of training, these collectives also have clear similarities to the emancipatory, 'anyone can do it' ethos that would characterise punk.

Open and collective social forms were enabled through choices to live, work and create autonomously, without the mediation that often afflicted mainstream modes of production, work and life. A network of experimental art collectives around the country were inspired by well-known countercultural ones, such as Indica, Arts Lab and the UFO Club. The creative commune The Exploding Galaxy (initiated by the artist David Medalla, 1967) also proved inspiring to other collectives in their decided outsider status.

Following the Stanford Rivers Quartet, Vaucher and Rimbaud started the avant-garde, performance group EXIT (1968–72), which had up to twenty members at any given time. They toured the country meeting artists and musicians, including members of the radical and experimental art movement, FLUXUS, who they collaborated with for ICES '72 (International Carnival of Experimental Sound) held at the Roundhouse (London, 1972). Rimbaud describes EXIT with the in turn grandiose and self-deprecating humour that characterises his writing, as a 'small band of aspirant musicians blundering their way through ... a repertoire of avant-garde clichés'.[41] Many of the experimental sound and multi-media techniques developed by EXIT would, however, be adapted and refined by Crass.

It was at this time that Vaucher and Rimbaud went to visit Rimbaud's parents in the USA (his father had moved there for work). They stayed on, travelling in the country for three months. The trip was to prove inspirational and significant to the direction Vaucher would take with her work. Rimbaud recalls,

It was fantastic being with Gee in America because we were able to be classless. People couldn't tell the difference between Gee and me, so if we were talking to people they wouldn't just refer to me as being the articulate,

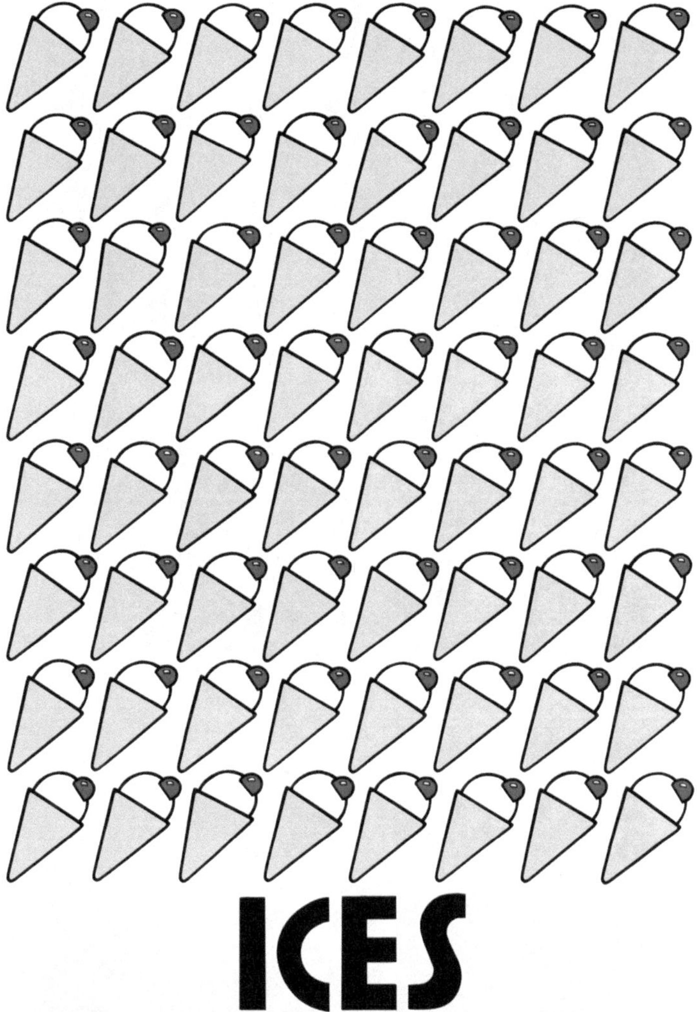

Figure 2.1 Gee Vaucher, Poster for ICES 72, 1972, gouache, 600mm × 400mm

upper class twit, as opposed to the ignorant, working class git. So I think that was illuminating for both of us really. And I think that really was inspiring for her. And almost from the moment we got back, she wanted to go back.[42]

During their absence, EXIT had continued to perform (involving a very young Steve Ignorant for one of their pieces).[43] On their return, Vaucher and Rimbaud continued to perform with various EXIT members, although they ceased to operate under that name. They became involved in works with the

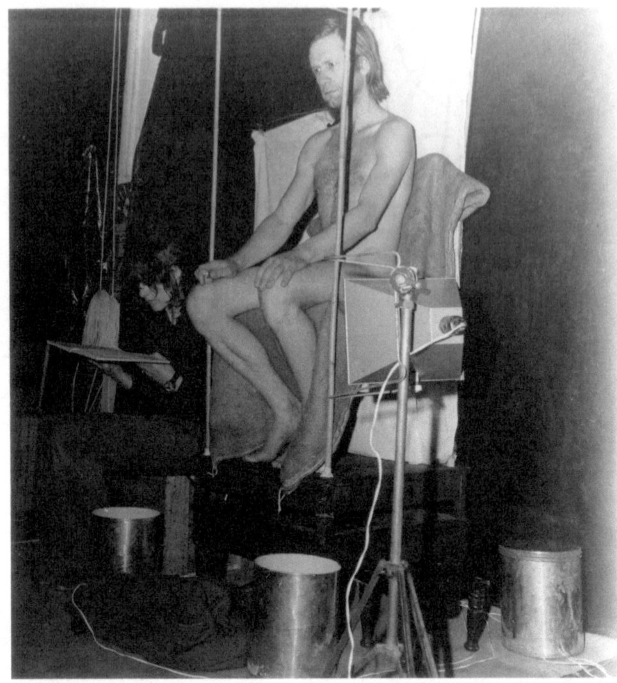

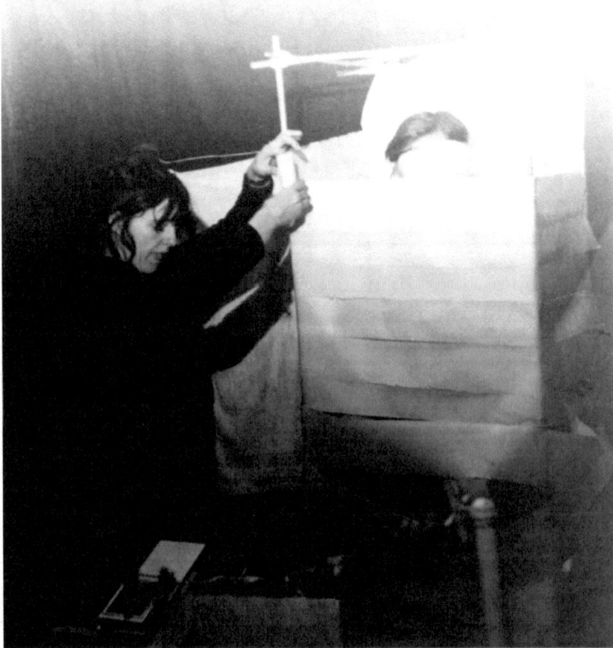

Figure 2.2 EXIT performance featuring Vaucher and Rimbaud, *Wrap Piece*, Museum of Modern Art, Oxford, 1973, photo

experimental artist, Anthony McCall, who was similarly immersed in FLUXUS culture through his friends and colleagues, as well as his partner, the feminist conceptual artist Carolee Schneemann.[44] Vaucher and Rimbaud had helped McCall find the location at North Weald airfield near Dial House for his performance piece for ICES, *Landscape for Fire*. Vaucher comments, 'He needed people to be able to do what he did, which at the time was burning petrol [laughs] which would be outrageous to do now.'[45]

FLUXUS were at the vanguard of a movement that rejected the gallery as the ideal space for presenting art, and this emphasis on collaborative work outside the control of the art world also characterised EXIT and other radical art collectives who pushed performance to extremes during the 1970s. One such outfit was COUM Transmissions (UK, 1969–76),[46] whose members included Genesis P-Orridge and Cosey Fanni Tutti. P'Orridge had formerly lived as part of the Transmedia Commune in Islington (London), which evolved from the Exploding Galaxy. He was particularly influenced by one of the founders of the group, the kinetic artist, Gerald Fitzgerald, and their focus on de-conditioning influenced the approach of COUM, Throbbing Gristle (which featured COUM members Fanni Tutti, Peter 'Sleazy' Christopherson and Chris Carter) and Psychic TV.[47] COUM was also influenced by Dada and, similarly to EXIT, challenged and undermined social values and norms.

COUM's emphasis on sexual transgression and subjective revolution differentiated them from the projects concerned with social change that Vaucher and Rimbaud were involved with; not least that of Dial House itself, which modelled self-sufficient communality. There also seem to have been predatory, exploitative and misogynistic elements to COUM and subsequent outfits that were not evident at Dial House.[48] Vaucher herself had little time for COUM's attempts to make a connection. As she recalls dismissively, 'They used to send artwork to me all the time. I hated it and burnt it.'[49]

Vaucher claims not to have fully grasped the concepts that Rimbaud derived for EXIT, which would often include theoretical ideas derived from Situationism and the like. She was instead inspired by street theatre and describes bringing the confronting aspect of this to performances. She enjoyed what she describes as people coming together to express something in a different way.[50] Among other projects she worked on with Rimbaud, in 1972–73 she created illustrations for a set of fifty poems he had written, entitled *Acts of Love*. These were assembled in an LP case, with no record in it. Vaucher recalls, 'It looked like there would be, but the idea was that if you pulled it out of a record collection to play, you would have to perform it yourself.'[51] The set would later be published when, in the aftermath of Crass, Rimbaud set the poems for music in 1984 (see Chapter 7, Figure 7.1).

On the surface it may look as if Rimbaud dominated their collaborative projects, with her often embellishing or responding to his ideas rather than initiating them, but to see Vaucher as somehow undermined by Rimbaud would be wrong. Rimbaud was uncomfortable with being ascribed guru status by the hippies who stayed at Dial House and, as such, Vaucher provided a much-needed counterbalance. She was unimpressed by the pretentiousness of the hippie scene and refrained from becoming involved in many of their conversations.[52] But she regularly challenged Rimbaud's intellectualism, arguing that images were more powerful than words; something he says he admires about her.[53]

As the 1970s progressed, darker forces at work within and against the counterculture became more apparent. The most obvious one related to problems of excess. On the issue of drugs and alcohol, Vaucher notes, 'I think it has a long-term corrosive effect and it just slows you down. "Chill out man". Yeah, chill out for too long, you get nothing done. Your life's just drifted by, which is fine if people are happy with that, it's fine. I just think it's a shame; so much potential lost.'[54]

Vaucher's experience of the damage done to individuals and its curtailment of their potential to create an alternative society created a 'lifelong dislike of the whole cornucopia of drugs'. From the very inception of Dial House, drugs were banned.[55] While this was seen as draconian by some, it was believed by others, including Vaucher, to be necessary to avoid the pitfalls experienced by other alternative communities. It is also the case that drugs and indecency were the primary means by which the authorities sought to undermine alternate communities. There was the high-profile drugs bust and sentencing of Rolling Stones members Mick Jagger and Keith Richards in 1967, following the *News of the World* expose. There were police raids on the underground press and trumped-up obscenity charges that descended into farce (the *Oz* Schoolkids trial, 1970, being a case in point). These raids were seen at the time as an orchestrated attack on the counterculture.[56] The headline of *Black Dwarf* (Front Cover, Vol 4, No 17) from 1969 declared,

> What a Bloody Nerve: Five free papers have been threatened by the police. 02: Six thousand copies burned. IT: office raided, private documents removed. Rolling Stone: gallery proofs examined. Black Dimensions: office raided, charges pending. Black Dwarf: three visits by Scotland Yard, threats of criminal libel.

Likewise, individuals involved in the counterculture and radical politics became the target of increasingly hostile forces. High-profile cases included the Mangrove Trial (1970), where Special Branch and the Home Office tried to undermine black radicals by falsely accusing them of running a drugs den.[57] The rise of the Bomb Squad coincided with the targeted criminalisation of the counterculture and led to a string of false convictions that were later overturned.[58]

Vaucher suggests that in the USA something even more sinister was afoot. 'Obviously, in the States it got crushed so badly by heavy drugs, which it's now known were fed into the system so that it would break it down … In the beginning it was always cannabis and marijuana. It was marijuana culture. Not like in the end, it was heavy, destructive drugs.'[59]

The movement in the States was also undermined by the Manson Murders and killing at Altamont (1969), both of which signalled the end of the hippie dream. But the rising hostility from the authorities towards the counterculture in Britain during the 1970s was to prove pivotal to the political and creative direction that Vaucher took.

Running alongside this shift in the counterculture was the development of the free festivals movement, and it was here that the anarcho-pacifist ideas that had gained ground during the 1950s and 1960s would make a decisive impact. Influential figures in the free festival scene had come from anarchist factions within the peace movement. For example, the controversial figure, Sid Rawle, aka Sidney William (1945–2010), had a background in the London squatting scene, and was a campaigner for peace and land rights, notably through his involvement with Hyde Park Diggers/Digger Action Movement.[60] Similarly, Bill 'Ubi' Dwyer, who also lived in London communes, was involved with Freedom Press and its associated *Anarchy* magazine, and organised the Acid symposium at Conway Hall (London) in 1971. In the wake of the inadvertently free festivals on the Isle of Wight and Phun City, Dwyer and Rawle among others had organised the Windsor Free Festival (1972), which went largely unnoticed. When it was staged again the following year, however, somewhere between 10,000 and 20,000 people attended.[61] Vaucher talks of how inspiring the event was, and as a result what a threat it was seen as by the authorities. This resulted in the violent suppression of the festival in 1974, after which Dwyer and Rawle were imprisoned to prevent its organisation in 1975. It was also around this time that the police began their controversial undercover operation, STUFF (stop the unlawful free festivals).[62]

It was in this context that Vaucher and Rimbaud would make their own contribution to the movement. In 1974, inspired by their friend Phil Russell (known in the scene as Wally Hope), Dial House functioned as a base for planning the first free festival at Stonehenge. The impetus behind the festival was a perceived need to prevent the deterioration of festivals through State management and commercialisation.[63]

Vaucher helped to make and print flyers for Stonehenge, including one that features drawings of pyramids and standing stones on either side of a picture of the Turin Shroud (see Figure 2.3). It also includes a well-known poem by e e cummings (1894–1962) and a reproduction of a photograph (photographer unknown) of Russell (aka Hope) talking about his vision for Stonehenge at Windsor Free Peoples Festival in 1973.[64] The reverse of the flyer includes imagery associating Stonehenge with Native American and Inuit dwellings, an incantation to the Buddha Amitabha, and Russell's well-known quote … 'EVERYBODY'S WALLY! EVERY DAY IS SUN DAY!'[65] This mantra was born when festival-goers all decided to answer to the name of a dog, Wally, who had gone missing years before at the Isle of Wight festival. The

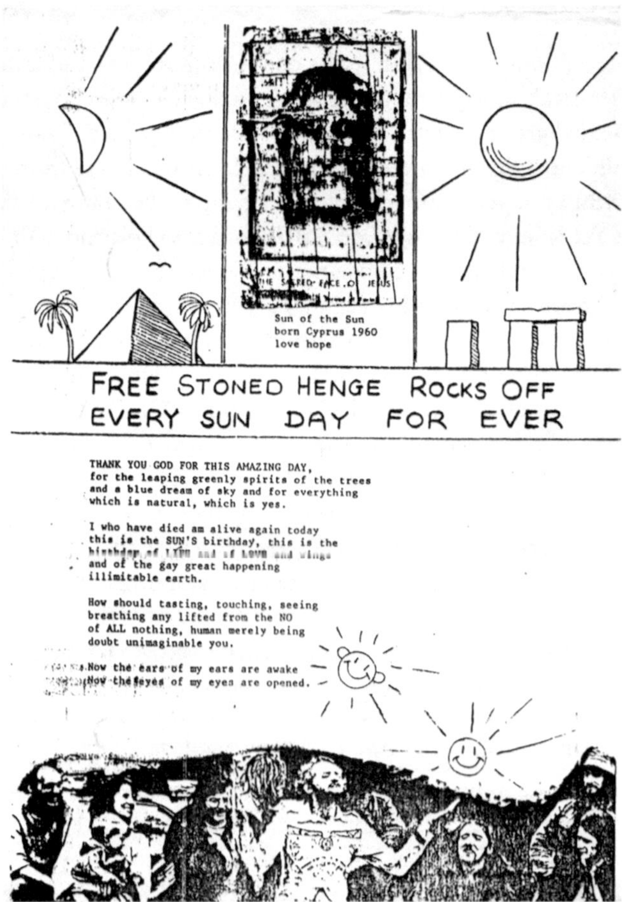

Figure 2.3   Stonehenge Flyer, front, 1974

adoption of the name Wally en masse was also a tactic, so that everyone, and hence no specific individual, would be held responsible for any activities deemed problematic by the authorities.[66] It also alludes to the idea that freedom comes from individuals all playing their part, with no hierarchy of leaders and followers. As such it can be seen as a precursor to Crass' iconic mantra, 'There is No Authority but Yourself'.

Vaucher had a mixed impression of Russell, noting, 'Pen I think found Wally very inspirational and I knew why, but I found Phil sexist. That was not unusual for the times, but I had a slight problem with that. Even so, he was a good guy, even if he hadn't come to terms with a certain area of understanding, i.e. women. But his heart was in the right place.'[67]

Russell's vision would prove inspirational to the scene that grew out of the first Stonehenge Festival, evolving from its hippie roots to incorporate young punks, who often lived in squats in cities, and in turn became what the media termed New Age Travellers in the 1980s. This movement culminated with the police assault on travellers, directed by Margaret Thatcher's government, at the notorious Battle of the Beanfield (1985).[68] Russell himself, however, would not live to see this come to fruition, and his death in 1975 had a profound effect on Rimbaud and Vaucher. The suspicious nature of his death following incarceration in a psychiatric institution was to play a key role in changing their attitude towards authority.[69]

Russell had first met Vaucher and Rimbaud when he came to visit Dial House with some friends from nearby Ongar, where he lived with Frank and Sylvia Hatfield. Russell's father had died when he was a child, and the Hatfields (two doctors) had been appointed by his official guardian, the BBC newsreader John Snagge, to oversee his care after his mother left for overseas. As Vaucher puts it, 'His mother had a lover who had tried to get rid of Phil. The guy [John Snagge] that understood that the son was in danger had been a friend of his father's. He took this to court. That's when we met him. He had been made a ward of court and taken away from his mother and put in the care of a family in a village close to Dial House.'[70]

After being arrested for possession of LSD following the hugely successful first Stonehenge festival in 1974, Russell was imprisoned and then transferred to Old Manor Hospital (Salisbury), a psychiatric institution. Here, he was indefinitely sectioned and given what was colloquially referred to as a 'mental cosh', whereby a patient was dosed so heavily with drugs they were barely conscious.[71]

Russell believed the doctors had excessively sedated him on purpose, telling him he should 'get off cloud nine sonny'.[72] News of his heavy sedation filtered through to Dial House, leading Vaucher to impersonate his sister,

Vanessa, in order to gain access to the hospital. She sat with him in the garden, from where she could tell they were under constant surveillance. She believed that the hospital authorities didn't want people to see how, in the two short weeks Russell had spent there, he'd become dangerously ill. At that point Vaucher and Rimbaud believed they had to get him out and started working on a rescue strategy. They went to great lengths to plan his escape along with a group of friends, enlisting legal advice, which found a loophole in the law on sectioning. However, Russell was too sick and too fearful of recriminations from the authorities to attempt it, so the plan was dropped.[73]

As a result, Russell was still incarcerated when the second Stonehenge Festival happened in 1975. It was a roaring success, or in Rimbaud's words 'everything that he [Russell] would have hoped it to be, except he wasn't there'.[74] Russell was released from hospital shortly after, in a terrible, zombie-like condition that was believed to be chronic dyskinesia, brought on by the excessive intake of the anti-psychotic drug Largactil.[75] Vaucher recalls, 'Finally he made his way back here [Dial House]. I do remember taking him by the arm and marching him up and down the garden to try and get his limbs to work, his arms to swing'.[76] They looked after Russell, giving him homeopathic remedies to try to counteract the impact of his medication.[77] Russell then turned up at the newly formed Watchfield Festival (September 1975) telling a friend, 'they've broken me'.[78] John Hoppy Hopkins (editor of *International Times*) and Sue Hall conducted the only known video interview with him at the festival, which reveals that despite his ordeal he was still committed to the free festivals movement and planning how to facilitate it.

He was two years away from his 30th birthday when he would inherit a considerable sum of money and land, but four days after the Watchfield festival he was found dead, having choked on his own vomit at the house of the Hatfields. The official verdict, following an inquiry which was postponed three times, was suicide, although this did nothing to dispel suspicions of foul play. As his guardian, Snagge, put it in the aftermath, 'All I can tell you is that an autopsy was held and there is no question of suicide.'[79] Rimbaud later noted, 'The court passed a verdict of suicide with no reference at all to the appalling treatment that had been the direct cause of it. Our inquiries convinced us that what had happened was not an accident. The state had intended to destroy Wally's spirit, if not his life, because he was a threat, a fearless threat who they hoped they could destroy without much risk of embarrassment.'[80]

Vaucher similarly believes that Russell's involvement with Stonehenge, combined with his naivety, as evidenced by him making a mockery of the authorities during a court appearance along with various other 'Wallies', meant he was seen unjustly as a threat.[81] However, she also recognises that the people involved in the movement were unaware of what they were up against. She notes,

> We didn't know the power of the State like we do now … The enquiries we were making and the answers we were getting were frightening. You know, we backed off. I wouldn't back off if it was now. But we were young and it was a bit too much to take on. There were a lot of things happening around here that just felt heavy and really weird, directed from the state and I think we pulled back.[82]

Vaucher is here referring to police she spotted surveying Dial House. She says, 'Police used to cruise by all the time. But you couldn't go anywhere. It's a dead end!'[83] Vaucher supported Rimbaud in the aftermath of this episode, when he became depressed and was drinking heavily.[84] During this period, he started work on a book about their experiences entitled *Homage to Catatonia*. The three illustrations that Vaucher created for it all feature claustrophobic interiors. Rather than representing the psychiatric institution in which Russell was incarcerated, these stifling interiors represent his family, and as such reflect one of Vaucher's recurring themes of familial oppression and its relationship to a pervasive violence in civilised society.[85]

In the first image in the series, Russell is depicted (as his nickname Hope suggests) as a boy bathed in light. His mother is the female figure depicted leaving the claustrophobic setting, while a male figure, representing Russell's stepfather, picks up the skipping rope (see Figure 2.4). Vaucher commented, 'This is the claustrophobia of being locked into this whole family, a rich ghetto family, and the child is under threat.'[86]

This whole affair encapsulates Vaucher's preoccupation with the idea that rather than providing sanctuary and support, the family can foster an environment that is corrosive for a child. Such ideas resonate with those espoused by R. D. Laing, which she had found so inspiring. In fact, the whole episode with Russell makes Laing's critique of destructive psychiatric treatment especially pertinent. While stationed at the British Army Psychiatric Unit at Netley (near Southampton) for his national service, Laing was disturbed by the routine use of treatments such as ECT and lobotomies to treat patients, observing that these seemed to be 'ways of destroying people and driving people crazy', rather than their professed purpose to treat and cure if possible.[87] While subsequently based at Glasgow's Gartnavel Royal Mental Hospital in the mid-1950s Laing had set up the Rumpus Room, where particularly disturbed patients were placed in pleasant surroundings and treated humanely by staff. This largely successful experiment became the basis for his book, *The Divided Self: An Existential Study in Sanity and Madness* (1960). Laing's radical approach

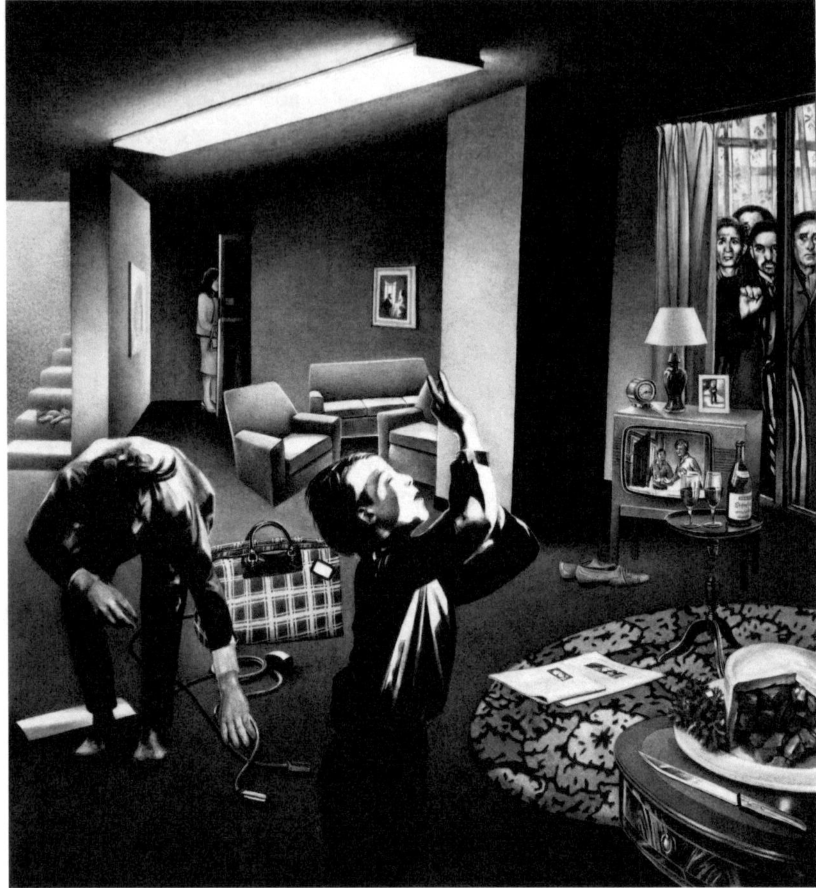

Figure 2.4   Gee Vaucher, *A Homage to Catatonia*, 1975, gouache, 180mm × 170mm

has drawn significant criticism from some quarters, while being hailed as visionary in others, in particular paving the way for patient-centred mental health treatment.[88] His ideas resonate with Vaucher's stress on practising personal autonomy rather than entrusting your wellbeing to an external institution, which will inevitably be compromised by its position as the dominant body imposing its own value system.

The second illustration in the series (Figure 2.5) continues the narrative of Hope's life. The representation of the ceiling light fixture as an overflowing ashtray reinforces the atmosphere of hedonism that pervades the scene. The illustration depicts Russell's mother returning to the house to find him holding

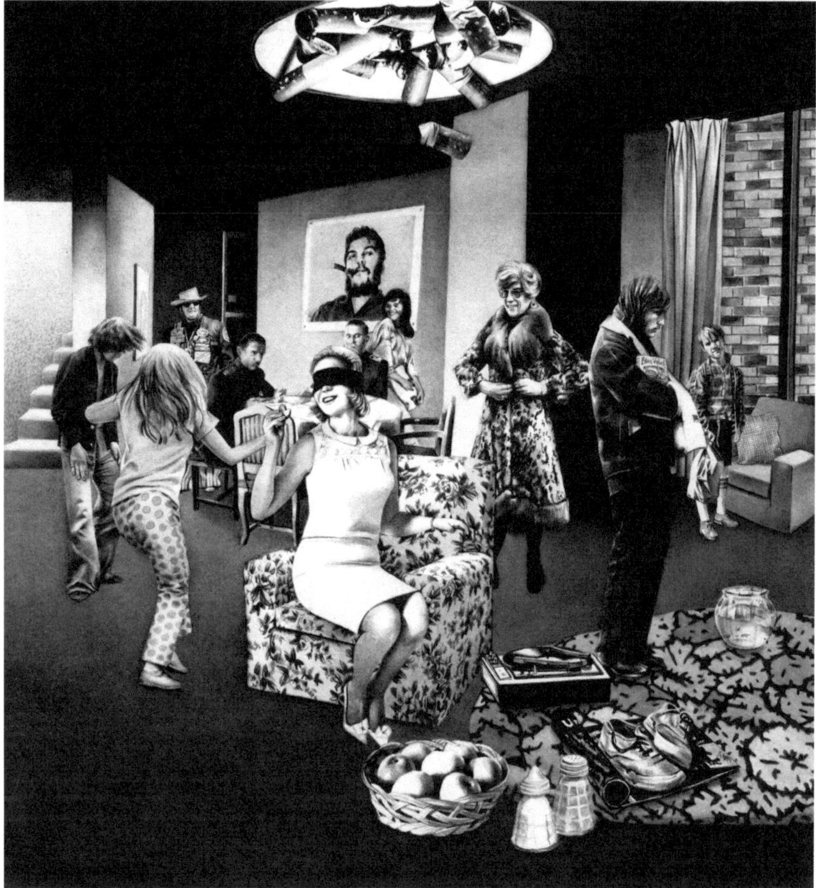

Figure 2.5   Gee Vaucher, *A Homage to Catatonia*, 1975, gouache, 180mm × 170mm

a party. Vaucher comments, 'She realised what had been happening. She had the police called because of the drugs, so I think he was sectioned.'[89]

The third image portrays a dysfunctional familial scene with the father tearing into his meat dinner with gusto while his daughter cries (see Figure 2.6). A placid looking couple watch, seemingly unsettled by the unfolding scene. One figure to the left is distraught, while another one flees the oppressive space through a portal. Vaucher clarifies that this corridor with no way out – again symbolic of their friend's family situation – is in fact a ship turned on its side. As such the illustration can be read at a perpendicular angle, something that viewers tend to miss.

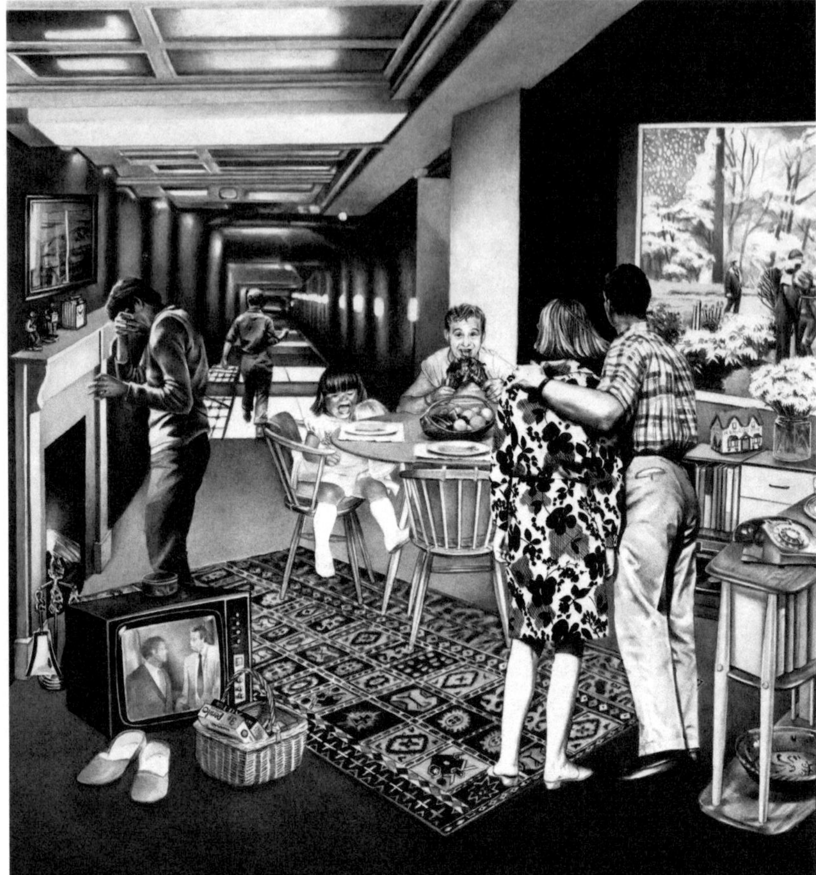

Figure 2.6   Gee Vaucher, *A Homage to Catatonia*, 1975, gouache, 180mm × 170mm

While all three illustrations are focused on Russell's harrowing personal story, they share Pop Art's ironic take on the consumerism of the 1950s and 1960s, sending up societal aspiration and the idealised family unit. However, the pessimistic tone and references to relational breakdown indicate a more cynical mood, reflective of the 1970s as it progressed.

The plan had been to publish the illustrations in Rimbaud's book on the incident, but he ended up destroying all his writing due to his fearfulness about the whole episode. He recalls, 'Over the year when I was working on the book, the place became progressively uninhabited and visitors ceased to come. There was a dark atmosphere. It was not a happy time.'[90]

As well as investigating the Wally Hope incident, Rimbaud had begun to look into the suspicious 'suicide' of another friend from the free festival scene, and had uncovered what he believed to be links between Essex police and Brighton drugs gangs. As well as the ongoing surveillance, he claims he received death threats from the police, and had increasingly dysfunctional interactions with old associates.

Vaucher would eventually publish the Homage to Catatonia images in the first issue of her self-produced publication, *International Anthem*, in 1977, but by this time she was living in New York, far from the increasingly paranoid atmosphere of Dial House. As Rimbaud recalls, 'Gee went off to try out living in America. I was left with her dog and a goat. Basically I was on my own here.'[91] In many ways, it felt as if the dream of Dial House had died. Ultimately, however, it was this episode that set them on a path that culminated in the formation of Crass.

Notes

1   See Jeff Nuttall's (1933–2001) important first-person account of the counterculture, *Bomb Culture* (1968). Nuttall also edited the anarchist publication, *My Own Mag* (1964–67) and contributed articles and cartoons to *International Times* and other underground press publications.

2   Countercultural figures with a background in CND included Jeff Nuttall, David Widgery, Barry Miles, John 'Hoppy' Hopkins and David Zane Mairowitz.

3   J. Nuttall, *Bomb Culture* (London: Paladin, 1968), p. 52.

4   Vaucher in interview with Binns, 2017

5   N. Walter, quoted in B. J. Pauli, 'Pacifism, Nonviolence, and the Reinvention of Anarchist Tactics in the Twentieth Century', *Journal for the Study of Radicalism*, 9:1 (2015), p. 86.

6   Nuttall, *Bomb Culture*, p. 53.

7   Writing in 1962, the British anarchist writer, speaker and activist, Nicholas Hardy Walter (1934–2000), heralded a call to mass direct action. Its purpose was to form part of a wider revolutionary project; or in his words, 'an anarchist insurrection without the violence' (from *Damned Fools in Utopia*, by Nicholas Walter, quoted in Pauli, 'Pacifism, Nonviolence', p. 86.

8   Pauli, 'Pacifism, Nonviolence', p. 85 with reference to Nicholas Walter's concept that large numbers of people engaged in civil disobedience through the C100 could undermine the functioning of the State.

9   The Vietnam Solidarity Campaign planned the demonstrations, which were organised around the International Socialists, which later became the Socialist Workers Party, in N. Fountain, *Underground: The London Alternative Press, 1966–74* (London/New York: Routledge, 1988), p. 60.

10 *The New Left Review* (edited by Perry Anderson from 1962) fostered a new student militancy that thrived on British university campuses from around 1967.

11 Radical political organisations that did not exclude violence included *The Weather Underground Organisation* (1969), known as The Weathermen, *The Black Panther Party*, 1966–82, *Black Mask* (1966) and *Up Against the Wall Mother Fucker* (1968) in the States, *The Angry Brigade* (1967–) in Britain and the *Red Army Faction (RAF)*, 1970–98 in West Germany.

12 See J. D, Taylor, 'The Party's Over? The Angry Brigade, the Counterculture and the British New Left, 1967–72', *The Historical Journal*, 58:3 (2015), p. 894 for an account of how the press contributed to a climate of fear over terrorism throughout the 1970s.

13 Voter turnout dropped marginally from 80.5% (1950s), to 76.45% (1960s). See www.electoralcommission.org.uk/ (accessed 21 June 2021).

14 Vaucher in interview with Binns, 2017.

15 P. Marshall, *Demanding the Impossible: A History of Anarchism* (London: Harper Perennial, 2007), p. 307.

16 Marshall, *Demanding the Impossible*, p. 307.

17 *The Society of the Spectacle* by Guy Debord was translated into English by Fredy Perlman et al. in 1970 (Detroit: Black and Red) while *The Revolution of Everyday Life* by Raoul Vaneigem was translated by John Fullerton and Paul Sieveking in 1972 (Practical Paradise). The collection of Situationist writing, *Leaving the 20th Century*, edited by Chris Grey, who had himself been a member of the SI, was published by Free Fall Publications (London) in 1974.

18 After 1999, *Black Flag* was produced occasionally until 2006. Since then, it has been produced annually.

19 *Direct Action* has had three eras: 1970–1978/79, 1984–87/88 (Direct Action Movement, Manchester) and 1996–present (Solidarity Federation).

20 Vaucher in interview with Binns, 2017.

21 This position was prominent in Raoul Vaneigem's influential book, *The Revolution of Everyday Life* (Traité de savoir-vivre à l'usage des jeunes générations) (Paris: Gallimard, 1967).

22 In *Bomb Culture* (1972) Nuttall highlights the lineage between avant-garde movements and the cultural underground of the 1960s. See also S. Plant, *The Most Radical Gesture: The Situationist International in a Postmodern Age* (London: Routledge, 1992).

23 E. Goldman, *Anarchism and Other Essays* (Auckland: Floating Press, 2008 [originally published in New York: Mother Earth Publishing Association, 1910]), p. 61.

24 See Richard Drinnon's Introduction to *Anarchism and Other Essays*, which was first published as a paperback in 1969.

25 See Goldman, *Anarchism and Other Essays*, p. 230.

26 The theoretical text, *Anti-Oedipus: Capitalism and Schizophrenia* by Gilles Deleuze and Félix Guattari (Paris: Les Éditions de Minuit, 1972), was influential in this respect, marking a decisive break with orthodoxies of Marx and Freud, in favour of libidinal drive as a precursor to revolutionary change.

27 Laing's ideas are set out in his book, *The Politics of the Family and Other Essays*, which was first published in 1969.

28 In particular, see Vaucher's series, *A Week of Knots or The Seven Daily Elements* (2013) which fuses the ideas of *Knots* (Middlesex: Penguin Books, 1973) by R. D. Laing with a series of collaged images by the surrealist artist, Max Ernst, entitled *Une Semaine de Bonte* (1934).

29 See F. Musgrove, *Ecstasy and Holiness: Counterculture and the Open Society* (Norfolk: Cox and Wyman Ltd, 1974), Introduction.

30 Musgrove cites authenticity as the value that was most prized by people within the counterculture. In Musgrove, *Ecstasy and Holiness*, p. 21.

31 Jeff Nuttall, for instance, was raised in a middle-class home and would later become an art teacher. Mick Farren, who edited the underground publication, *International Times* and played in the band, The Deviants, had a grammar school education and was on course for a 'straight' profession in advertising/graphic design (M. Farren, *Give the Anarchist a Cigarette*, London: Pimlico, 2001, p. 11). Richard Neville, editor of the underground publication *Oz*, had a secure and materially comfortable upbringing in Australia and was headed for a career in advertising (R. Neville, *Hippie Hippie Shake*, London: Bloomsbury, 1995), p. 9.

32 P. Rimbaud, 'A Very Private Person' in S. Shukaitis (ed.), *Gee Vaucher: Introspective* (Colchester: Firstsite, published in collaboration with Minor Compositions, 2016), p. 15. Also see R. Binns, 'Freedom, Desire and the Questioning of "isms", in Gee Vaucher's Early Designs (1975–79)' in S. Shukaitis (ed.) (2016), *Gee Vaucher: Introspective* (Colchester: Firstsite, published in collaboration with Minor Compositions, 2016), pp. 44–66.

33 Many of Bookchin's ideas on this subject are set out in his essay, M. Bookchin, 'Ecology and Revolutionary Thought' (1965), in M. Bookchin, *Post Scarcity Anarchism* (Edinburgh/Oakland/West Virginia: AK Press, Working Classics Series, 2004), pp. 19–41.

34 Bookchin, 'Ecology and Revolutionary Thought', pp. 24–25.

35 See S. Shukaitis 'The Door to the Garden: Gee Vaucher and the Cultivation of Artistic Counterculture' in S. Shukaitis (ed.), *Gee Vaucher: Introspective* (Colchester: Firstsite, published in collaboration with Minor Compositions, 2016), p. 14.

36 S. Ignorant, *The Rest is Propaganda* (Norfolk: Dimlo Productions, 2020, 3rd edn), p. 125.

37 Shukaitis, 'Door to the Garden', p. 16.

38 Vaucher in interview with Binns, 2017. Rimbaud notes that Vaucher's private nature is intrinsic to her autonomy in his essay, 'A Very Private Person', pp. 30–44.

39 Vaucher in interview with Binns, 2017.

40 Vaucher in interview with Binns, 2021.

41 P. Rimbaud, *Shibboleth: My Revolting Life* (Edinburgh: AK Press, 1998), p. 57.

42 Rimbaud in interview with Binns, 2021.

43 G. Berger, *The Story of Crass* (Oakland: PM Press, 2009), p. 38.

44 Berger, *The Story of Crass*, p. 33.

45   Vaucher in interview with Binns, 2021.

46   Confirmed by Vaucher in interview with Binns, 2013.

47   S. Ford, *Wreckers of Civilisation: The Story of COUM Transmissions and Throbbing Gristle* (London: Black Dog Publishing, 1999), pp. 112–14.

48   Cosey Fanni Tutti's autobiography, *Art, Sex, Music* (London: Faber & Faber, 2017) highlights the misogynist violence and control freakery she was subjected to by Genesis P-Orridge. The exploitative practices of the cultish wing of the band Psychic TV, The Temple of Psychic Youth that had P-Orridge at its helm is highlighted by Dan Siepmann in 'Unholy Progeny: Psychic TV and Witch House at the Crossroads of Occultism in the Information Age', *Journal of Musicological Research*, 37:1 (2018), pp. 81–104, and 'Groupthink and Other Painful Reflections on Thee Temple ov Psychick Youth', *Popmatters* (27 September 2019). At www.popmatters.com/genesis-p-orridge-groupthink-2640631583.html?rebelltitem=9#rebelltitem9 (accessed 14 July 2020).

49   Vaucher in email conversation, April 2021.

50   Vaucher in interview with Binns, 2017.

51   Vaucher in email conversation, April 2021.

52   Rimbaud, *Shibboleth: My Revolting Life,* pp. 53–54.

53   Rimbaud, *Shibboleth: My Revolting Life,* p. 51. Also see Rimbaud, 'A Very Private Person', pp. 30–44.

54   Vaucher in interview with Binns, 2017.

55   Vaucher in email conversation, April 2021.

56   See Farren's account of raids on *International Times* in 1967 and 1969 in *Give the Anarchist a Cigarette,* p. 109.

57   See R. Bunce and P. Field, 'Mangrove Nine: the court challenge against police racism in Notting Hill', The *Guardian* (9 November 2010). Available from www.theguardian.com/law/2010/nov/29/mangrove-nine-40th-anniversary (accessed 1 September 2017).

58   This is highlighted by Taylor, 'The Party's Over', p. 893.

59   Vaucher in interview with Binns, 2017.

60   Sid Rawle was known and increasingly alienated from the scene for behaving in a sexually predatory way towards young girls. See C. J. Stone, 'Review: Travelling Daze a book about New Age Travellers by Alan Dearling & Friends', *Hub Pages* (16 December 2017). Available at https://hubpages.com/literature/Travelling-Daze (accessed 14 August 2020).

61   G. McKay, 'The Free Festivals and Fairs of Albion', in G. McKay, *Senseless Acts of Beauty: Cultures of Resistance since the 1960s* (London/New York: Verso, 1996), p. 16.

62   See P. Sedazzari, *Everyone's Wally* (2015), which estimates that STUFF began then, although the exact date is unknown due to official secrecy. See See E. Laxton and M. Pritchard, *Busted* (1978) for ex-undercover policeman, Martin Pritchard's insider account of STUFF.

63 See McKay, 'Festivals and Fairs of Albion' pp. 11–45 for an account of free festivals in Britain during the 1970s, which he argues provided a continuum with 'cultures of resistance' during the preceding and subsequent decades. In *When the Lights Went Out: Britain in the 1970s* (London: Faber and Faber, 2009), pp. 248–253, Andy Beckett describes attempts made by the Conservative MP, Mark Woodnutt, and eight other Tory MPs to bring in legislation that would prevent festivals.

64 W. Dean, 'Free Stoned Henge Rocks Off', *Wally Hope's blogspot* (8 June 2011). Available at http://wallyhopes.blogspot.com/2011/06/free-stoned-henge-rocks-off.html (accessed 12 June 2021).

65 Dean, 'Free Stoned Henge Rocks Off'.

66 Sedazzari, *Everyone's Wally* (2015).

67 Vaucher in interview with Groß, 2002.

68 See A. Worthington, *The Battle of the Beanfield* (Berwickshire: Enabler Publications, 2013) for an authoritative and in-depth account of this traumatic event, its background and the aftermath.

69 Rimbaud recounts his anger and distrust following the death of Wally in *Shibboleth: My Revolting Life*, p. 67. Vaucher recalls her side of the story in interview with Sedazzari, 2015.

70 Vaucher in interview with Binns, 2017.

71 See N. Goodwin, 'Wally Hope – A Victim of Ignorance', *Squall*, Issue 11 (Autumn, 1995), 28. Available at https://squallmagazine.com/f/f11–28-wally-hope.html?fbclid=IwAR3xMOtqquwAZU0yH3h9Aojw5rEKtHXbpX6r6zkjy9_YeJ-2DuXODgL6AI0 (accessed 4 August 2020).

The film, *Everyone's Wally*, discloses the form that Russell filled in that complained to the National Council of Civil Liberties (NCCL) about the seriously excessive use of drugs being used for his sedation.

72 Reported in Sedazzari, *Everyone's Wally*.

73 Rimbaud in Sedazzari, *Everyone's Wally*. Also see Vaucher in interview with Paolo Sedazzari, 2015.

74 Rimbaud in Sedazzari, *Everyone's Wally*.

75 Reported in Sedazzari, *Everyone's Wally*. In his article, 'Wally Hope – A Victim of Ignorance', Goodwin also notes that an independent doctor recognised Russell's condition to be chronic dyskinesia following his release from the hospital.

Rimbaud in Sedazzari, *Everyone's Wally*.

76 Vaucher in Sedazzari, *Everyone's Wally*.

77 Wally Dean (aka Dean Phillips), in telephone conversation with Binns, July 2020.

78 Mary Guyver in Sedazzari, *Everyone's Wally*. While the ban on the free festival at Windsor remained, in 1975, Roy Jenkins of the new Labour government (1974) provided a site for the festival at Watchfield (Oxfordshire).

79 This quote from John Snagge appears in newspaper articles, 'Cult Leader Wally Dead', The *Guardian* (2 October 1975) and 'Leader of Stonehenge Wallies Dead', The *Daily Telegraph* (2 October 1975). In the film *Everyone's Wally* (Sedazzari).

80 P. Rimbaud, *Last of the Hippies: An Hysterical Romance* (Oakland: PM Press, 2015), p. 88. This text was included as part of the album packaging for the Crass album, *Christ the Album* (1982). Rimbaud also covers the episode with Russell [aka Hope] in his book, *Shibboleth: My Revolting Life*, pp. 64–69. For an account of Crass members' involvement with Wally Hope and his influence on the free festivals movement, also see Berger, *The Story of Crass*, pp. 42–55.

81 Vaucher in interview with Sedazzari, 2015.

82 Vaucher in interview with Sedazzari, 2015.

83 Vaucher in interview with Sedazzari, 2015.

84 Wally Dean (aka Dean Phillips), in telephone conversation with Binns, July 2020.

85 All confirmed by Vaucher in interview with Binns, 2017.

86 Vaucher in interview with Binns, 2017.

87 D. Kynaston, *Family Britain: 1951–57* (London: Bloomsbury Publishing Plc, 2009), p. 97.

88 M. Paton, 'R.D. Laing: Was the Counterculture's Favourite Psychiatrist a Dangerous Renegade or a True Visionary?' *Independent* (30 November 2015). Available at www.independent.co.uk/life-style/health-and-families/rd-laing-was-the-counterculture-s-favourite-psychiatrist-a-dangerous-renegade-or-a-true-visionary-a6755021.html (accessed 28 March 2021).

89 Vaucher in interview with Binns, 2017.

90 Rimbaud in interview with Binns, 2021.

91 Rimbaud in interview with Binns, 2021.

New York, political photomontage and the underground press

Throughout the late 1960s and early 1970s, Vaucher lived communally at Dial House, working with Rimbaud and various others on a number of collaborative art projects and becoming involved in the free festivals movement. It was also during this period that she undertook her first work as a commercial illustrator. She and Rimbaud created book covers and illustrations for children's books, for the publisher White Lion Press. Rimbaud recalls, 'The guy who ran it was a friend of my brother's and my brother suggested to him that Gee might be interested in that kind of work, which she was.' One of their joint designs was for a reprint of *Mystery of the Blue Tomatoes* by Jennie Hawthorne. Inspired by Jasper Johns, it featured the distinctive circle and stencil lettering that would later become the blueprint for the Crass Records singles design. Another future member of Crass, Bronwen Jones (or Eve Libertine as she would later be known), also did some work for the publisher, and Rimbaud attests that 'it was our bread and butter for four or five years'.[1] Towards the end of this period, Vaucher was commissioned to produce the artwork for a children's book, *Ace of Diamonds* (1974). Here her nascent design language, featuring closely observed human and animal behaviour and interaction, can be observed (see Figure 3.1).

While these images incorporate surreal elements, they are grounded in a social-realist observation of everyday life, here centred on New York street scenes. In the end the publisher rejected the series, commissioning another, more cartoonish, set of images from another illustrator (Mike Jupp).

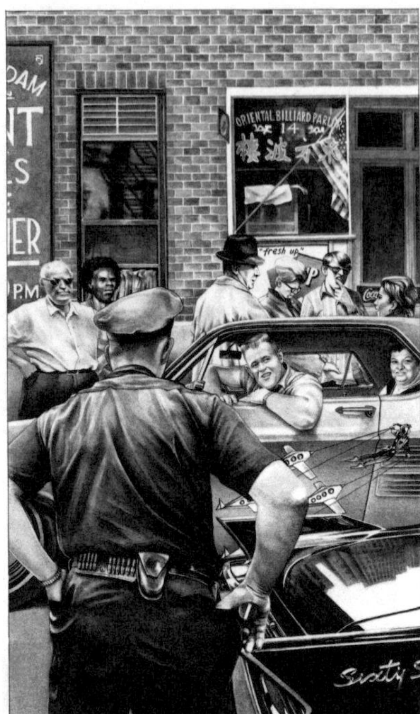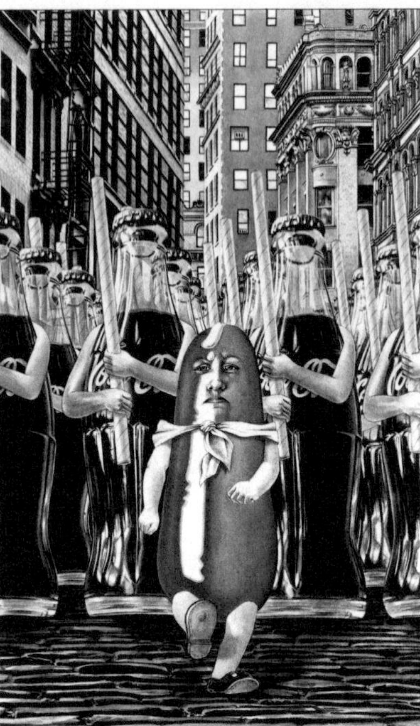

Figure 3.1   Gee Vaucher, Illustration for *Ace of Diamonds*, 1974, gouache, 210mm ×
130mm

Her next foray into commercial illustration work involved a dramatic life
change. She had become increasingly disillusioned with working for art editors
in the UK, who 'tended to use the illustrator as a tool for their own usually
boring ideas', and decided to move to New York to try working in 'the belly
of the beast'.[2] This also marked the end of what Rimbaud describes as their
'singular relationship'. He comments, 'I have to say I didn't particularly want
her to, because we were in a sort of active relationship at that time and I didn't
really want to see that challenged. At the same time I had to support the idea
in her terms of finding herself, or finding the self she got on so well with in
America, which was denied here.'[3]

The move ultimately played a key role in her finding her voice, both as
an illustrator and independent artist. She comments, 'I needed to find myself
a bit more, away from Dial House, away from – I wouldn't say away from Pen,
but I needed to find myself, my own way. We'd been hanging out together
since we were sixteen, and I'd learnt a lot, but ultimately I was fed up with
doing artwork for magazines and books here in the UK that had no "bite".'[4]

She moved there initially as an old school friend of Rimbaud's, also a good friend of hers, offered her somewhere to stay, but the move lasted longer than she had intended. Despite the city being in dire straits economically, Vaucher found the left-leaning, creative environment liberating, while the cost of living, including rent, was cheap. She decided to try to find work by starting at the top, calling the art editor at the *New York Times* where she fixed up an appointment with ease. She says, 'In those days you actually got to sit down with an art editor and show your portfolio of work; a situation that's denied to aspiring young illustrators today, that's for sure.'[5] She elaborates, 'It was not a 'drop off' situation as it is now. The *New York Times* was in Times Square then, a massive place. It was here that I got my first commission, illustrating a political piece involving a school photo-shoot scandal.'[6] She found that the art editors granted her creative licence, on her terms. From the start, she refused to produce the usual rough sketches (not trusting the editors' imagination), but took away the story, and completed the finished picture before showing anything to them. She adds, 'Somehow it worked.'[7]

Vaucher worked at this time under her birth name Carole, and along with the *New York Times* and *New York Magazine*, created illustrations for a host of publications including *Rolling Stone, Ebony, Crawdaddy* and *High Times*. She covered a range of contemporary social situations and news stories, including controversial topics that sat well with her personal interests. 'Hite Report' (*New York Magazine*, gouache, 1976) for instance featured a woman being interviewed on the telephone about female sexuality in relation to the incendiary research conducted by the feminist and sex educator, Shere Hite. Her illustration, 'Creativity on Drugs' that accompanied a book review (*High Times Magazine*, gouache, 1978, 150mm × 160mm) featured Salvador Dalí, Walt Disney, Robert Michum, Quana Parker, Frederico Fellini, John Lennon, Patti Smith and Jackie Chan, all of whom were reputedly on drugs when they did their most famous work. In Disney's case this was his film, Fantasia, which he allegedly created under the influence of peyote. Many of her illustrations explored the social and psychological dynamics of everyday lives (see for instance 'Broken Family' in the *New York Times* and 'Death in the Family' in *EBONY Magazine*, both in gouache, 1978). Vaucher's images illustrated the subject being reported, while at times sending it up through the use of exaggeration or bringing in discordant features. In this way, she used humour to expose inconsistencies in the subject or in its representation. Her illustration for a *New York Times* article entitled 'It's English Hospitality – For Friendship and a Fee' commented on the phenomenon of British people hosting tourist parties for Americans, drawing attention to the performative aspect of their roles (see Figure 3.2).

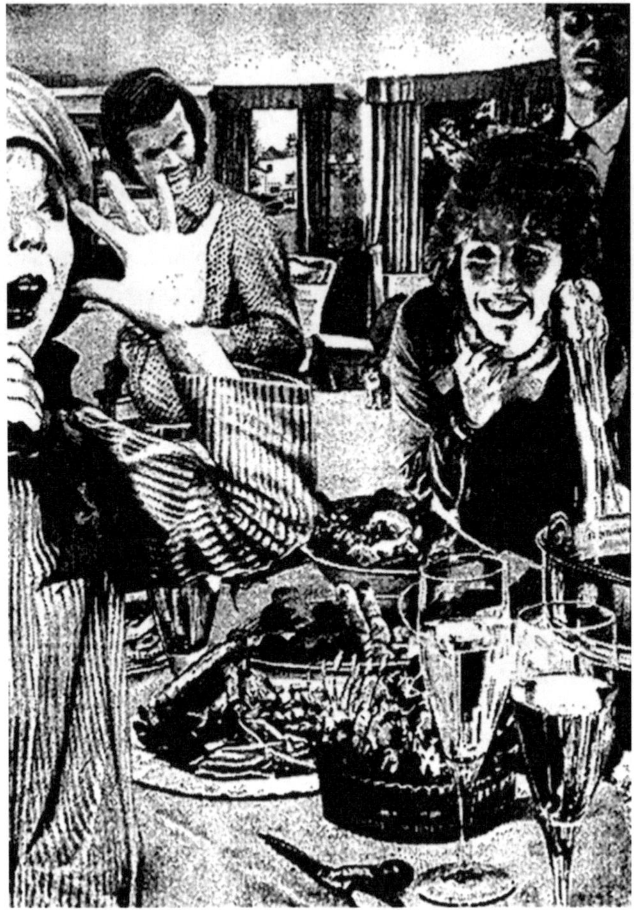

Figure 3.2   Gee Vaucher, 'An impression by Carole Vaucher of a surprise party given American visitors by their English hosts'. Illustration for *New York Times*, 8 June 1977

As such, Vaucher's magazine illustrations shared characteristics with her earlier series *Homage to Catatonia* and *Ace of Diamonds*. They featured the dynamics of human interaction, often set within a claustrophobic environment and commenting on the family unit or social aspiration. The same use of satirical humour and/or irony was used to expose human insincerity, hypocrisy or corruption. Her treatment of seemingly innocuous subjects such as the family, celebrity culture or the music industry were as subject to satire as more serious ones such as Watergate, the Mafia or the Nazi sympathising mass murderer, Freddie Cowan.[8]

With overtly political subjects, her preoccupation was often the abuse of power or corruption. Vaucher notes,

> In New York, I was seen as a political illustrator from the start, so the problem of keeping my own views out of a piece of work became harder as time went on. An article concerning Billy Carter, who was accused of making money off the back of his brother, Jimmy Carter (President at the time), was deemed to be a step too far, so I agreed to remove the offending part. After that I vowed to myself that I would never do any more removing again.[9]

It was also during this period that Vaucher started using collage in her work. Faced with unreachable deadlines, she started adding collage components to her paintings to speed things up (see for example colour insert, Plate 2). As she notes, 'I'd never tried it before as it felt like cheating. Since then I've never stopped collaging.'[10] It is perhaps ironic that it was the pressures of commercial work that had this freeing effect on her process, but the extent to which she embraced this change is plain to see in her output from this time on. She comments, 'Whatever it takes to illustrate what you're trying to say, I'll use it. I'm a plagiarist. I'll use anything – whatever it takes. I mean, all art is plagiarism anyway.'[11]

One notable commission for *Rolling Stone* magazine involved her illustrating a review of a film soundtrack. *Sgt Pepper's Lonely Heart's Club Band* was a misguided attempt by Hollywood to capitalise on The Beatles' legacy (see colour insert, Plate 2). Rather than involving any of the band's members, the film starred the Bee Gees, newly revitalised after embracing disco, and Peter Frampton, whose 1976 album Frampton Comes Alive! had recently become the best-selling live album of all time. The film was poorly received, as was the soundtrack, which featured contemporary covers of tracks from The Beatles' Sgt Pepper (1967) and Abbey Road (1969) albums. Vaucher, along with Rimbaud, had adored The Beatles, and latterly identified the (pre-disco) Bee Gees themselves as symptomatic of the sterility of the pre-punk mid-70s music scene. Added to that very personal connection to the subject matter, the job gave her an opportunity to engage with pop artist Peter Blake's iconic sleeve for the original Sgt Pepper album. While in the original, The Beatles are set back behind a drum kit, nestled into the crowd, here the Bee Gees and Frampton are foregrounded, perhaps reflecting the hubris of the project, and are reminiscent in some way of the presidential statues at Mount Rushmore. They are smiling smugly as they stare out of the picture, but Vaucher has rendered them as wallpaper, with flaps of it peeling away to reveal the emptiness below. She has similarly had fun with Blake's montage, replacing his cast of pop cultural figures with her own. Vaucher's cast includes members of The Beatles,

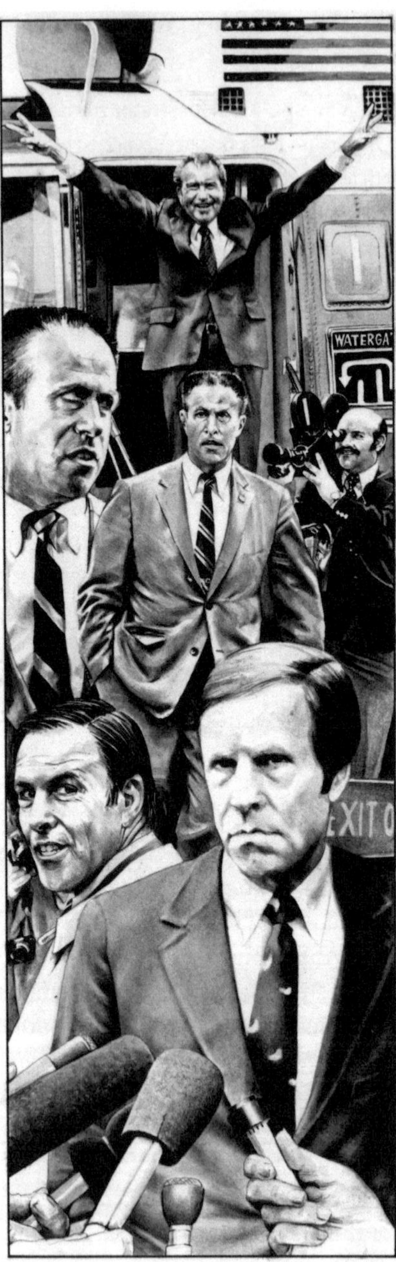

Figure 3.3　Gee Vaucher, Illustration for book review on Watergate, *New York Magazine*, 1977, gouache, 240mm × 80mm

alongside Sophie Loren, Idi Amin, Roman Polanski, James Callaghan, John D. Rockefeller, a woman screaming at the Ohio university shooting, the Queen, a torture victim, Mickey Mouse, Patti Smith (again), John Travolta, George Washington, the Duke of Edinburgh, Gore Vidal, Yves St Laurent, Arnold Schwarzenegger and Mick Jagger, plus an assortment of everyday folk.[12]

The Sgt Pepper project is symptomatic of how she brought her own aesthetic and sensibilities to bear on her commercial work, but it was always an awkward marriage. Even in that context, she was uncompromising in terms of her vision, so when her illustration for a *New York* magazine article entitled 'Attack on Gays – Central Park' (1978) was rejected due to its supposed explicit content, rather than re-working it, she realised it was time to leave commercial illustration work behind.[13]

Alongside her commercial commissions, Vaucher had been working on her own creative projects, the most significant of which was to be her self-produced journal, *International Anthem* (1977–81). She was inspired by the burgeoning punk scene in downtown New York, noting, 'Punk was at CBGB's every night, so when I'd finished a commission I'd just nip round there. It was a great time.'[14] Vaucher describes the scene as exciting and multifarious; pinpointing the radicalism that many felt the hip culture hangover from the former decade had lost. She comments,

> You know, from that particular arena a lot of walls came down for a lot of people and I think that was one of the most important things. Many people from that scene have gone on to do weird and wonderful things that one wouldn't naturally see as 'punk', but to me punk is to do with the spirit, not how you look. To me that spirit was also the most important thing about the hippies – taking control of your life.[15]

She adds that this spirit is about transcending parameters that are internally and externally set, noting, 'I mean, when you start to question yourself, you very soon hit a wall. It can be painful, but with courage it can also be exciting. A vibrant thing that's happening ... finding yourself.'[16] She also observed, 'Later, punk became deeply political in the USA, especially with the Dead Kennedys, Fugazi and other bands. But at that time it wasn't really political. For me it was only notable in Patti Smith's work. In the UK, punk was different. It was about the class struggle.'[17] This was the same year that Crass was founded in the UK, and heralded the rekindling of her creative partnership with Rimbaud, who sent polemical text for inclusion in *International Anthem*. She comments, 'Earning enough money for the first time in New York enabled me to do my own newspaper, something I'd had in mind for a long time as it meant I could make it a vehicle for my own work and the work of people I respected.'[18] In this endeavour she built on the legacy of the underground press, which had sprung up in London during the 1960s, to document and contribute to the emerging counterculture. For the pioneers of the 1960s, creating underground publications had entailed an active choice to foster culture in opposition or as an alternative to dominant society. However, despite the sense of egalitarianism that accompanied the cultural expansion of the time, the underground press was also notably elite; produced by a host of well-connected (often Oxbridge) graduates and successful professionals, intermittently backed by wealthy financiers and supported by celebrities.[19]

Despite these elitist associations, the underground press publications were often produced collaboratively rather than along individualistic lines, with the aim of sharing knowledge, developing ideas and fostering community. Technical advances in printing and cheap production meant that the process was newly accessible to these fledgling publications.[20] They often used cheaper materials, relatively amateur binding techniques, and were printed in monochrome, or with a restricted colour palette, which often resulted in a raw or gritty look. The message conveyed was more important than the production quality. In fact, the publications deliberately rejected the glossy, anodyne aesthetic of mainstream magazines in favour of an original, imaginative or punchy design better suited to what they wanted to express. In these ways, the alternative media being developed at that time was DiY in the sense this term has come to mean, in particular since punk.

In a strategy that would be taken up by Vaucher and her contemporaries, the underground press functioned not to report on reality, but to transform it. Graphic design, illustration work and radical writing all occupied a central role in this endeavour. Graphic design served to undermine official representations through the use of rhetorical techniques such as détournement. These methods were quick and accessible (using a simple method of cut 'n' paste) for artists to use to convey their critique and vision of an alternative world.

Reality was shaped via the alternative media in other ways. Psychedelia, for example, which flourished in the pages of the *San Francisco Oracle* (US) and *Oz* (UK), deliberately flouted design conventions. Art Director Martin Sharp produced psychedelic posters of Bob Dylan and Jimi Hendrix for *Oz*, as well as album graphics and book covers for related bands. His assistant Jonathon Goodchild (who would later take over from Sharp as art director) developed the swirly, amorphous aesthetic that provided the publication with its distinctive style. Mind altering drugs, LSD and marijuana had a profound influence on this aesthetic, as many artists worked under their influence. The observation by William Burroughs that de-conditioning is dependent on the ability to 'turn the word into a useful tool instead of an instrument of control in the hands of a misinformed and misinforming press'[21] summarised the approach of those involved in shaping culture.

While the underground press was concerned with re-shaping reality, the liberation it heralded was principally geared towards white, heterosexual men. The sexual revolution entailed freedom from certain traditional gender constraints and the androgynous appearance of hippies provided one manifestation of this. However, the counterculture and its attendant magazines were also inflected with the discriminatory and pejorative attitudes towards sex and women that prevailed more widely. Prior to second-wave feminism, which only really took hold in Britain in the 1970s, women generally had a subordinated position within the counterculture. As with the supposedly free and subversive avant-garde art movements of the earlier twentieth century, women tended to be relegated to the position of muse, sex object or drudge.[22] Similarly to the *Situationist International*'s use of sexualised representations of women, the underground press often featured images that reiterated the sexual subjugation of women seen in mainstream society, rather than offering anything that constituted an alternative. This was partly due to the preponderance of female rather than male figures, depicted as hippie 'pin-ups' for male viewers, as well as cartoon strips featuring sexual violence against women that risked being celebratory as well as satirical. This was most pronounced in US publications such as *Other Scenes* by comic artists like Robert Crumb, where blatant misogyny was prevalent.

International Times set out to express a liberating voice on all matters, including sex, which were subject to societal ignorance, repression and hypocrisy. To this end, the paper featured 'pretty girls' and pin-ups as a staple component of their output. The 'girls' were presented as unambiguously symbolic of sexual liberation without any awareness these images represented a male, heterosexual ideal of liberation imposed upon women. Similarly, the notorious 'Schoolkids' edition of *Oz* magazine featured material that could be seen as sexually exploitative of underage teenage girls under the guise of challenging repression in mainstream society. It was for reasons such as these that Marsha Rowe, describing the impetus behind the groundbreaking feminist magazine she started in 1972 with Rosie Boycott, stated '*Spare Rib* became a product of the counterculture and a reaction against it'.[23] As such, feminists criticised the liberation that the counterculture heralded for men, often at women's expense, while recognising that it inadvertently spurred the rise of feminism.

Indeed, second-wave feminism in the United States and Europe built on the progressive rhetoric and ideals associated with wider political movements for civil rights and equality, which characterised that era. The women's movement, which took on these tenets, while challenging women's oppression both within

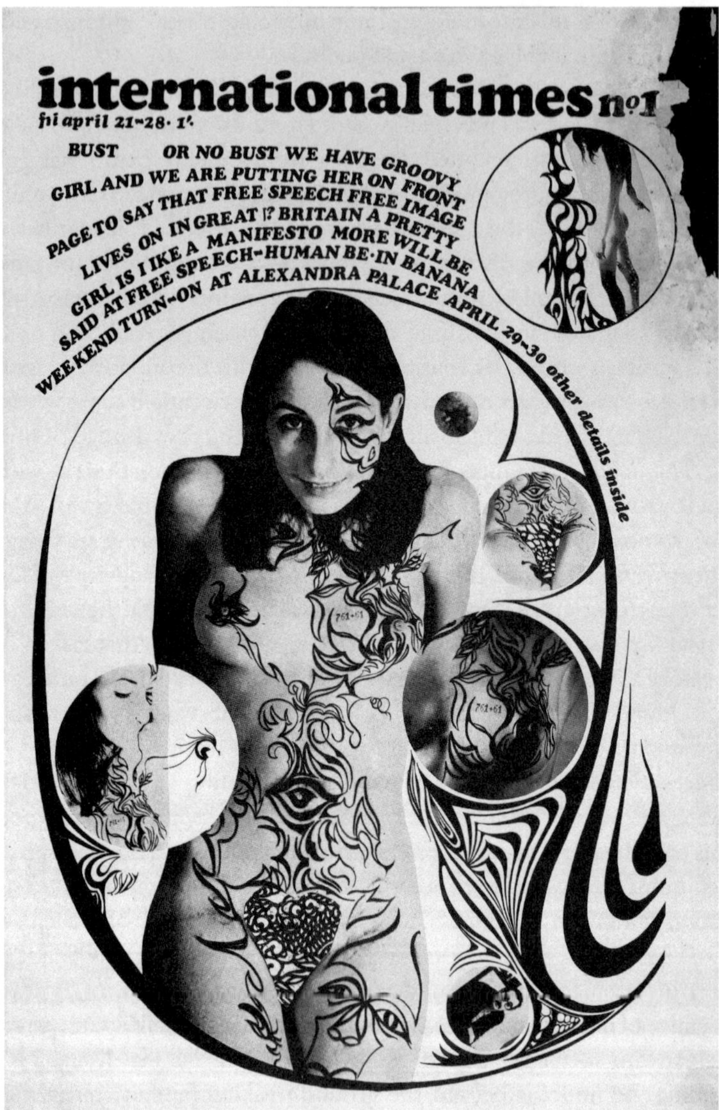

Figure 3.4   Cover, *International Times*, Issue 11, 21 April 1967

radical political and countercultural spaces as well as mainstream society, fed into artistic and cultural milieus during the 1970s. Despite Vaucher not being specifically affiliated with the movement, she nonetheless supported many of its fundamental ideals. During the second half of the 1970s, Vaucher's work became preoccupied with issues of female oppression and exploitation. Indeed, the pin-ups that she created for *Pent-Up* (1975) and *International Anthem* (1977–84) can be seen to provide a riposte to the misrepresentation of female sexuality in men's magazines and the underground press, both of which were granted licence through the sexual revolution of the preceding decade.

Pent-Up (1975) is a play on the title of the men's magazine *Penthouse*, and the series aimed to confront male preconceptions by offering a female point of view (see Plate 3, colour insert).[24] The intention was to publish the images as a facsimile of *Penthouse*, but this proved impossible due to the prohibitive costs of full colour printing. In one striking image, the female figure (see Figure 3.5) appears as an object of desire for the watching crowd, particularly the man with the ice cream (a recurring figure in the series that was based on a photo that she took at a local summer fete). Vaucher's image comments on the ubiquity of the female form when presented as an object of male desire, while simultaneously indicating the opportunities for female sexual agency in such situations. Her pin-up embraces her sexuality, in a self-possessed manner that is at odds with the submissive desire to please the (male) viewer that characterises representations of women in men's magazines (and the underground press). As such, her use of pin-ups is comparable to that of the female Pop Artist Pauline Boty, who celebrated female sexuality, while criticising the imposition of a masculine paradigm for its appreciation. This contrasts with the uncritical redeployment of pin-ups from consumer magazines by Pop Artists such as Richard Hamilton and Peter Blake.

Vaucher's images show female sexuality as a source of freedom and power rather than subordination, as is predominantly the case with pornographic imagery. In Vaucher's words: 'Erotica rouses; pornography sucks.'[25] Accordingly, her pin-ups subvert the construction of female sexuality via a male dominated media. In interview, Vaucher articulates her views on this subject,

> I had a friend; some would say she was a prostitute, she would say she was a high-class escort who had her regular customers. I had another friend who was a dominatrix; she had her regular customers and she ruled the roost. They were both very much in control of what they chose to do and were independent. But I've seen other women who are using their bodies through coercion, desperation and working for pimps. You could say that some were in control because they made that choice. But to me that's not ultimate control; they have chosen to do what they do because they had to, very often this being the last attempt at surviving.[26]

Nonetheless, Vaucher refuses to see these women as victims. She comments, 'These women have chosen this "trade" even though they may hate it, often to keep themselves, and their kids, fed. I see them as really strong because

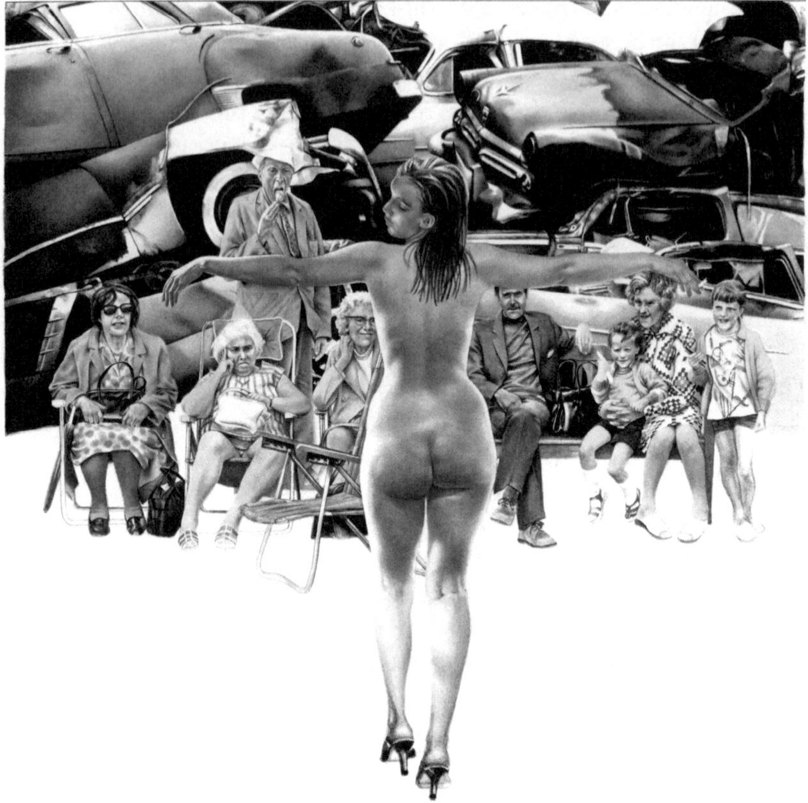

Figure 3.5   Gee Vaucher, Illustration for *Pent-Up* magazine, 1975, gouache (colour), 190mm × 190mm

that choice is in fact a strength to me, not a weakness. There's no "poor soul" there; only the situation.'[27] In this way, she refused to adhere to the anti-pornography line that became prominent within the women's movement towards the end of the 1970s, while not belittling the exploitative reality on which it was hinged.

In this, her work had some parallels with that of overtly feminist artists at the time. In her authoritative account, *Pin-Up Grrrls*, which explores how women have appropriated and reclaimed the pin-up throughout its 150-year history, Maria Elena Buszek points out how the use of the pin-up in the 1970s encapsulated the changing sense of womanhood brought about through feminism's second wave.[28] While some artists' work reflected the essentialist qualities that bound all women together, many were also exploring ways in which 'womanhood' was a social construction. These ideas would become more readily identified through later, third-wave feminism, but clearly mirror Vaucher's perspective. There is no monolithic woman as such, and her pin-ups indicate that such identities are constructed, rather than innate.

The emphasis on gender as the basis for oppression in radical feminism was also alien to Vaucher, who never felt she was defined this way. While she felt strongly that women's voices had historically been repressed, and was proud to be a part of an era in which that was being challenged, she felt no affinity with the idea that men should be excluded from the conversation. She comments, 'Feminism in the seventies wasn't the same as it is now and what I found alienating was one of the chants, "all men are rapists".'[29] She has acknowledged that this may be coloured by the fact that, overall, her experiences with men were positive. She comments,

> I've been flashed at, touched up, but nothing I couldn't handle ... When I was growing up it seemed like every girl was flashed at at least once, it seemed like a rite of passage. I'm not saying it's right, but you would have to find your own way of dealing with it. I've never been raped. I've never been badly groped. I've never been sexually abused by my parents. I didn't have any of that, so I came from another angle of thinking, what must that feel like? What must be the damage caused? I can only imagine it. I can't say that I could ever fully understand the depth of such an experience. I could only observe that for each woman it was different. Some women come to terms with it in a positive way. Some women, you kind of knew, were going to use it as a crutch for the rest of their life and that made me sad and I thought; I don't know how I can help.[30]

Interestingly, despite her reservations about this development within the women's movement, it was at this time that she developed a more intense and polemical stance against the sexual exploitation of women. The cover of *International Anthem 1* (see Figure 1.3) shows an idealised 1950s family unit, with deformed features, above a typeset caption reading '*HISTORY IS HIS STORY. MANSLAUGHTER IS MAN'S LAUGHTER*'. It then opens with a letter seemingly written by someone who has all the markers of societal success. This is juxtaposed with a poem by Rimbaud (which would later form the basis of the Crass song 'End Result'), which slams human consumption, mindless lives and institutionalised violence towards those who don't fit the dominant mould. What follows is Vaucher's image of a female pin-up, bent over, naked in heels, threatening a baby with a hammer, while school children look on (see Figure 3.6).

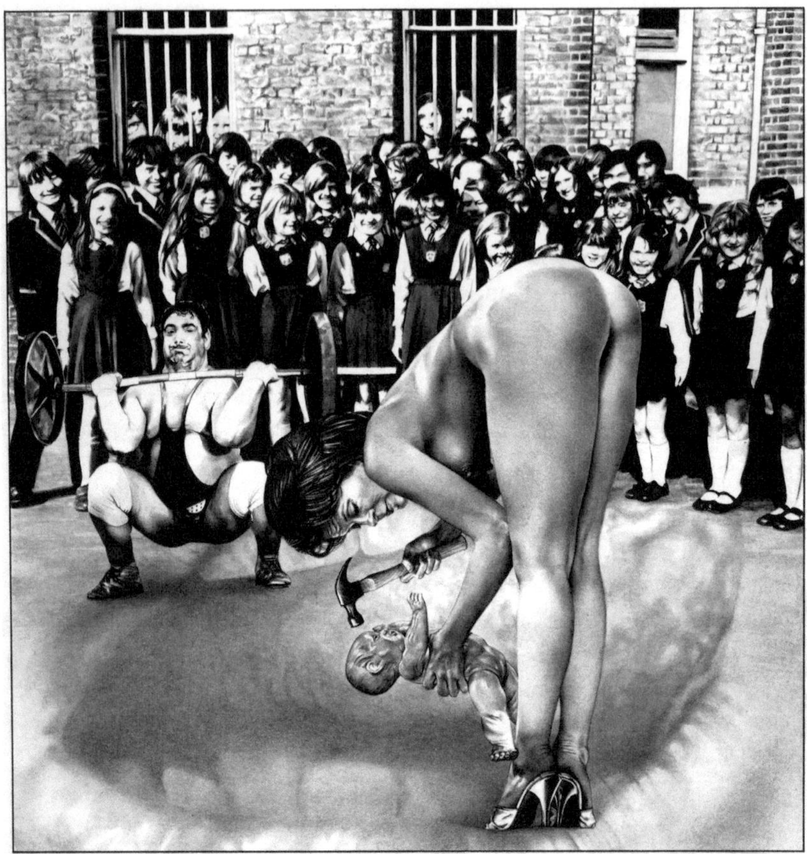

Figure 3.6 Gee Vaucher, Illustration for *International Anthem 1: Education*, 1977, gouache, 210mm × 200mm

This image highlights the frustration inherent to the dichotomous roles of mother and sex object that were often ascribed to women at that time. The face of Vaucher's pin-up registers indifference, at odds with the eagerness to please that characterises their usual presentation in men's magazines. The children's sadistic amusement at her threatening to smash the baby's head with a hammer seems to comment on the cycle of institutionalised violence, extending this concept beyond educational institutions to encompass the family. The faded image of a lascivious mouth appears on the ground, further referencing pornographic culture. It also lampoons the male role model for boys through the inclusion of the strongman caricature. However, this figure is not imbued with the depth, agency or complexity granted to the pin-up.

While Vaucher had started using collage at this time, she still predominantly painted her illustrations. It's testament to the skill of her art process that her work is often assumed to have been created using photomontage and collage techniques even when it's entirely painted. In 2015, for example, Vaucher discovered that her contemporary, Peter Kennard, was presenting her work to classes he taught as Head of Photography at the Royal College of Art as fine examples of photomontage. She met with him at the college and showed him a couple of original pieces. She reports his amused response, 'Ah, my students have been going away from here year after year thinking it's photomontage, and it's not.'[31]

The image of the woman with the baby and a hammer provides a clear example of how easily this misunderstanding can occur, while also showing how her painting process gives her greater control over the representation. Vaucher used a different source for the face of the pin-up to the one used for its body. Due to Vaucher's dexterity as a painter, the figure appears as a single entity, but the result of having used two disparate sources is visually jarring. It conveys messages that are at odds with the usual way the audience receives such strongly coded images. Vaucher's ability to alter the original source in this way is further pronounced with the schoolchildren, whose faces register mocking glee at the act of violence they watch. The effect is at once familiar, in the depiction of a typical group of schoolchildren in the traditional, British educational mould, and yet disconcerting. Vaucher explains,

> You've gone from a group of kids standing in front of you and the photo being taken; to seeing the photo that's been taken of the real kids; to a photo that's been printed in a book; from a book into a painting. So you can see it's like Chinese whispers, it's that slight change all the time. There's also a different reality when a photo is used, maybe it's an official photo for a school magazine; the next time it's used for who knows what, advertisements, the local paper, and so on, the ambiance and quality changes again. If I was to just look at the photo of the kids, it would say something very different to if I saw it reproduced next to a naked figure, an advert for a car, the local jumble sale, or it might have a news item next to it about a murder. Each time it's used in a different context it will say something different to each one of us.[32]

Alongside critiques of societal coercion, women's subordination within patriarchal society, State and militaristic violence, and religious control, *International Anthem 1* also articulates a loosely speaking anarchist-feminist perspective that is intrinsically linked with anti-militarism. Rimbaud writes in one of his lengthy tracts, 'Because society trains its men to be heroes, fools who die in the mud of the trenches, and treats its women as delicate flowers, to be fucked, screwed, abused, raped and ruined, so perverted are the logics, the floor has become a primarily male domain.'[33]

Similarly to Vaucher, Rimbaud uses shock and obscenity in his writing to provoke the reader out of complacency, and make apparent what is disturbing about social conformity. His writing is intense, providing a searing critique of human relations inflected with socially endorsed violence. A collage by Vaucher commenting on the banality of war and State sanctioned violence and its relation to social obedience follows on the next page (see Figure 3.7). It features the famous photograph by Nick Utt (1972) of a naked girl fleeing Napalm bombing in Vietnam juxtaposed with visual references to the Second World War. The image is overlaid with newspaper cuttings featuring negative press coverage of punk, and comments on unruly youth made by Margaret Thatcher (who was then the leader of the opposition to James Callaghan's Labour government). Vaucher's assemblage lambasts 'the establishment' and its media for promoting State violence, carnage and war while misreading and denouncing punk for its supposed violent tendencies. This is presented as a pretext to justify State authoritarianism, and so the cycle continues.

Vaucher's images from this period often evoked the peace movement agit-prop of the preceding decade. During Nixon's administration (1969–74), the protest movement against the Vietnam War made frequent use of photo-montage, reproduced on placards, banners and flyers and displayed at marches and protests. News photographs printed in the popular press were combined with text in ways that undermined or subverted the original message. As such, this graphic material critiqued the media narrative and its ability to influence public opinion as well as protesting against the war itself.

Feminists were at the forefront of the peace movement in the States at this time, and instrumental to forming a critique of patriarchy that linked militarism with misogyny and violence towards children.[34] Martha Rosler's prominent series, *Bringing the War Home* (1966–72) combined reportage photos of the Vietnam War taken from *Life* magazine with images of aspirational American homes, reproduced in *House Beautiful*. Rosler said that photomontage was the ideal medium for her egalitarian message, which was 'pitched against' what she referred to as 'the mythology of everyday life' in which 'all the things that were supposed to be separate from one another actually were not in any way separate but intertwined practices'.[35]

Vaucher similarly juxtaposed images of militarist violence with the petty tyrannies of domesticity, and her illustrations for later issues of *International Anthem* and Crass would critique patriarchal power at a macro and micro scale, from the major institutional level to familial oppression within the home. Rosler was also an early example of a new wave of radical artists who

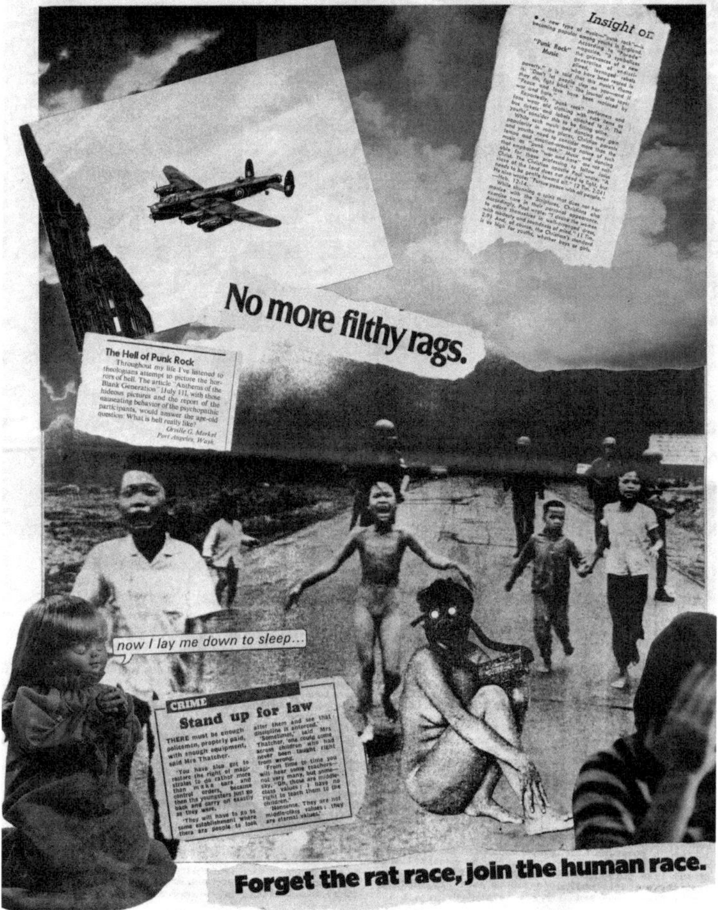

Figure 3.7   Gee Vaucher, Illustration for *International Anthem 1: Education*, 1977, collage

wanted their work to serve some social and/or political purpose as opposed to being displayed as artefacts in a gallery. Rosler said, 'At the time it seemed imperative not to show these works – particularly the anti-war montages – in an art context. To show anti-war agitation in such a setting verged on the obscene, for its site seemed more properly "the street" or the underground press, where such material could help marshal troops and that is where they appeared.'[36]

Rosler and the feminist movement, as well as a range of political artists working in Britain during the 1970s, challenged the falsehoods constructed by the mass media narrative and patriarchal institutions, including art galleries.

The American art critic Lucy Lippard observed that socio-political art flourished more in Britain than the United States because left-wing movements and parties that artists could join or collaborate with were firmly established there at that time.[37]

Richard Hamilton (b. 1920) and his far younger contemporary Peter Kennard (b. 1949) both appropriated material from the mass media, to comment on war and political events as well as their mediation through the press. Both Hamilton and Kennard produced artistic responses to news reports of the fatal shooting of four students by National Guardsmen at Kent State University, Ohio during a campus protest about the invasion of Cambodia by South Vietnamese and US forces in 1970. *Kent State* (1970) by Hamilton is based on a photo the artist took of a television report that shows an injured student at the site of the shootings. Rather than disseminating the work through the exhibition circuit, he issued several thousand prints of the image at low cost to maximise the reach of its politicised message.[38] Kennard also created copies of his image, *Kent State* (1970), featuring one of the dead students, which he flyposted around London to commemorate the victims and to show solidarity with the movement in the States. Such strategies practised by various political artists and activists at that time provided a precedent for Vaucher's practice of flyposting her political designs for Crass later in the decade. In their intention to undermine messages disseminated by powerful institutions, and construct an alternate narrative, such political work can be understood as 'anti-propaganda'. However, while radical artists frequently situated themselves outside mainstream institutions during the 1970s, they often believed there was scope for their reform rather than rejecting them out of hand. Their position was essentially left wing and progressive, which was at odds with the outlook in Dial House, and Crass' political perspective in the 1980s.[39]

The existence of a progressive infrastructure in the UK also meant that left-wing artists could often access State patronage for their endeavours. Vaucher was quite distinct in this respect through working as a commercial illustrator, and then self-funding her more radical work. While she didn't court public patronage, the anarchist ideas her work contained situated her outside the value system that was supported by State institutions at the time. Along similar lines, Rimbaud left his teaching post at art school, shortly after initiating Dial House as an open house, due to his disillusionment with its institutionalising aspects.

Whatever their positioning with regards to mainstream institutions, the work of all these artists had a function in the 'real' as opposed to art world. Similarly to Rosler, Kennard highlighted the way photography was used in the media to mask the interconnectedness of seemingly disparate subjects.

He observed that unlike photography, photomontage could show the terrible connections between things, for example capitalism and the war machine, and outcomes such as children dying needlessly in the developing world for want of medical attention. The power of photomontage was therefore seen as its ability to bring seemingly disparate elements together to create a third meaning.[40]

Vaucher deploys a comparable approach. By combining the image of the napalm attack with reporting that scapegoated rebellious youth (Figure 3.7), she made apparent what was hidden through the collusion between the mainstream media and institutions of 'the system'. Similarly, the juxtaposition of the praying Caucasian doll with Vietnamese children running from a napalm attack highlights the disparity in outcomes between the victims of war and comparatively privileged and protected children in the West. The newspaper caption, 'Forget the rat race, join the human race', encapsulates the theme of humanity that transcends societal stratifications.

What distinguished Vaucher and Kennard was that they would reach mass audiences beyond the art gallery in the late 1970s and 1980s. For Kennard this was via his designs that were displayed on placards, banners and flyers for CND, and for Vaucher this was through her work for Crass. In this they built on the legacy of Rosler and other 1970s radical artists, who were themselves following a precedent set by Dada.

Vaucher's decision to disseminate her artwork in *International Anthem* as opposed to a gallery setting was also mirrored in Kennard's regular contribution of political photomontages to left-wing and underground press publications.[41] In this, their work reflected the approach of the Berlin Dadaist photomontage pioneer John Heartfield, whose work engaged with an audience in Germany (1924–33) via the popular socialist magazine *AIZ*.[42] German Dadaists including Heartfield and Hannah Höch used photomontage and collage with political intent, to advocate communism and pacifism. These photomonteurs rejected the primacy of aesthetics in image making, instead giving priority to meaning. They re-appropriated material from bourgeois culture and political propaganda in order to critique it.

In keeping with later punk designers including Vaucher, Dadaists also utilised shock as a tactic. Heartfield's specific aim was to subvert the dominant ideology being propagated by the Weimar Republic and the Third Reich to reveal the social inequities and class antipathies that mass media propaganda tried to obscure. Within the context of the polarised politics of the 1930s, many avant-garde artists aligned themselves with the left, which advocated for equitable and progressive outcomes. Heartfield took propagandist photographic images and rendered them uncanny through distortion or juxtaposition with new elements. This was particularly effective as a political weapon with his critique of Hitler and National Socialism.

Although Vaucher's work had a clear precedent in the work of male Dadaist artists, the strongest parallels are with the work of their female contemporary, Hannah Höch. Höch's early collage and montage work, produced in the 1920s and 1930s, had a satirical acumen akin to Vaucher's. Höch employed a deliberate process of alienation in her collages, while Vaucher enjoyed reeling the viewer in, only to deliver a shock once they recognised the obscene content they were engaging with.[43] Vaucher and Höch also both operated in overwhelmingly male environments where their contributions were often not recognised. In Vaucher's case, this was to some extent due to the anonymity of her work with Crass and her deliberate avoidance of mainstream exposure. However, there may well also have been sexism at play in her work taking so long to receive the recognition it deserves (see Chapter 7). Höch existed in an exclusively male, Berlin Dada environment that actively excluded her.[44]

Both artists were particularly attuned to patriarchal oppression. Höch's focus was on the gap between the rhetoric and reality of the New Woman promoted in Weimar Germany. She saw a disconnect between the promotion of this liberated figure in the media, where she was shown to assume prominence in the workplace and public life and enjoy sexual freedom, and the reality of women's domestic lives, in which they were overwhelmingly expected to be subservient to the patriarch of the house. This reflected the attitude of male avant-garde artists, who ostensibly stood for freedom and equality between the genders. In practice, however, they overwhelmingly assumed their own role as a 'genius', while assigning all domestic duties and a supportive role to women.[45]

It should however be noted that, as with Vaucher, a retrospective feminist reading of Höch misses the nuance and complexity of her observations. Throughout this book, I argue that Vaucher's illustrations critique patriarchal power, while resisting disempowering women by portraying them as victims because of it. With Höch, it is the reality of the New Woman in Weimar Germany who embodied both freedom and oppression that provided the basis for her comment. This is distinct from a straightforward exposé of gender-based inequality. As Maud Lanvin writes in a thought-provoking essay, 'Höch's montages both celebrate and critique (to different degrees in different works) the myths of the New Woman.'[46]

Both Höch and Vaucher were working at a time of great societal change, and it is perhaps no surprise that interest in the Dadaist photomontage artists of the 1930s was revived during Vaucher's time, with major exhibitions being staged in Britain throughout the 1970s. Prior to this period, the work of the

Dadaists had been sidelined in British art history.[47] Sadly, it took until 2015 for the first major retrospective of Hannah Höch's work to be staged at the Whitechapel Gallery (London), reflecting how important women working in such genres are often the last to receive recognition.

Dada, and Heartfield, in particular, proved highly influential to the politically motivated photomontage work of artists including Peter Kennard and the photographer Jo Spence (1934–92), who used documentary photography to encompass feminist and socialist themes. It also had a significant impact on punk graphics. Heartfield's photomontage, *Hurrah, the butter is all gone!* (1935), was used on the cover of the 7" single, 'Mittageisen (Metal Postcard)', by Siouxsie and the Banshees (Polydor, 1979) and to illustrate Lucy Toothpaste's analysis of the patriarchal basis for fascism in the Rock Against Racism fanzine, *Temporary Hoarding.*[48] His work continued to appear on the covers of work by post-punk, hardcore and new wave bands, but ultimately, it was through the original work of punk designers including Vaucher and her contemporaries Jamie Reid and Linder Sterling that Dadaist strategies found their way into the new milieu of punk.

Notes

1 Rimbaud in interview with Binns, 2021.
2 Vaucher in email correspondence, June 2021.
3 Rimbaud in interview with Binns, 2021.
4 Vaucher in interview with Binns, 2017.
5 Vaucher, panel discussion at Firstsite, Colchester, 1 December 2016.
6 Vaucher in email correspondence, April 2021.
7 Vaucher in email correspondence, April 2021.
8 See Vaucher's Illustration that accompanied an article about a Mafia boss, *New York Magazine* (gouache and collage, 1977), Shooting of Sieff, *New York Magazine* (watercolour and collage, 1976) and Freddie Cowan, *New York Magazine* (watercolour, 1977).
9 Vaucher in email correspondence, April 2021.
10 Vaucher in email corresondence, April 2021.
11 Vaucher in interview with Binns, 2013.
12 Vaucher in email correspondence, Jan. 2021.
13 Vaucher in email correspondence, Dec. 2016.
14 Vaucher in interview with Binns, 2017.
15 Vaucher in interview with Groß, 2002.
16 Vaucher in interview with Groß, 2002.
17 Vaucher in interview with Groß, 2002.
18 Vaucher in interview with Binns, 2017.

19 Cambridge graduates included Ed Victor, who founded *Ink* in 1971; the co-founder of *International Times* (started in 1966), John 'Hoppy' Hopkins and Australians Germaine Greer and Clive James who wrote for *Oz*. Editors and contributors throughout *International Times's* duration were from mixed backgrounds, although they usually had a university education. The production and editorial team at *Black Dwarf* (founded in 1968 by self-made media man, Clive Goodwin) included Oxford graduates Sheila Rowbotham, Dan Jones and Tariq Ali. Later on, Oxford graduate and Cambridge economist Bob Rowthorne (a member of International Socialists who then moved towards the Communist Party) also joined the editorial board. Others on the board (such as David Mercer) had more ordinary backgrounds. *Friends/ Frendz* also featured a range of graduates, including several from Oxford (Jerome Burne, Johnathon Green and various others intermittently).

20 See G. Kaplan, *Power to the People: The Graphic Design of the Radical Press and the Rise of the Counter-culture, 1964–1974* (Chicago: University of Chicago Press, 2013), Introduction, for information on the advances in print technology that made publishing affordable and accessible to a wide demographic during the 1960s.

21 W. Burroughs, 'Academy 21: A Deconditioning', *San Francisco Oracle*, 1:10 (1967), p. 21, referred to in Kaplan, *Power to the People*, p. 81.

22 This was overwhelmingly the case with underground press publications, despite some notable exceptions, including Germaine Greer (*Oz*) and later on Sheila Rowbotham (*Black Dwarf*). See N. Fountain, *Underground: The London Alternative Press, 1966–74* (London/New York: Routledge, 1988), pp. 42–54 for analysis of the roles assigned to women within this milieu.

23 M. Rowe (ed.), *Spare Rib Reader* (London: Penguin, 1982), p. 15.

24 G. Vaucher, *Crass Art and Other Pre Postmodernist Monsters* (Colchester: Firstsite, published in collaboration with Minor Compositions, 2nd edn, 2014), p. 18.

25 Vaucher in email conversation with Binns, April 2021.

26 Vaucher in interview with Binns, 2017.

27 Vaucher in interview with Binns, 2017.

28 M. Buszek, 'Our Bodies/Ourselves: Pin-Ups in the Wake of Women's Liberation', *Pin-Up Grrrls: Feminism, Sexuality and Popular Culture* (Durham, NC: Duke University Press, 2006), pp. 268–311.

29 Vaucher in interview with Binns, 2017. Texts such as *Sexual Politics* by Kate Millett (New York: Doubleday, 1970) and *The Dialectic of Sex: The Case for Feminist Revolution*, by Shulamith Firestone (New York: William Morrow and Company, 1970) helped to move feminism away from its embeddedness within ideas of progressive socialism towards radical feminism with its basis in gender and psychoanalytic interpretations.

30 Vaucher in Interview with Binns, 2017.

31 Vaucher in interview with Binns, 2017.

32 Vaucher in interview with Binns, 2018.

33 P. Rimbaud, *International Anthem 1: Education* (1977), pp. 9–10.

34 One well-known example is the anti-Vietnam war poster entitled *And Babies?* (Art Workers' Coalition, 1970) that combined a famous reportage photo of corpses of

women and children, who were victims of the My Lai massacre, together with red lettering that quoted a news interview between CBS interviewer Mike Wallace and the American soldier Paul Meadlo who participated in the massacre.

35 M. Rosler, 'Place, Position, Power, Politics', in M. Rosler, *Decoys and Disruptions* (Cambridge, MA: MIT Press, 2004), p. 355.

36 Rosler, 'Place, Position, Power, Politics', p. 355.

37 J. A. Walker, *Left Shift: Radical Art in 1970s Britain* (London: Taurus, 2002), p. 9.

38 Walker, *Left Shift*, p. 26.

39 See Walker, *Left Shift*, for a comprehensive account of a movement of radical, left-wing artists and collectives that incorporated a strong political and social consciousness during the 1970s.

40 P. Kennard, *Images for the End of the Century: Photomontage Equations* (London: Journeyman Press, 1990), Afterword.

41 While Vaucher self-published *International Anthem* as a vehicle for her more radical work, Peter Kennard published his political montage work in publications including *Workers' Press* and *International Times*.

42 *Arbeiter-Illustrierte-Zeitung* or *AIZ* (in English, *The Workers Pictorial Newspaper*) was founded in Berlin in 1925 and moved to Prague when Hitler took power in Germany in 1933. In 1936 it changed its name to the *Volks Illustrierte* (*The People's Illustrated*). It collapsed in 1938 shortly before the Nazi invasion of Czechoslovakia.

43 Vaucher, in interview with Binns, 2013. On Höch's strategy of alienation, see D. F. Herrmann, 'The Rebellious Collages of Hannah Höch', in D. Ades, E. Butler and D. F. Herrmann (eds), *Hannah Höch* (London: Whitechapel Gallery and Prestel, 2014), pp. 8–16.

44 In 'Hannah Höch, Dada and the "New Woman"', D. Ades, E. Butler and D. F. Herrmann (eds), *Hannah Höch* (London: Whitechapel Gallery and Prestel, 2014), pp. 22–23, Dawn Ades outlines the exclusion Höch faced, such as lack of exposure in Dada magazines. At the First International Dada Fair she was the only female exhibitor. The artists John Heartfield and George Grosz had opposed her inclusion, but they were overruled.

45 Herrmann covers this issue in relation to the Berlin Dadaists in 'Collages of Hannah Höch', pp. 8–16, while accounts of such behaviour within the Surrealist movement in France, and by the artist Picasso towards the women in his life, are well established.

46 M. Lavin, 'The Mess of History, or the Unclean Hannah Höch', in D. Ades, E. Butler and D. F. Herrmann (eds), *Hannah Höch* (London: Whitechapel Gallery and Prestel, 2014), p. 89.

47 Walker, *Left Shift*, p. 71.

48 L. Toothpaste, 'Sex vs Fascism', in *Temporary Hoarding*, Issue 7 (1979), p. 4.

- 4 -

Towards the definition of a punk aesthetic

While Vaucher was based in New York at the time that she produced the first issue of *International Anthem*, the magazine's content was much more reflective of punk in the UK than its incarnation in the States. She comments,

> I think punk was very British. Some people say it came from America, a certain form of punk did … but what happened here was an incredible response to what was happening in the UK at that time. Politically there was nothing going on. It wasn't bland; it was too serious for that. I just think of it as a very positive reaction to the atmosphere in Britain at that time. [1]

The social and economic context of the UK in the 1970s has often been identified as the source of the nihilism that permeated punk.[2] Rather than inheriting a notion of social progress that enabled movements for freedom and equality to emerge and influence government, first-wave punk allegedly believed there was 'no future'.[3] This dystopian outlook reflected the changing social and political terrain of the 1970s. This was a period characterised by social tension, industrial unrest and fear of terrorism. The future for young people was uncertain due to the as yet unacknowledged economic restructuring from an industrial to a service economy. This resulted in traditional male identities built around class, employment and political allegiances being destabilised. Feminism also affected the expectations of women, with increasing numbers joining the workplace, while family breakup became more prevalent. In keeping with other post-war youth subcultures, punk opened up a space where young people contested outdated social constructs and expectations, as well as playing out the problems they faced.[4] The rise in unemployment, for example, became a prominent feature of early punk lyrics, although an active rejection of traditional work was as prevalent as any concern for this issue.[5]

The sense of nihilism within punk was also manifest in society at large. Much of this related to alienation and desolation, especially among the inhabitants of the vast sprawling estates and high rises that were by then often in a state of neglect. This setting, interspersed with traffic arteries and intersections (major road building providing another feature of post-war planning) eroded a sense of community and a relationship to the natural environment. Punk developed an aesthetic that was stark and gritty, often depicting urban decay as symptomatic of a wider sense of dystopia. Added to this was the fear engendered by the prevalence of televised violence, which reached people due to mass private ownership of television sets for the first time. News footage of war and conflict became commonplace, while political violence, from direct action protest to terrorism, was also a regular feature, inducing fear and a sense of helplessness in the viewer.[6] Macho violence also permeated popular TV series such as *The Sweeney* and *The Professionals*, which reflected and/or encouraged its establishment as a social norm. A sense of social estrangement was also cultivated by the rise in individualism and consumerism, which saw upwardly mobile individuals and their families abandoning the inner cities for the suburbs or nearby counties; a phenomenon known as 'white flight'.

Vaucher's illustrations for *International Anthem 1* often reflected these prevailing concerns, and frequently referenced Northern Ireland. The illustration in Figure 4.1 includes an armed British soldier, tank and the Catholic banner display, 'Queen of the most holy rosary'. It reiterates the dichotomous presentation of women in the media as homemakers, through items such as slippers, curtains, the carriage clock and wedding photo, and simultaneously objects of lust and derision through the image of the pin-up, which looks like it has been taken from the Readers' Wives section of a men's magazine. Echoing the strongman motif that appears in some of her earlier work, an allusion to contemporary masculinity is provided in the grappling men on the ground. The whole assemblage is set against a backdrop of derelict housing that characterised cities across the UK, and in a heightened sense in the case of the warzone that existed in Northern Ireland.

The emphasis on urban and social deprivation in Vaucher's image was already prominent within punk culture. Left-wing bands, notably The Clash, featured a declinist visual language as symptomatic of an uncaring capitalist society, while also using this to bolster their street credibility.[7] Vaucher's work

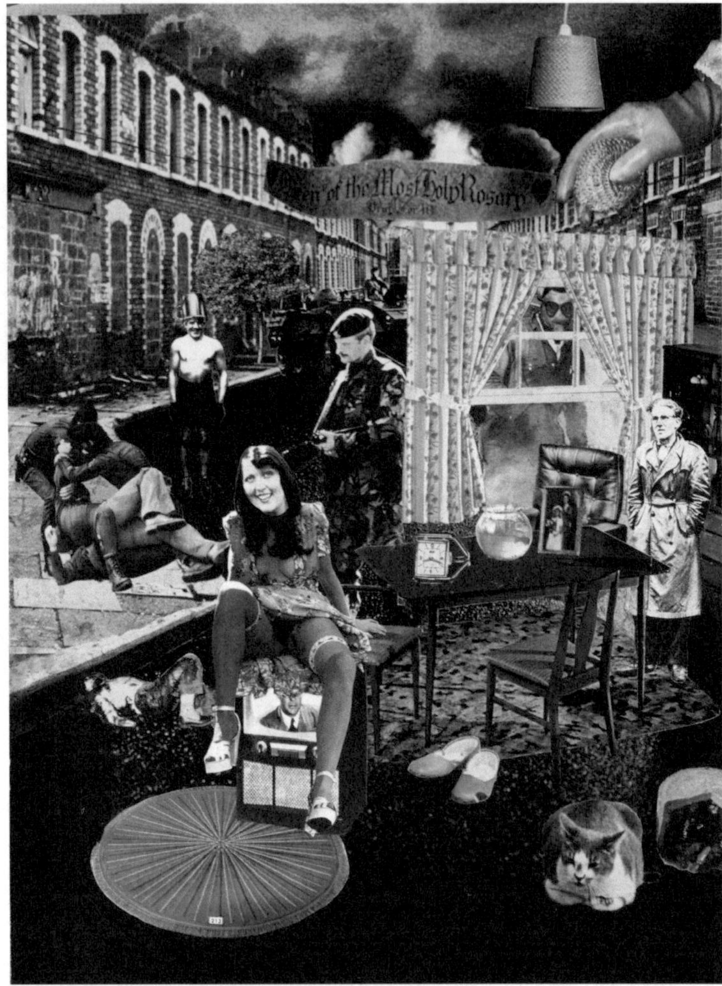

Figure 4.1   Gee Vaucher, Illustration for *International Anthem 1: Education*, 1977, collage 420mm × 300mm

reflects this sensibility, but her outlook is more concerned with creating alternatives than reforming the 'system'. Despite its sense of gritty realism, her image incorporates surrealist elements, including the man with a tin pot on his head, the lampshade in the sky and the hand looming in holding a kitchen sink scourer. Overall, the image appears as a visual stream of consciousness containing manifold references to the contemporaneous environment.

It should be stated that while a state of decline is commonly associated with Britain in the late 1970s, historical analyses have overall been too restricted in their portrayal of the decade. This was in part initiated at the time, as the concept of decline was articulated by both left- and right-wing proponents to support their distinct agendas. For the left this was to attack the failings of capitalism. They criticised the cuts in public expenditure brought about by Callaghan's government obtaining a loan from the IMF in the face of the sterling crisis, the perceived erosion of civil liberties signalled by the implementation of the Prevention of Terrorism Act and increased police violence.[8]

A particularly virulent narrative of Britain in decline was promoted by right-wing politicians and commentators, with scant analysis of the economic situation to back it up. Politicians, authors and journalists allied with right-wing think tanks associated with the New Right, such as the Institute of Economic Affairs,[9] set out to undermine the liberal democracy of the post-war decades, and more specifically the legitimacy of trade unions.[10] The concept of economic decline was allied to notions of societal, moral and imperial failure, to create a sense of panic, suggesting society was on the verge of collapse. This paved the way for the combination of reactionary Victorian values and an aggressive, new individualist ideology aligned to monetarist economic policy that would underpin the Thatcher government.

In the years leading up to Thatcher's election win, the economic situation in Britain fared a lot better than the generators of a declinist ideology claimed. The widely touted rise in unemployment that characterised the decade, for example, paled into insignificance by comparison with the situation in the 1980s.[11] The situation had declined relative to the 1950s and 1960s on various economic indicators, including inflation, public spending, public borrowing and growth, but despite the 'poor man of Europe' rhetoric, Britain fared no worse and was often in a stronger position than comparable countries.[12] British people also experienced a better sense of wellbeing during this decade than was subsequently the case.[13] Significantly, under Callaghan's Labour government, Britain was more equal than it had been before or has been since.[14]

Despite this, widespread poverty existed, particularly in the inner cities, which had begun to be emptied out by the 1970s. The decaying built environment, however, created the ideal conditions for people who wanted to develop alternative social structures, projects and organisations. Many of those involved in the creation of these radical living environments were grown-up hippies who had avoided becoming 'casualties' of the 1960s. While increasingly interacting and overlapping with 'straight' society, many strove to retain the sense of authenticity that was integral to the counterculture.[15] By the mid-1970s, an estimated 20–30,000 people throughout London squatted and rehabilitated thousands of empty properties that were earmarked for demolition or redevelopment.[16] Squatting was legal and members of Crass, as well as those who constituted their significant support network, often lived in these squatted environments. Crass vocalist Steve Ignorant recounts, 'These squats made living in London affordable for musicians, artists and families who otherwise couldn't have done it, and allowed them to live the same sort of creative, imaginative lives we were trying, in our small way, to have at Dial House.'[17]

These squats were the precursor to housing co-ops, and eventually councils provided squatters with rent books in their properties until they needed to use them.[18] Land and buildings could also be bought up relatively cheaply and transformed into arts venues, community facilities and projects. London boroughs such as Hackney and Islington hosted a thriving network of radical or alternative print shops, arts organisations, community theatres, bookshops and cafes that hosted projects and workshops for local, working-class communities.[19] The Labour councils were amenable towards such projects, which were funded generously before the cuts that were implemented by the Thatcher administration.

Punk culture was similarly facilitated through the ability of its progenitors and participants to live cheaply in squats, and the infrastructure created by their countercultural predecessors often supported them in their endeavours. Left-wing, independent co-operatives, such as Better Badges and the Islington Bus Company, largely staffed by older hippies, provided cheap services and a supportive environment in which young punks could print and publish their fanzines (more conventional printing companies often proved hostile to what was seen to be controversial content). Independent outlets, such as the record shop Rough Trade (1976–) and the bookshop Compendium (1968–2000), sold punk fanzines, while record labels Beggars Banquet (1973), Stiff (1976) and Small Wonder (1977) recorded and distributed punk music.

By the autumn of 1977, the independent record labels formed an alternative, nationwide, distribution system.[20] These labels allowed punk bands to record for free and press and distribute records in their thousands. However, the common presumption that an ideological commitment to independence was integral to punk from the outset is open to question. There are examples of bands, such as Desperate Bicycles, who were committed to this ethos, but many punk bands just worked independently until the opportunity arose to sign to a major label. Buzzcocks, for example, who are often cited as key originators of punk DiY for releasing their four-track debut EP, *Spiral Scratch*, on their own New Hormones label (January 1977), subsequently signed to United Artists.[21] However, while releasing music on independent labels started for pragmatic reasons for many punk bands, it quickly developed into an ideology of autonomy that would find its logical conclusion in Crass.

There was therefore a progressive and ideological element to first-wave punk from its inception. Rather than simply being symptomatic of decline and impoverishment, punk exposed the gap between the promise and the reality of idealistic liberalism. Culturally, the hippies and the whole progressive liberal consensus they embodied were becoming tiresome, particularly to a younger generation. In its rejection of this agenda, punk could appear synonymous with individualism, and individualised expression was indeed integral to punk. However, this was more akin to anarchist ideas on de-conditioning than to an expression of preferences within a consumerist ideology. Punk was explicitly anti-consumerist in its DiY ethic, as well as in the focus of its sentiments and lyrics.[22]

Following the furore created around McLaren, Westwood and the Sex Pistols on the Kings Road and via the Bromley Contingent in 1976, punk was taken up by disaffected teens, claiming their own disenfranchisement. However, by placing value on concepts such as freedom and rebellion, punk had more in common with the imperatives behind the counterculture than might be expected. The radical element to hip culture that involved iconoclasm and subversion (as expressed via the underground press), and attacking bastions of societal control, was seen again in punk. Rather than a complete repudiation of the 1960s, punk can in many ways be seen as a reconnection with its radicalism.

Punk also provided a space in which women could make a decisive impact. The rock music world of the 1960s overwhelmingly saw women as sex objects and/or foils for its male stars. Punk women often refused to passively subscribe to such roles. Female writers, including Jane Suck (*Sounds*), Julie Burchill (*NME*) and Caroline Coon (*Melody Maker*) were instrumental to defining its music and culture. The Sex Pistols' circle included a host of women, such as Jordan and Soo Catwoman, who embraced a confrontational, subversive look that was at odds with preconceived ideas on femininity. For some women, including singer Siouxsie Sioux, this meant embracing their own power or ability to intimidate. Pauline Murray (Penetration) and Chrissie Hynde (the Pretenders) both refused to adopt a 'feminised' look in order to practise their music. Gaye Advert (the Adverts), Poly-Styrene and Laura Logic (both X-Ray Spex), and the Slits all played with, transcended or subverted gendered looks and expectations. However, it's worth noting punk's disavowal of progressive politics also encompassed feminism. Lucy Toothpaste, who started the feminist punk fanzine *Jolt* (1977), and also wrote for *Spare Rib* and the Rock Against Racism 'zine *Temporary Hoarding*, commented,

> I never got one Punk woman in any of my interviews to say she was a
> feminist, because I think they thought the feminist label was too worthy, but

the lyrics they were coming out with were very challenging, questioning all the messages we'd been fed through *Jackie* comics. Punk made women feel they could compete on equal terms to men.[23]

In this respect, the 'feminist' critique offered by Vaucher had a strong connection to punk. In Figure 4.2, Vaucher uses a 'punk' element of shock in her depiction of the Prime Minster, Jim Callaghan, receiving oral sex from a fantasy figure. Similarly to the Dadaists, who reacted against rationalist justifications for the insanity of war, the values of civilised society are here undermined through the use of satirical humour. The act of fellatio is watched aghast by a young woman with a disfigured face (a victim of Hiroshima), while a homeless man stands by impassively. Again, the setting is the claustrophobic interior of the family home, evoking the envrionments depicted in her earlier *Homage to Catatonia* series (1975) on the death of Wally Hope (see Figures 2.4–2.6).

The conventions of punk graphics were rooted in the visual language of political protest and dissent and alternative culture. The use of rhetorical forms of humour, including satire, parody and irony, had a precedent in the graphic language of *International Times* and *Oz*. Similarly, the influence of peace movement agit prop and Situationist graffiti was evident in the use of stark monochrome, or two-colour stencils (full-colour printing was often too costly).

As with Vaucher, many of the originators of the punk aesthetic were from high art backgrounds, and deliberately took on a lowbrow aesthetic. Trained designers such as Barney Bubbles, Jamie Reid, Linder Sterling and Malcolm Garrett brought their distinct vision to bear in developing punk's visual style.[24] Reid was commissioned to create graphics for the Sex Pistols, while Garrett produced posters and record sleeves for Buzzcocks, and Bubbles worked as a senior designer for the Stiff Records label (alongside Chris Moreton) – notably for Ian Dury & the Blockheads, the Damned, and Elvis Costello. Sterling contributed a collage to the iconic design for the Manchester punk band, Buzzcocks's first major label single, 'Orgasm Addict' (1977). Many of these key progenitors of the aesthetic were also immersed in the culture they were representing. Alongside her iconic Buzzcocks image, for example, Sterling produced graphics for *The Secret Public* (1978), the arty, Manchester-based fanzine she created with Jon Savage. She also contributed to the feminist fanzine, *City Fun* (1978–84), which reported on the post-punk Manchester music scene.

Jamie Reid's designs played an essential role in constructing punk's visual identity and had a major mainstream impact through his association with the Sex Pistols. His independence as a designer facilitated the striking visual language that he cultivated. The famous design for the cover of the

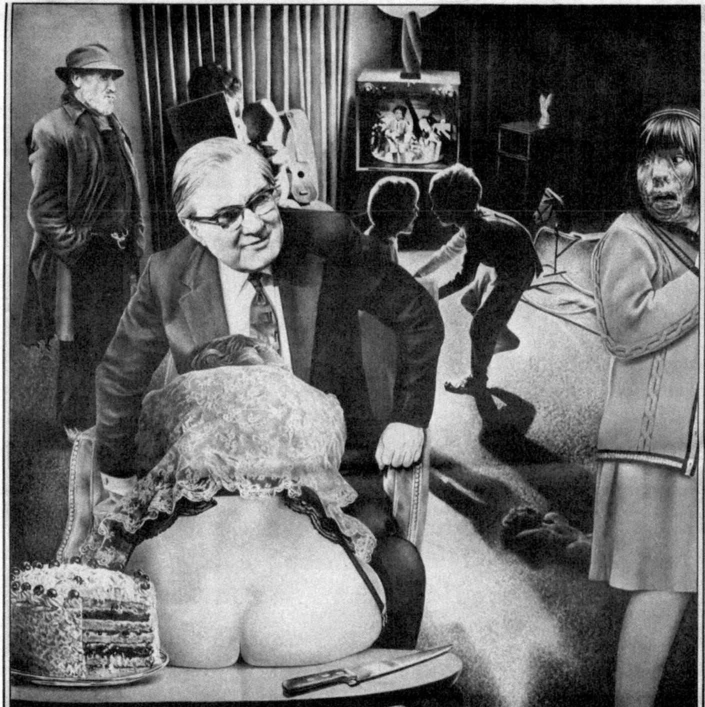

Figure 4.2 Gee Vaucher, Illustration for *International Anthem 1: Education*, 1977, gouache, 230mm × 230mm

'God Save the Queen' 7" (1977) subverted the most iconic representation of British imperial power. Together with Helen Wellington-Lloyd, who produced the Pistols' early flyers, Reid made wholesale use of the avant-garde technique of détournement, taking visual elements and text from sources including advertising, newsreel footage and notably the ransom note motif, re-presenting them to create new meaning. Reid's work was subversive, satirical and iconoclastic, using humour to send up vaunted British institutions of power as well as the music industry itself. He had a history as an agent provocateur within the radical underground of the 1970s, where he created visual material in an agitprop style for the political print studio, Suburban Press (London, 1971–75).

Reid and Vaucher shared an anarchistic outlook, valuing personal and political autonomy rather than conventional career structures. Similarly to political photomontage artists such as Peter Kennard, Vaucher and Reid were influenced by the merging of art and life seen in the 1960s that culminated with Paris '68.[25] On his intentions with the *Suburban Press* magazine, Reid noted, 'From rather naive beginnings, it very quickly settled into a shit-stirring format, with thorough research into local politics and council corruption, mixed with my graphics and some Situationist texts.'[26] Both Reid and his art-school friend Malcolm Mclaren were connected to the English branch of the Situationist International, King Mob, and Reid also produced the graphics for *Leaving the 20th Century: Incomplete Work of the Situationist International* (Free Fall Press, 1974), edited by former Situationist Chris Grey. The book was to have a significant influence on his thinking.[27]

Reid's concern with corruption via political institutions and processes was mirrored in Vaucher's critique, expressed in *International Anthem* (particularly issues 3 and 4, produced after Margaret Thatcher's election in 1979) and Crass. Reid and Vaucher also both sought to unite art with a political critique of power for instructional purposes. Reid set out to decode and simplify the jargon of the Situationist International to widen accessibility to their ideas.[28] One example was a *Suburban Press* campaign which sent up government advice through the creation of stickers advising *Save Petrol, Burn Cars, Keep Warm this Winter, Make Trouble* and *This Store Welcomes Shoplifters* plastered in public places, which he later reused for Sex Pistols material.[29] Crass would similarly take their design language to the street, spray-painting stencilled anti-war messages as graffiti on the London Underground and attacking sexist advertising on billboards.

Reid and Vaucher also shared an ethos of co-operation to foster mutual support within their respective milieus. Suburban Press functioned as a community press and facilitated the printing of various left/libertarian publications.[30] As an independent record label, Crass Records aimed to create a mechanism for like-minded bands to record and distribute their music as well as engendering a wider anarcho-punk movement (see Chapter 5).

However, there were some contradictions between Reid's stated intentions and the way his projects functioned. Suburban Press was criticised for setting out to make a profit.[31] There were also inherent inconsistencies in Reid and Maclaren's 'anarchist' intention to counter-exploit the music industry, something that would be exposed by Crass and used to further their version of anarchism (see Chapter 5).

There are also differences in their methods. While, as a graphic designer, Reid brilliantly re-presented material from the media, pop culture and other sources to subvert and create new meaning, as an illustrator, Vaucher meticulously painted many of her creations. As such she used a fine art technique and process, whereas Reid exemplified the technique of pillaging and cut 'n' paste graphic design that came to be associated with punk. Collage was also employed by Linder Sterling, whose assemblages featuring female torsos taken from pornographic imagery juxtaposed with domestic appliances from women's magazines brought an explicit feminist outlook into punk design. Sterling recalls her approach,

> It was like doing a peculiar jigsaw puzzle. I had two piles of magazines
> – trashy men's stuff and trashy women's. I noticed that in both, women were
> high-profile. Men's magazines were filled with pictures of women. And the
> invisible man was present by his absence. I was fascinated by the fact that I as
> a woman was supposed to be in all these worlds, I was represented in two
> separate male/female views of the world. These montages became an explicit
> diary of my feelings at that time.[32]

The posters, flyers and record sleeves that Sterling worked on for Manchester bands Buzzcocks and Magazine, were often created under assumed names, such as Anxious Images.[33] She also produced material for Factory Records and the Hacienda nightclub, as well as photomontages and collages for fanzines. Similarly to Reid's *Suburban Press* and Vaucher's *International Anthem*, her magazine *The Secret Public* (1978) provided a model for the DiY ethic integral to punk. She and her co-creator, Jon Savage, produced 1000 copies as the second product released on Buzzcocks' New Hormones label. It was distributed through the Rough Trade shop in West London and other independent outlets.[34]

Sterling often featured smiling mouths wearing red lipstick in her punk collages; most notably in place of nipples on the oiled torso of a woman with an iron for her head in her most famous image, which featured on the iconic cover (and poster) of Buzzcocks' second single, 'Orgasm Addict'.[35] The smiling mouth motif also appears, entirely coincidentally, on the cover of Vaucher's second edition of *International Anthem* (1979) (see colour insert, Plate 4).[36] This re-appropriated a reportage photograph of a soldier, taken during the Korean War in 1950, by the American photojournalist David Douglas Duncan (1916–2018), encircling it with smaller snapshots of civilised society taken from lifestyle magazines. The garish mouth introduces a discordant element to the otherwise monochrome image, perhaps highlighting the disparity between the two worlds presented in the mass media.

Sterling was part of a younger generation to Reid and Vaucher (born in 1954, as opposed to 1947 and 1945 respectively). As such she had not soaked up the heady atmosphere of change prevalent in the 1960s. Instead of a background in the counterculture or radical politics, Sterling was a trainee lawyer and worked as a journalist for the music magazine, *Sounds*. Accounts of the Manchester punk scene Sterling was involved with portray an exciting and diverse, often transgressive, environment. The politics of identity comes across as an overriding factor, something that is reflected in her work.[37] In this she differs markedly from Vaucher, whose work rarely engages with identity politics. What they had in common, though, was their critique of women's circumscribed presentation in the media and pornography. As symptomatic of punk more widely, their work provided an affront both to civilised society and the progressive liberal consensus.

Sterling's work, symptomatic of the Manchester punk scene, was meant to be disturbing, featuring sex and violence as part of that transgression. She juxtaposed nude, female torsos, often submissively positioned and/or bound, with domestic appliances, often in place of the head, to disturb the pleasure of the (presumably male) viewer. She here disturbed the dichotomy between sexless housewife and mother used to sell domestic goods and women for whom sex is fetishised to the point that they are the commodity itself (pornography). This is strongly reflective of Vaucher's approach in a host of images (see, for instance, Figure 3.6), which focus on this dichotomy. Other than the juxtaposition with domestic appliances, Sterling's female torsos are presented as they would be in pornography. The obliteration of the faces via appliances contributes to their de-personalisation – even alienation. By contrast, Vaucher's pin-ups inhabit their roles, or subvert them due to their personalisation.

In much the same way as Vaucher, Sterling's critique of the representation of women in the media has a notable precedent in the work of Hannah Höch. All three artists were commenting on politics and gender disparity in a fast-changing world. They incorporated a far more extensive range of female imagery into their collages and photomontages than other (male) Berlin Dadaists or punk/anarcho-punk designers respectively. Perhaps reflecting on their ubiquity within illicit society, the pin-up provided a staple element in the work of all three, while for Sterling this was the overriding feature.

Sterling and Vaucher's work was created over fifty years later, in the light of punk and the women's movement, and added new emphases to Höch's concerns. Whether referencing the false promise of marriage as a gateway for women's happiness or their fate as prey for murderous men, in the second edition of *International Anthem* (tellingly subtitled Domestic Violence), the message seems unambiguously one with strong correlations in contemporaneous

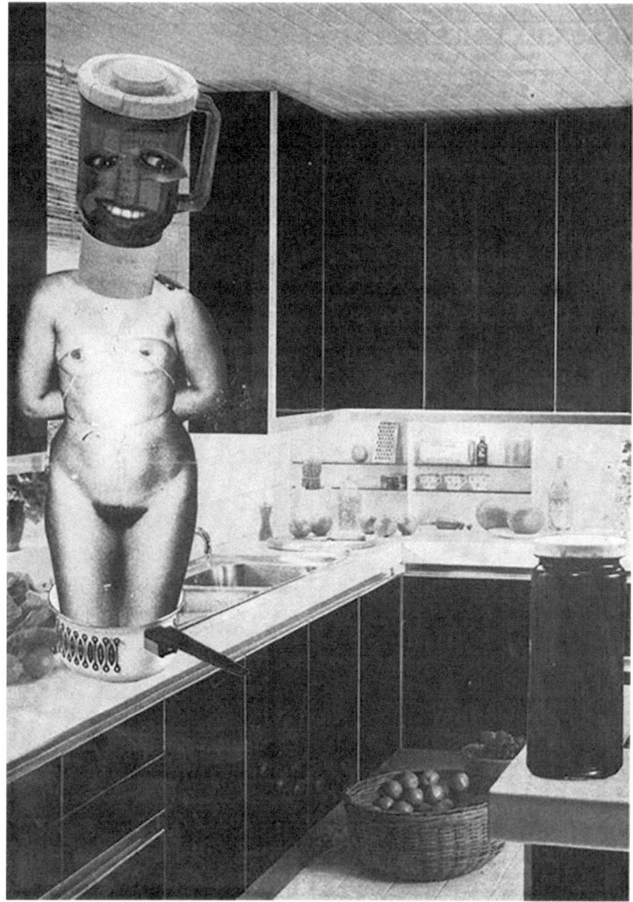

Figure 4.3   Linder Sterling, Untitled in *The Secret Public*, 1978, photomontage, 271mm × 195 mm

feminism. In Vaucher's representation in Figure 4.5, the lower half of a naked woman with her legs spread apart is situated under a crashed car. The text asks *Are you really a lady killer?* Vaucher commented, 'Of course, things happened on the front seat with your girlfriend and I suppose it was connecting sex with a death machine.'[38]

Sterling and Vaucher both presented the home as the location for patriarchal violence. Both also attacked romance as a false relational form, promoted through the media to engender social conformity within a heterosexual paradigm. In Figure 4.6, Vaucher juxtaposes an idealised representation of an innocent, young bride with imagery representing the harsh reality of the life

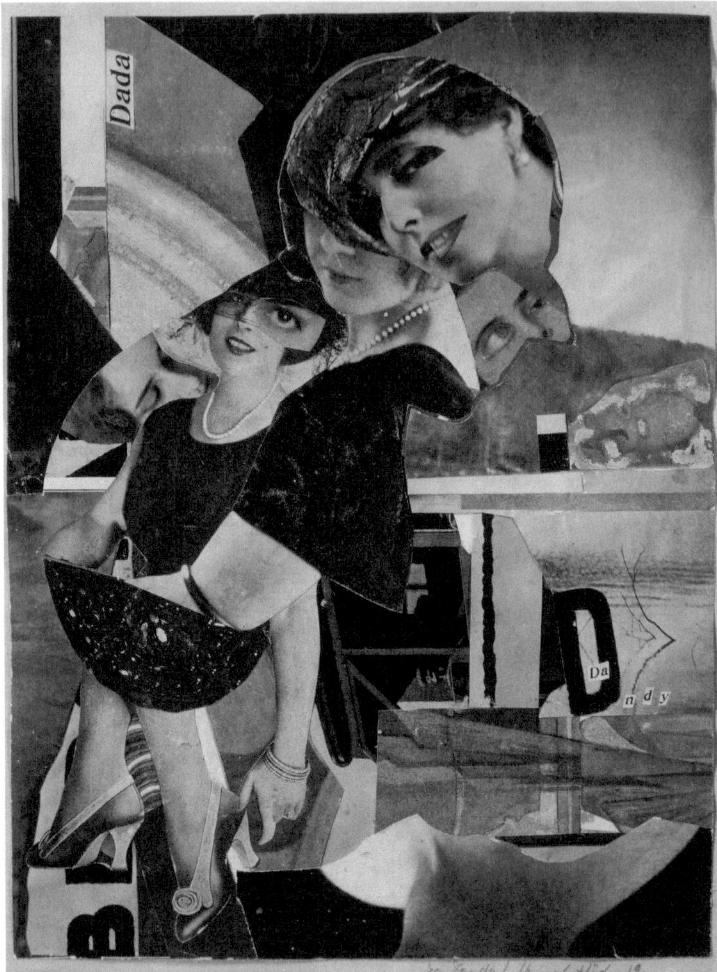

Figure 4.4   Hannah Höch, *Da Da Dandy*, 1919, collage

ahead of her. The disparity between idealism and realism is further highlighted through the juxtaposition of an aspirational male figure, pristine girl and ornamental stand holding cakes with the run-down street scene featuring scruffy, but free-looking children and a soldier (again referencing events in Northern Ireland). This image utilises a visual strategy common in punk graphics of collaging the eyes of the (male) figure, to disrupt and unsettle the viewer.[39]

In fact, the obliteration of facial features, including the eyes, through collage is a recurring trope in *International Anthem*. In Plate 5 (see colour insert), the

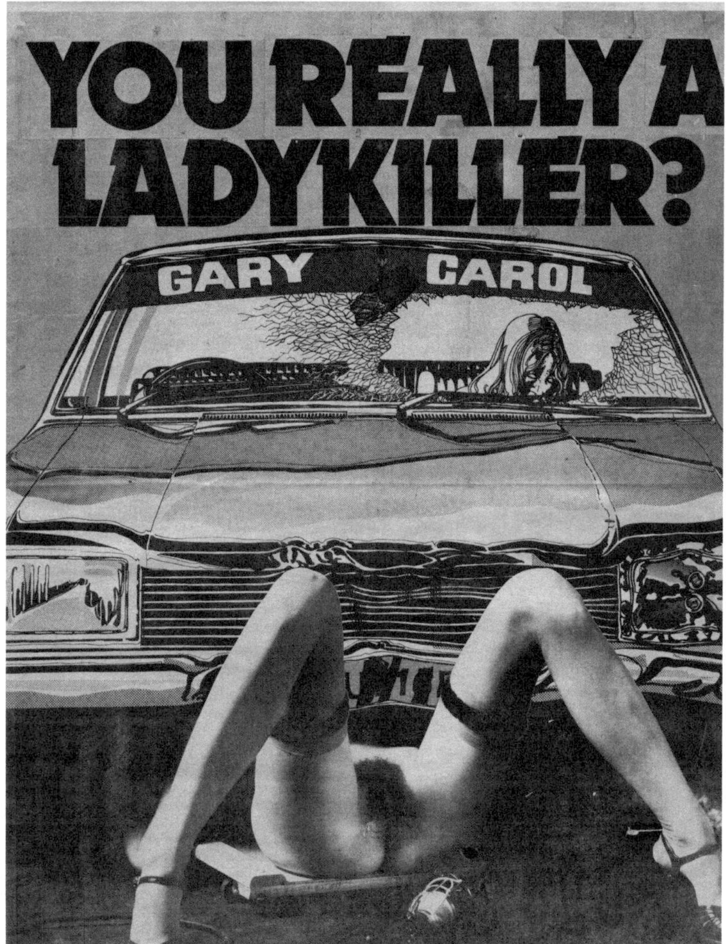

Figure 4.5   Gee Vaucher, Illustration for *International Anthem 2: Domestic Violence*, 1979, collage

male figure is an eerie composite of two faces blended into one, while the eyes of the female figure are superimposed with a magazine cut-out. Brandon Taylor featured this image prominently in his book on the history of collage, noting how, as with so many of Vaucher's images 'the scene is one of "normality" gone crazily awry'.[40] Taylor is noteworthy in being the first academic to engage with her work from an art historical as opposed to punk perspective.

Another illustration from *International Anthem 2* (Figure 4.7) likewise appropriates the signifiers of idealised domesticity that circulated in lifestyle magazines and advertising to subvert their intended messages. On the marital

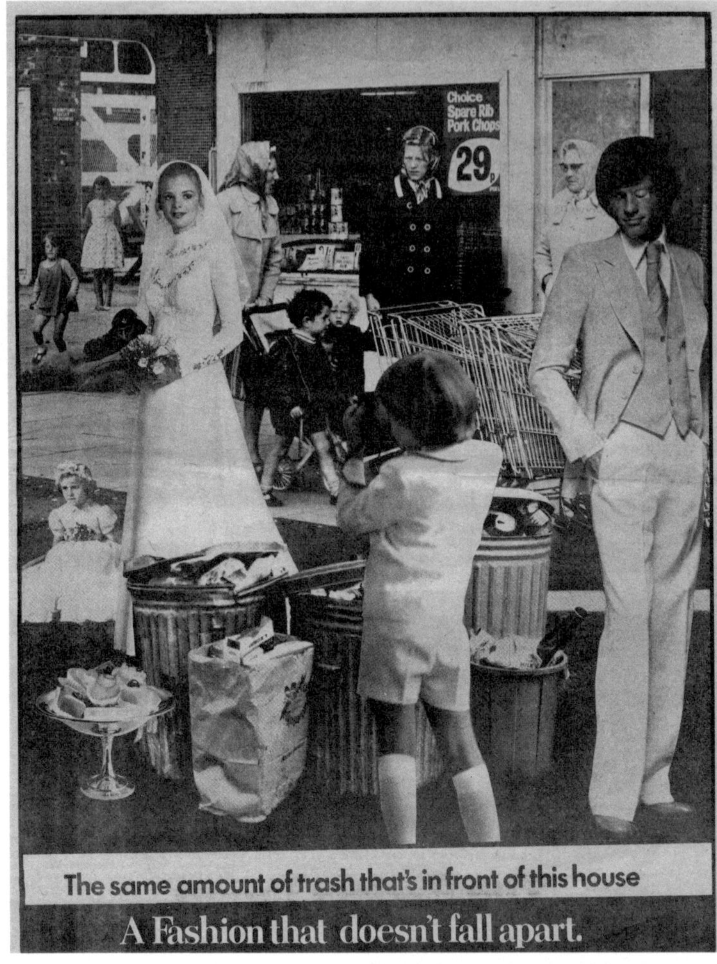

Figure 4.6   Gee Vaucher, Illustration, *International Anthem 2: Domestic Violence*, 1979, collage

bed is a baby confronting a trussed-up chicken, with pornographic connotations. The smiling, archetypal all-American male figure is at odds with the child he holds who is crying with his hands over his ears. The female figure seems to gaze fixedly towards new horizons. These painful and jarring unions contrast with the idealised portrayal of romantic love shown on the TV. Vaucher's perspective, as well as her mood, personality and feeling, are imbued in this image. She observes, 'Always, the painter might get up to paint and realise that life has taken a different turn since yesterday, or you might be in another

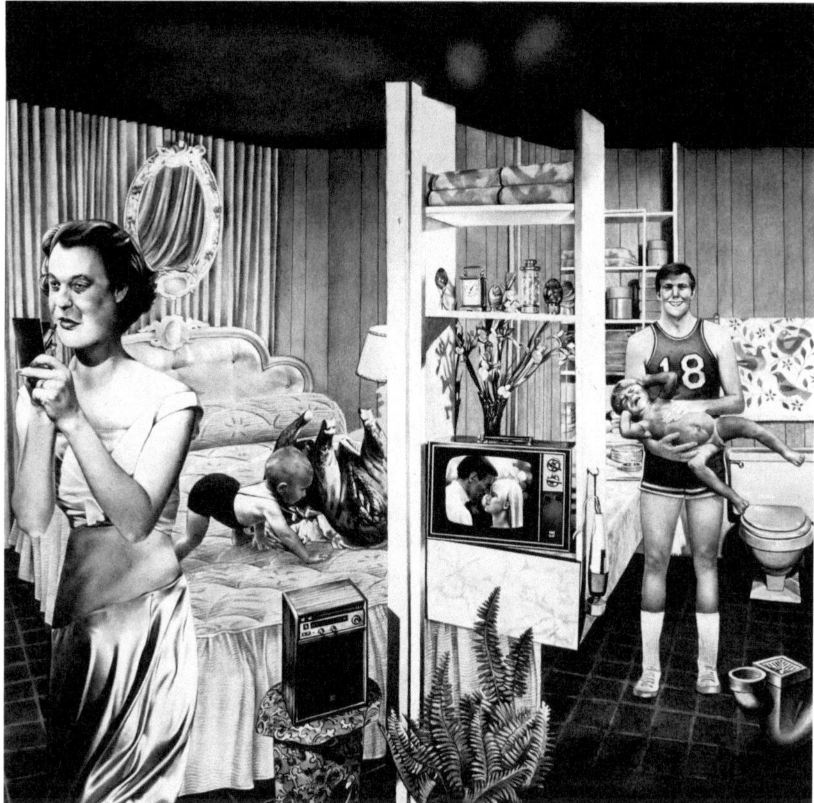

Figure 4.7 Gee Vaucher, Illustration for *International Anthem 2: Domestic Violence*, 1979, gouache

mood today. Everything plays a part in how you're going to express something. You're looking at the same photo every day, and you may not interpret it the same way every time, because of what's happening in your life.'[41]

Vaucher's artistic as opposed to technical process is most obviously manifested in the face of the female figure applying lipstick, which was actually created by combining male and female features.[42] This illustration measured just 30 × 29cm in total, so it was painted using very fine brushes, requiring immense skill and dexterity. The merging of different body and facial elements from different people, genders and even species would become a recurring trope in her work.

International Anthem 2 also contained material reflecting her preoccupation with war and militarism. The collage in Figure 4.8 brilliantly expresses the correlation between female subordination and male violence and war. While

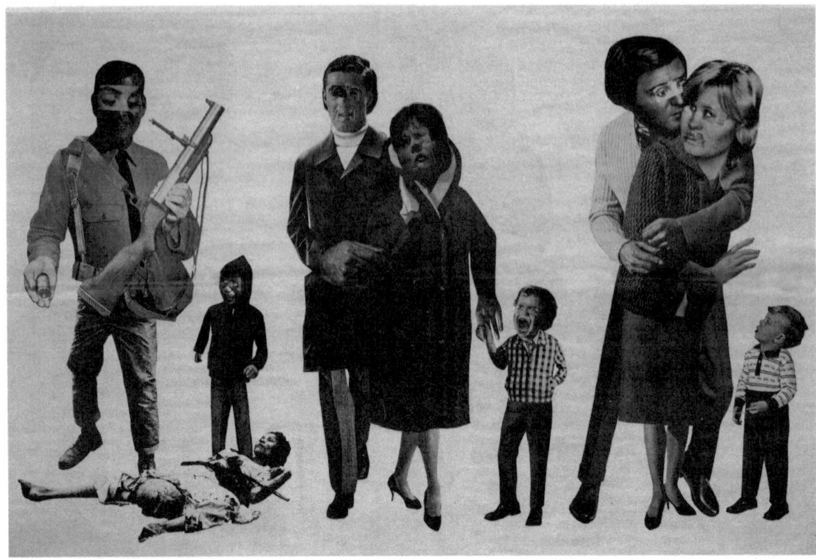

Figure 4.8   Gee Vaucher, Illustration for *International Anthem 2: Domestic Violence*, 1979, collage, 540mm × 350mm

this image illustrates female subservience within a patriarchal family unit, the male and child figures seem equally unhappy in their roles. This is reflective of a key concern of Vaucher's, which is to explore the ways in which both genders are exploited by the patriarchy through the societal expectations placed on them. The outcome of women rearing boys to be good patriots is illustrated through the inclusion of a corpse, a victim of war, which is disturbingly incongruous.

Vaucher, Sterling and Reid all utilised their underground newspapers and fanzines as vehicles for the development of their punk design language. Indeed, Reid reworked much of the material he developed at *Suburban Press* for the Sex Pistols. Sterling developed her method of juxtaposing images of sexually objectified or domesticated women and their accompanying appliances from magazines, via *The Secret Public*, prior to her iconic image for Buzzcocks. Along similar lines, Vaucher developed her aesthetic via *International Anthem* prior to and alongside her work with Crass. All three publications featured an independent ethos and gritty, unpolished aesthetic, featuring run-down urban scenes that became integral to the visual language of punk.[43] What was absent from both Reid and Sterling's work in the punk milieu, however, was a concern with the effects of social and political injustice. This was true of the aesthetic of first-wave punk more widely, obsessed as it was with the aesthetic of nihilism and societal decay; but all that was about to change, initiated by the impact of Vaucher's work for Crass.

Notes

1   Vaucher in interview with Groß, 2002.

2   One well-known author who makes this equation is Jon Savage, who positions punk emanating from an avant-garde, revolutionary place (via the inner circle of McLaren and Sex Pistols on the Kings Road) but becoming confronted with the 'brick wall of England's decline' in 1978, in J. Savage, *England's Dreaming: Anarchy, Sex Pistols, Punk Rock, and Beyond* (New York: St Martin's Griffin, 2002), p. 480.

3   This famous line is taken from the track, 'God Save the Queen' (7" single) by Sex Pistols (1977).

4   Dick Hebdige's influential book, *Subcultures: The Meaning of Style* (London: Routledge, 1979) following *Resistance Through Rituals: Youth Subcultures in Post-war Britain* (London: Hutchinson [for] the Centre for Contemporary Cultural Studies, University of Birmingham, 1976) by Stuart Hall and Tony Jefferson, argued that subcultures provided space for political resistance to an overarching capitalist ideology.

5   Examples of punk tracks highlighting unemployment include 'Career Opportunities', featured on the debut album of The Clash, *The Clash* (1977), 7" single, 'Right to Work' by Chelsea (1977), 7" single, 'Boys on the Dole' by Neville Wanker and the Punters (1978) and the 7" EP 'I Love the Dole' by The Exits (1978). There are also references to, or mentions of, life on the dole on the 7" 'Life' (Alternative TV, 1978), 12" 'Gobbin' on Life' by Snuff Rock (1977), 7" 'I Don't Wanna' by Sham 69 (1977), 7" 'Smithers-Jones' by The Jam (1979), 7" 'New Wave Love' by The Dole (1978) and 7" 'B.1.C' by UK Subs (1978).

6   See J. D. Taylor, 'The Party's Over? The Angry Brigade, the Counterculture and the British New Left, 1967–72', *The Historical Journal*, 58:3 (2015), p. 885.

7   Well-known examples include the rear cover of the 7" single, 'White Riot' and both front and rear covers of 'Remote Control/London's Burning' (live) 7" single, both by The Clash, 1977, and the front and rear covers of their album, *The Clash*, 1979, as well as the front cover of the album, *This is the Modern World* by The Jam, 1977.

8   See S. Hall (author), Brian Roberts (contributor), John Clarke (contributor), Tony Jefferson (contributor) and Chas Critcher (contributor), *Policing the Crisis: Mugging, the State, and Law and Order* (London: Macmillan 1978) and C. Moores, 'From Progressive to Radical: The 1970s and a Crisis of Civil Liberties', in C. Moores, *Civil Liberties and Human Rights in Twentieth Century Britain* (Cambridge: Cambridge University Press, 2017), p. 166.

9   Peter Jay at *The Times* and Samuel Brittan at the *Financial Times* are cited to have been influential by J. Tomlinson in *The Politics of Decline: Understanding Post War Britain* (Oxford: Routledge, 2000), p. 89. For further analysis of this affair, see B.

Jackson and R. Saunders (eds), *Making Thatcher's Britain* (Cambridge: Cambridge University Press, 2017).

10   In *The Politics of Decline*, pp. 58–59, Tomlinson mentions Correlli Barnett's *Audit of War* (1986) and Martin Wiener's book, *English Culture and the Decline of the Industrial Spirit*, 1850–1980 (1981) as influential in shaping how Thatcher's policies were presented as rescuing Britain from a long period of decline.

11   The average 2.03% rate of the 1960s increased to 4.3% in the 1970s, while in the 1980s it was 10.61% (J. Denman and P. McDonald, 'Unemployment Statistics from 1881 to the Present Day', *Labour Market Trends* (1 January 1996). Available at http://terencebunch.co.uk/articles/globalisation-the-united-states-empire-the-rise-of-thatcherism-and-the-uks-descent-into-dependency/unemployment-statistics-from-1881-to-1995-the-government-statistical-service-uk.pdf (accessed 18 June 2021).

12   See Tomlinson's analysis with reference to figures released by the OECD, in *The Politics of Decline*, pp. 91–93. On pp. 93–94, Tomlinson also highlights how problems such as inflation and spending were dealt with pretty effectively by Callaghan's Labour government in the latter years of the decade.

13   See A. Beckett. *When the Lights Went Out: Britain in the 1970s* (London: Faber and Faber, 2009), p. 4.

14   In *When the Lights Went Out*, Beckett, p. 410 refers to the Gini coefficient, which measured the lowest level of income inequality for British households in 1977, while the amount of British people living below the poverty line was at its lowest level in 1978.

15   In his sociological study, *Ecstasy and Holiness: Counterculture and the Open Society* (Fakenham: Cox and Wyman Ltd, 1974), p. 21, F. Musgrove cites authenticity as the value that was most prized by people within the counterculture.

16   C. Wall, 'Sisterhood and Squatting in the 1970s: Feminism, Housing and Urban Change in Hackney', *History Workshop Journal*, 83:1 (2017), p. 79. Available from https://doi.org/10.1093/hwj/dbx024 (accessed 12 September 2020).

17   S. Ignorant, *The Rest is Propaganda* (Norfolk: Dimlo Productions, 2020), p. 137.

18   Vaucher in email correspondence, April 2021.

19   Former employee and volunteer with the community printers and centre, The Islington Bus Company, in the late 1970s, Bob Gilbert, in conversation with Binns, 2017. For further discussion on the independent, co-operatively run print shops that emerged in the city during the 1970s, see J. Baines, 'The Freedom of the Press Belongs to Those who Control the Press', in N. Carpentier, P. Pruulmann-Vengerfeldt, R. Kilborn, R. Olsson, H. Nieminen, E. Sundin and K. Nordenstreng (eds), *Communicative Approaches to Politics and Ethics in Europe* (Tartu: ECREA & University of Tartu Press, 2009), pp. 113–127.

20   Savage, *England's Dreaming*, p. 417.

21   See R. Bestley, 'Design it Yourself? Punk's Division of Labour', *Punk & Post-Punk*, 7:1 (2018), pp. 7–24 for an analysis of the extent to which punk bands practised an ideal of independence. Also see R. Bestley and A. Ogg, 'DiY Punk' in R. Bestley and A. Ogg (eds), *The Art of Punk* (London: Omnibus Press, 2012), pp. 106–124.

For further reading on this subject, see A. Ogg, *Independence Days: The Story of UK Independent Record Labels* (London: Cherry Red, 2009).

22 Poly-Styrene of X-Ray Spex (1976–79) in particular was preoccupied with this theme. Many of the tracks she wrote for the album *Germfree Adolescence* (1978), including 'Art-i-ficial', 'Warrior in Woolworths', 'Identity', 'Genetic Engineering' and 'Germfree Adolescents' contain lyrics that send up the banality of consumerism and individualism.

23 Lucy Toothpaste (aka Whitman) quoted in Savage, *England's Dreaming*, p. 418.

24 Barney Bubbles (b. 1942) worked as an assistant for design company Michael Tucker & Associates from 1963, before joining The Conran Group as a Senior Graphic Designer in 1965. Malcolm Garrett (b. 1956) studied typography at the University of Reading (1974–75) and graphic design at Manchester Polytechnic (1975–78). Linder Sterling (b. 1954) studied Graphic Design at Manchester Polytechnic (1974–77). Jamie Reid (b. 1947) attended Wimbledon Art School (1962–64) and Croydon Art School. (1964–68).

25 P. Kennard, *Images for the End of the Century: Photomontage Equations* (London: Journeyman Press, 1990), Afterword, specifically mentions Paris '68 having an impact on him. Also see J. Reid and J. Savage, *Up They Rise: The Incomplete Works of Jamie Reid* (London: Faber and Faber, 1987) pp. 13–15. F. Vermorel, *Vivienne Westwood: Fashion, Perversity and the 1960s Laid Bare* (New York: Overlook Books, 1996), pp. 173–178, covers its influence on Malcolm Mclaren.

26 Reid and Savage, *Up They Rise*, p. 35.

27 J. A. Walker, *Left Shift: Radical Art in 1970s Britain* (London: Taurus, 2002), p. 41.

28 Reid and Savage, *Up They Rise*, p. 38.

29 Reid and Savage, *Up They Rise*, pp. 42–43.

30 Reid and Savage, *Up They Rise*, p. 36.

31 Reid and Savage, *Up They Rise*, p. 37.

32 Sterling in 1997, quoted in O'Brien, L, 'The Woman Punk Made Me', in R. Sabin (ed.), *Punk Rock: So What? The Cultural Legacy of Punk* (London: Routledge, 1999), p. 191.

33 P. Jones, 'Anxious Images: Linder's Fem-Punk Photomontages', *Women: A Cultural Review*, 13:2 (2002), p. 162.

34 J. Savage, 'The Secret Public', in L. Bovier (ed.), *Linder Works, 1976–2006* (Zurich: JRP/Ringier, 2006), p. 9.

35 The cover features Sterling's collage alongside typesetting by Malcolm Garrett.

36 Vaucher in email correspondence, April 2021.

37 See the account of this scene provided by Sterling, 'Northern Soul', in L. Bovier (ed.), *Linder: Works, 1976–2006* (Zurich: JRP/Ringier, 2006), pp. 16–48.

38 Vaucher in interview with Binns, 2017.

39 This visual strategy is seen in Jamie Reid's design for Sex Pistols 7" single, 'God Save the Queen' (1977) and appears throughout Linder Sterling's designs for *The Secret Public* as well as being a feature of punk graphics more widely.

40 B. Taylor, *Collage: The Making of Modern Art* (London: Thames and Hudson, 2006), p. 205.

41 Vaucher in interview with Binns, 2018.

42 Vaucher in interview with Binns, 2018.

43 The declinist aesthetic evident in *The Secret Public* was largely cultivated through the collages of Jon Savage, something he also utilised in his fanzine, *London's Outrage*, which regularly featured run-down urban landscapes.

Crass art and the birth of anarcho-punk

In 1979, Vaucher returned to Dial House (Essex), in the UK, to live and work as part of Crass. She was excited by the prospect of Crass as it gained momentum and played a supportive role in its development. She had organised four gigs for the band in New York City in 1978 and paid half the costs of their flights with the money she made from producing three illustrations for *High Times*. The band raised the remainder by selling paraphernalia Vaucher had collected at Dial House over the years and from their own pockets.[1] Vaucher recollects,

> I avoided booking the obvious. I said I'm not going to book CBGBs or Max's (Kansas City). I booked the Puerto Rican Club (Lower East Side, 2nd Ave) and the Polish Club (14th St). We did the Puerto Rican Club with James Chance and the Contortions. One of the people connected with the Contortions lived in the same building as me, so I was acquainted with that lot.[2]

Performing with one of the main acts of New York's downtown No Wave music scene provided a contrast to the band's early experiences in the UK. Ignorant found the performance by James Chance to be very contrived, as reflective of the arty, New York scene.[3] Vaucher notes, 'I don't really think that the people knew what we were going on about (laughs), because I really don't think punk in America was, at that time, anything to do with politics and what was coming out of Britain.'[4]

It was also at this time that Vaucher encountered Johnny Lydon, very much the worse for wear. She describes him looking 'very small and vulnerable', slumped asleep on the ground in the freezing cold, outside CBGBs in January/ February 1979 (just before she left New York for England). She got him to his feet, and a group of girls pointed to where he was staying nearby. She got him back safely. However, she recalls,

> I just remember spending the next hour or two making sure he didn't get raped as he lay semi-conscious on the bed. One of the girls definitely wanted to tell everyone she'd fucked Johnny last night! She gave up in the end and they all left. I wrote 'if he needed any help' and my telephone number on a piece of paper and stuck it in his jacket pocket and left. Thinking back on it, I suppose I was a bit naive, sex and drugs and rock and roll and all that, he missed his chance, I should have left them to it.[5]

Crass had been formed a year previously, when a young Steve Ignorant, inspired by seeing The Clash, wanted to form a punk band. He'd been going to Dial House since the mid-1970s, having been brought there by his older brother, Dave, who visited regularly.[6] During a visit in 1977, Ignorant showed Rimbaud a song he had written ('Do They Owe Us A Living', released on the Crass' album, *Feeding of the Five Thousand*, 1978) and broached the idea with him, and that night Crass was formed. This initial pairing set the tone for the band, which combined an older generation who'd grown up with the counterculture, with a younger generation inspired by punk. Many members of Crass had previously lived or spent time at Dial House and had helped out with their earlier endeavours.[7] Eve Libertine, for example, had lived with Vaucher in Stanford Rivers Hall, while logo designer Dave King had performed with EXIT at ICES in 1972.[8] Despite all having a strong connection to Essex, the various members also came from divergent class backgrounds, which similarly marked them out from many of their contemporaries.

The ensemble came together in a haphazard and organic way. One of Rimbaud and Vaucher's old hippie friends, Steve Herman, signed up to be the guitarist, and a young art student visiting Dial House, Andy Palmer, offered to play rhythm guitar. In true punk style the band agreed, despite him never having played before. Steve Ignorant claims that even by the end he hadn't learned to play a single chord. Joy de Vivre, who lived locally and often visited the house, and was also Palmer's art school friend, joined on vocals, along with Rimbaud's then-girlfriend, Bronwen Lloyd Jones (henceforward known as Eve Libertine). The line-up was completed when Phil Free replaced Herman on guitar, and Pete Wright joined on bass. These latter two members, along with Palmer and Crass filmmaker Mick Duffield, were involved in the

London squat scene, which would prove fertile territory for the band in years to come.[9]

Vaucher's return to Dial House marked the start of an incredibly intense and prolific few years, in which she produced a vast body of powerful work that defined the band's visual and political identity and proved highly influential to post-punk graphics. Rather than living and working independently as a successful freelance illustrator, she resumed her position as an artist, living and working in a communal environment. She recalls, 'I just wanted to come back and pursue what I really felt I'd started with the newspaper.'[10]

While Vaucher was excited at the prospect of returning to Dial House, she eventually had to build a shed at the bottom of the garden, as the band's practice room was next door to her studio and it was impossible for her to hold a brush steady once they started rehearsing.[11] She would work independently, only coming together with the band to get the gist of the next album.[12] Rimbaud later estimated that she produced 90% of Crass' visual material,[13] but it was the interplay of ideas within the communal environment that elicited her creative response as an artist. She comments, 'In the truest sense of the word, we shared the overall experience and there was no separation.'[14]

Dial House provided a rural retreat that fostered the creative energy of Crass, in a way that was unusual for a punk band. Vaucher comments, 'We were in a very privileged position. I mean we were living in a house where we hadn't paid rent for a long time and were living as a group in a very beautiful place.'[15] Noting the insecurity for young punks, who often lived in squats in the city, she observed, 'I couldn't have done what I did without a studio to come back to … I mean, this place was absolutely fundamental to Crass being able to go on for as long as they did.'[16]

Despite enjoying life at Dial House, at times Vaucher found living with up to sixteen people, including children, difficult.[17] She also acknowledges her propensity for irritability, noting, 'Well, obviously I was much younger and hopefully I've become a better person. I suffered from impatience, because I move quite quickly. There was a member of the band who moved quite slowly and it would just drive me nuts. I was always on at something and possibly annoyed people. It was a big learning curve for everyone and I like to think we have kept learning.'[18]

Several members of Crass have since acknowledged that they found Vaucher's intolerance a challenge,[19] but Ignorant recalls everyone pitching in and having a real consideration for one another's needs and boundaries.[20] This was reflective of the high level of personal accountability that characterised life at Dial House. Vaucher comments, 'I think that even before people come here they know they are expected to share and help out … They will pick up their dirty cup, take it to the sink and wash it.'[21]

Crass was run along open and democratic lines, with different members taking the initiative in different areas. Each member had the right to veto a decision they weren't happy with, but they rarely did. Vaucher recalled, 'Well, if a song was written that someone felt very strongly against then it was dropped, full stop. But that only happened once. I don't remember which one. It was just bad. People laughed about it, but just said no way. It was their first attempt.'[22]

Crass also went to great lengths to maintain their collective values in the public realm. Rimbaud, who wrote the largest share of the band's lyrics, and exerted the most influence on the direction they took, nonetheless maintained a low profile as their drummer. They appeared onstage in black, genderless attire, rejecting the tendency for female performers to be valued on the basis of their looks. This wasn't a puritanical denial of female sexuality; performances by Libertine and de Vivre were both visceral and empowering. It was instead a rejection of the commodification of female sexuality that prevailed in the marketing strategies of the music industry. It also meant that Crass' output, rather than personnell, took centre stage. The exception was Ignorant, who had an unmissable presence. This enabled him to forge a vital connection with their young, punk audiences. Crass' ethos meant they strove to communicate in a nonhierarchical way with their audiences. Eve Libertine recalled,

> We were anonymous onstage, but the house was open … what could someone get from Steve or me in the spot-light? Only that we were stars. But they could come to the house; they can see us doing what we're doing. And anyone could come to the house, *anyone*. And people came. They camped in the garden, they lived there, or they came with their fanzines … a day taken up with people we would never see again, talking about *anything*.[23]

Crass were hugely supportive to their fans, in a way that was highly distinct, if not unique, for a band. They felt personally indebted to answer fan mail, particularly from distressed individuals. While they shunned the mainstream media, they were committed to providing input and support to punk fanzines and bands and had done hundreds of interviews for punk-zines by around 1980. Mike Diboll, who created the potent anarcho-punk-zine, *Toxic Graffiti* (1978–82), was one of a host of producers that were in part inspired by Crass.[24] Diboll spent a lot of time at Dial House during this period, 'practically living there from 1980–early 1981'. He recalls,

> I wasn't an artist in the day. This was one of the things that I developed through my involvement in Dial House in the early days of Crass, under the

tutelage of Gee and others, which really helped. I learnt the basics of collage, cutting and scalpel use and physical image manipulation. She also showed me techniques, including the creative use of silkscreen and 'Gestetner' type duplicators, and so on. At one point they gifted me a small silkscreen press and a duplicator.[25]

The explosion of punk fanzine culture was to be enabled by the advent of low-cost photocopying, but Rimbaud and Vaucher's backgrounds in independent publishing meant they also had experience in the earlier technologies that had enabled the underground press.

The perception of Crass as genuine – marrying their politics with their life choices as well as their resolute independence as an outfit – provided a model that proved hugely inspirational. This cemented their relationship with their audience in a sense more akin to a cult than a band. Vaucher notes, 'A lot of people perceived that we cared. And that was good enough for me; because we did … I think a lot of people felt that we were actually singing to them personally; and we were. Okay, they might be in the crowd, but I think what we were doing touched people, and the politics of it all went from there.'[26]

Crass also felt responsible for the effect they had on their audiences. Their live performances incorporated multi-media projections produced by Vaucher and Mike Duffield. Vaucher also produced banners and backdrops to drape around the stage. The films featured brutal imagery of nuclear explosions, Nazi soldiers, concentration camp inmates and war victims, which, combined with their sound, formed an assault on the senses. They also handed out fanzines, leaflets and other printed matter, overall providing the sense of a clandestine experience. Rather than disappearing afterwards, the band hung around. Vaucher notes,

> We didn't think it was right to confront people with so much on stage and then just leave them to it. What we were saying and the imagery we were showing could be quite distressing for some, especially for the very young people. We thought it was important to be there, to have the time to sit down with the audience, straight after a gig, and at least try to answer some questions and try to reassure people.[27]

In their desire to maintain autonomy from mainstream production, and therefore promotion and recognition, Crass took control in numerous ways. Rimbaud and Vaucher had originally set up Exitstencil Press in 1970 to publish their creative material. This included leaflets and flyers for EXIT, and they now used it to produce material for Crass and issues of *International Anthem* (1977–84) that were given away for free at gigs or sold for a minimal cost.

Again, the legacy of the underground press and radical print shops that produced Marxist, feminist and anarchist material can be seen in the DiY and self-help approach adopted by Crass. During the 1970s, these print shops had enabled local communities to use their facilities and practised positive discrimination to ensure they were prioritising excluded demographics including working-class, female, ethnic minority and elderly communities. Crass likewise encouraged participation in the creation of culture by various people including those from disenfranchised communities.[28]

Often the independent print shops produced material that was intended to be the 'collective expression of a movement' as opposed to work credited to a single artist or designer.[29] In keeping with this approach, Vaucher published *International Anthem* anonymously, while she attributed her work for Crass to the collective, or was credited as G Sus. As well as providing a blasphemous pun, this could (as with the title of Crass' album *Bullshit Detector*) allude to an intention to 'sus' out, i.e. identify fakery. It also references a guitar chord.

Crass Records provides the most prominent example of how Crass took charge of their creative production. Crass had released their first record, *The Feeding of the Five Thousand*, on the Small Wonder label in 1978 and Rimbaud talks enthusiastically about both the model they provided and their support of the band.[30] However, when the label sent the album off to Ireland to be pressed, the workers at the factory refused to include the track 'Reality Asylum' on the record due to its blasphemous content. The band responded by removing the track, replacing it with silence and renaming it 'The Sound of Free Speech'. This incident convinced the band that they needed to set up their own label to avoid any repeats.[31] This allowed them to promote and sell their self-produced records at a discounted rate. In a move that would become ubiquitous in succeeding years, when they self-released 'Reality Asylum' on the 7", 'Reality Asylum'/'Shaved Women' (1979), the cover read, 'Pay no more than 45p' (singles at that time cost 80–90p).

While the majority of first-wave punk bands had adopted the 'DiY' approach for pragmatic reasons (see Chapter 4), Crass chose this route as it enabled them to express themselves without compromise. They lived by their principles, refusing an offer of £50,000 to sign with major record label EMI in 1978.[32] They further promoted independence in a political sense as resistance to the capitalist mode of production.[33]

Despite the lack of mainstream support, Crass were highly successful at subcultural branding and distribution, selling 20,000 copies of their second album, *Stations of the Crass*, within two weeks of its release. Many report Crass to have sold a quarter of a million copies of certain albums, with more than a million unit sales across their discography.[34] Undoubtedly, the skill, training and experience of Vaucher and Rimbaud as graphic designers was an essential part of their success. The iconic Crass symbol designed by Dave King, which combines ancient religious elements, the cross and the snake, to form a distinct stencil, was also essential to solidifying their 'brand'. King had created it for the cover of Rimbaud's 'journal of dissent', *Christ's Reality Asylum* (1977), produced just before the formation of Crass. Rimbaud sent the book to Vaucher in New York, where she reproduced the image in the first *International Anthem*. She notes, 'Somehow, it stuck with the band and the rest is history.'

Crass were in this sense professional in an area of DiY punk cultural production that was often characterised by amateurism. In effect they conceived a successful corporate idea, marketing and distribution strategy,[35] and in this sense some have seen them as exemplars of entrepreneurship as opposed to political resistance.[36] Regardless of the extent to which Crass circumvented the functioning of a capitalist economy, however, their independence facilitated the dissemination of ideas that criticised the commodification of culture as well as societal and political power imbalance. This resonated with their young, politically aware, subcultural audience, and increasingly they gave that demographic the opportunity to release their own material.[37] In addition to their own music, Crass Records released music by Poison Girls, DIRT, Zounds, Flux of Pink Indians, Conflict, The Cravats, Rudimentary Peni, Anthrax, Omega Tribe and Annie Anxiety among numerous others. These bands shared a broad ideological outlook with Crass that would become known as anarcho-punk. Correspondingly, punk fanzines reacted, not only through the dissemination of Crass' ideas into the wider anarcho-punk sphere, but also to the other bands' varied emphases on issues such as vivisection, nuclear energy, war and organised religion. The preoccupation with animal rights shown by bands such as Flux of Pink Indians and Conflict, for example, helped to install this as an important issue within the scene.[38]

Again reflecting their awareness of the power of cultural branding, Crass had a specific requirement that all record sleeves use a monochrome palette (although Vaucher acknowledges they couldn't have afforded to use colour, even if they had wanted to),[39] and Rimbaud also insisted the designs adopt the distinct circle design he and Vaucher had initially used for a commercial book cover in 1974 (see Chapter 3). Many bands also adopted Crass' strategy of including an extensive range of information sheets, booklets, flyers, postcards and patches, which all played a part in cultivating their identity and disseminating their perspective and ideology.

Often the bands learnt the requisite skills from releasing their first record on Crass Records before setting up their own label, which Crass often also helped to facilitate. Following the release of their music on Crass Records,

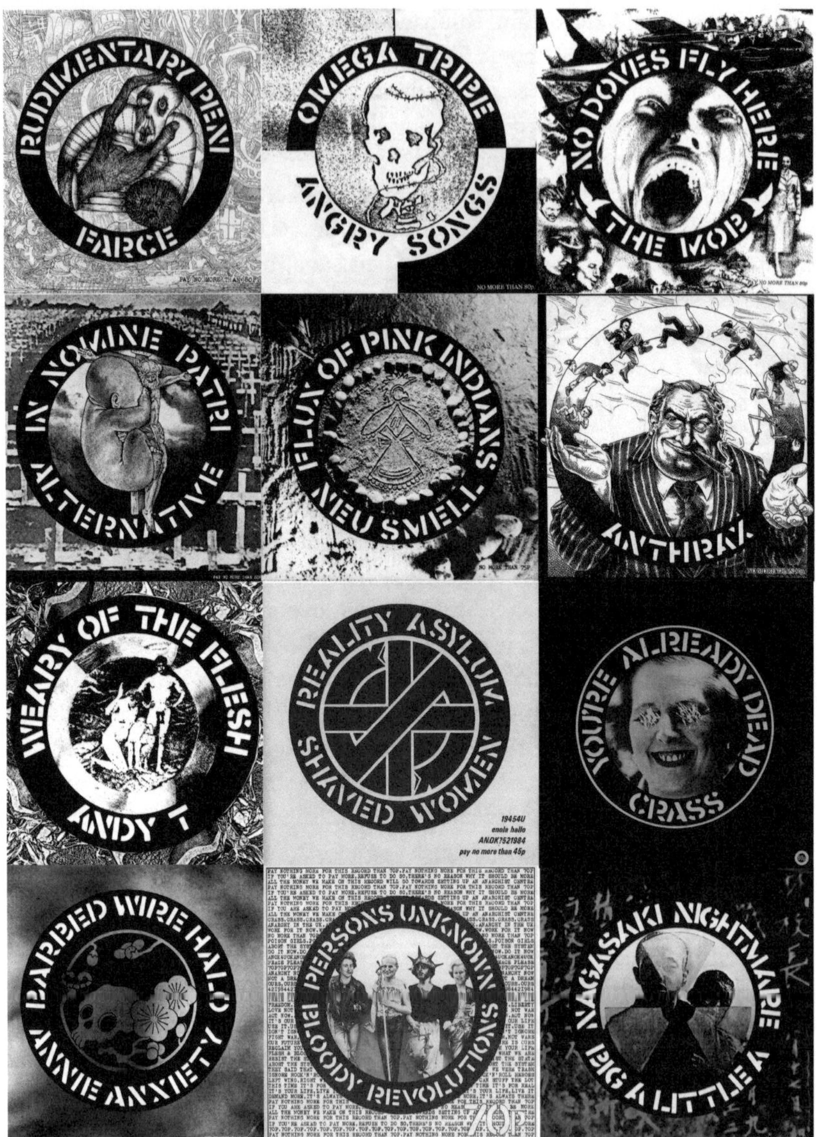

Figure 5.1   Crass Label 7" Single Covers

for example, Conflict set up the Mortarhate label, which released music by bands including Hagar the Womb, Icons of Filth, Lost Cherrees, the Apostles, Exitstance and Stalag 17. Similarly, anarcho-punk band Flux of Pink Indians set up Spiderleg (1981) following the release of their first EP, *Neu Smell*, on Crass Records. Flux released their own music on Spiderleg, as well as records by punk bands including the System, Amebix, Antisect and Subhumans. Subhumans subsequently set up their own Bluurg label, releasing music by more bands in the genre. Later, Derek Birkett (bass player) of Flux would set up the indie label One Little Indian (now renamed One Little Independent), which had major success in the late 1980s and 1990s with record releases by bands including Björk, The Shamen, Skunk Anansie and Chumbawamba. Crass Records became the model for an ideologically driven DiY ethic in punk in the UK, while it also proved influential to punk movements including hardcore and riot grrrl in the US during the 1980s and 1990s.[40]

Crass were inspired by the potential of punk as a grassroots, revolutionary movement and this was perhaps expressed most clearly in the rhetoric, aesthetic and DiY approach displayed in punk-zines. While the underground press of the 1960s had created culture, in the sense there was a gap in the 'market' (for want of a better word) to fill, by the late 1970s the publishing scene included music papers *Melody Maker*, *New Musical Express* and *Sounds*. These had vastly larger distribution and were prioritised by the increasingly powerful music establishment. It was these very papers that punk fanzines reacted against as elitist and pretentious. Instead, first-wave punk fanzines (1976–78), had attempted to create something authentic and in sync with disaffected kids.[41] Their emergence was facilitated by access to cheap black and white photocopying for the first time. As with their countercultural predecessors, punk-zinesters created culture by and for themselves, and against the grain of dominant culture. However, unlike their countercultural predecessors, they were often untrained kids, from relatively unprivileged backgrounds.

The rough 'n' ready aesthetic of the zines was therefore often driven by necessity, and this was something that Crass adopted and refined from the outset. Their first record, *Feeding of the Five Thousand*, contained an insert that matched this cut 'n' paste zine style, featuring text interspersed with fairly crude collages, often with newspaper cuttings overlaid. The album proved so popular that it was re-pressed six times during Crass' short lifespan, and in 1980 received a complete overhaul when it was released for the first time on Crass' own label with the new title *Feeding of the 5000 (The Second Sitting)*. The artwork for this release still featured Vaucher's immersive bombsite image (see Figure 1.2), but incorporated Crass' trademark fold-out design plus a host of new artwork, much of which reflected one of Crass' key preoccupations – the alliance of anarchy with peace.

As discussed in Chapter 1, Vaucher's pacifism originated in the context of her youth, where the horrors of the Second World War hung over her generation's childhood, many of whom, like her, had grown up playing in the rubble of urban bomb sites. Rimbaud's anti-militarism also stemmed from his childhood, formed in opposition to what he saw as corrupt values foisted on his father as a military man and bastion of civilisation.[42] They and other members of the band who had grown up under the influence of the counter-culture and anti-Vietnam protests, brought these preoccupations with them to the band.

This set a new tone within punk, which had previously construed anarchy as a revolt against social norms, while rejecting anything as hippie as 'peace'.[43] One of the new inserts for the *Feeding ...* re-release featured their slogan, 'Fight War, Not Wars' (see Figure 5.2), rendered in the stencil lettering Crass used for their graffiti campaigns, and which has been endlessly reused in punk visual culture.[44] Also featured are CND, anarchy and peace symbols and the Crass logo. The insert to their (double) album, *Stations of the Crass* (1979), also reflected their pacifist stance in its graffiti, stencil lettering and on tracks such as 'Demo(N)Crats', which chants the 'Fight War, Not Wars' slogan over a backdrop of explosions.

Crass were distinct from most other punk bands in having what could loosely be termed a philosophy, arising from their lived as opposed to theoretical anarchism. This immediately distinguished them from the anarchy as posturing (using Situationist-inspired shock tactics) that characterised the Sex Pistols.[45] While members of Crass were inspired by first-wave punk, they built their outfit on the premise that they offered a more authentic version of punk than the one implied by the trajectory of the Sex Pistols and their 'No Future' stance.

The predominant narrative is that the Sex Pistols' activities constituted détournement of the music industry. This was achieved through their attack on its essential vacuity, along with all other bastions of a hierarchical society. They posed enough of a threat for their music to be banned from radio airplay and the TV (*God Save the Queen* reached number one in the charts regardless). They sought to turn the tables on the industry through exploiting it for profit, while simultaneously undermining its essential purpose, to create banal pop to enthrall the masses. However, the 'exploitation' of the music industry by the Sex Pistols for profit implied collusion. Contrary to McLaren's self-generated myth that the Pistols began at year zero, negating all the 'pretend' radicals within rock and pop who came beforehand, they were arguably instead a sensationalist diversion, who were subversive and inspirational to a young, disaffected demographic for a brief period of time, before they became

Figure 5.2 Crass, Illustration on first inside flap to Crass' album, *The Feeding of the 5000 (Second Sitting)*, Crass Records, 1981

subject to implosion and, along with other big-name bands, commodification. Reflecting this, Vaucher notes, 'For me punk totally lost its impact and in a very short time, as it was consumed by the usual fashion designers and big companies.'[46]

This narrative was also increasingly prevalent in the rhetoric of punk-zines, which decried the corruption implicit in this process in bands they considered to be sell-outs. Crass adopted this narrative with a vengeance. Ignorant's searing intro to the song 'White Punks on Hope' (1978), for example, lambasts The Clash while setting out Crass' statement of intent.

> They said that we were trash
> Well the name is Crass, not Clash
> They can stuff their punk credentials
> Cause it's them that take the cash.

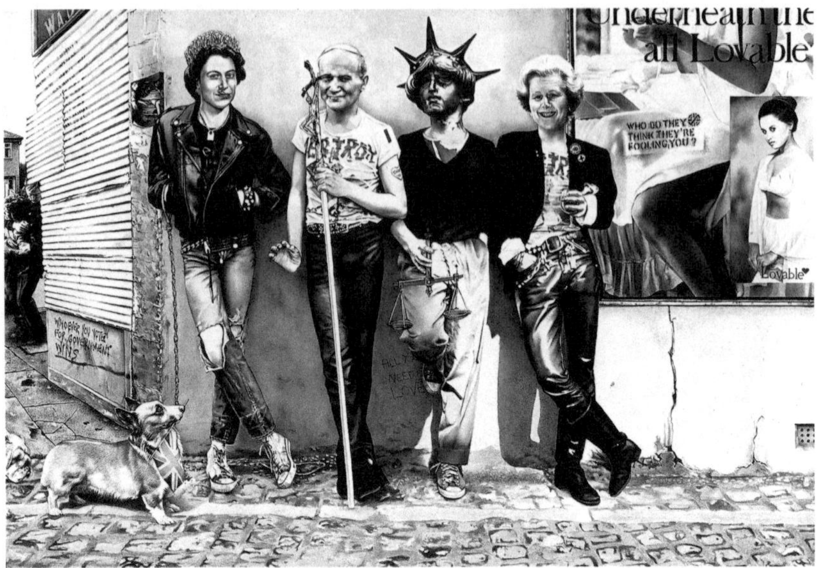

Figure 5.3 Gee Vaucher, Fold-out poster for Crass/Poison Girls 7" single, 'Bloody Revolutions'/'Persons Unknown', Crass Records, 1980, gouache, 430mm × 290mm

Crass pilloried the Sex Pistols and The Clash for displaying an affinity with their audience through punk fashion, rhetoric or antics, while simultaneously being signed to major record labels (EMI and CBS respectively), whose express purpose was to monetise their output.

The 7" single 'Persons Unknown'/'Bloody Revolutions' included a fold-out poster design by Vaucher that also featured on the front cover (see Figure 5.3). The image takes the famous shot of the Sex Pistols posing as rebellious idols and re-fashions it to cast them as establishment figures: the Queen (Sid Vicious), the Pope (Steve Jones), Justice (Paul Cook) and Thatcher (Johnny Rotten). By doing this, Vaucher mocks their faux-rebellious stance, presenting them as compromised by their collusion with 'the system'. This representation can also be seen to herald the end of Western philosophical belief systems, here embodied in its institutions of monarchy, religion, the law and government.

Despite her rapid disillusionment, Vaucher had found the 'initial punch' of punk, sparked by the Sex Pistols, 'incredibly exciting; in particular, the powerful symbolism of its clothing, safety pins and subversive use of icons, including the swastika'.[47] In this illustration, she borrowed the image of the Queen with a safety pin through her nose from Reid's famous design for the 'God Save the Queen' 7". Her inclusion of the corgi (the Queen's favourite pet), with the Union Jack in its teeth, at her feet, subtly undermines emblems of Britishness. This contrasts with the blatant iconoclasm of Reid's deigns, notably his Union Jack in tatters, emblazoned with the words 'Anarchy in the UK' in ransom note lettering, for the Sex Pistols 7" single of the same name (1976).

While Vaucher's image satirises the Sex Pistols as establishment figures, it simultaneously subverts the establishment figureheads by depicting them as rude, insubordinate and self-indulgent. This use of humour to attack hypocrisy, particularly that employed by the powerful, is reminiscent of the use of satire by renowned figures such Thomas Rowlandson, Issac and George Cruikshank and James Gillray in the late eighteenth and early nineteenth centuries. Here Vaucher symbolically inverts all that these figures profess to be. The figureheads are all slouching and wearing punk attire, while the supposed rebels are shown to be establishment figures in punk clothing. Both authority and anti-authority figures are superficial in their appearance and behaviour, which masks their true allegiances with the views and practices they profess to oppose.

Vaucher painted the elements that make up this illustration from photographs, amalgamating the bodies of the Sex Pistols with the heads of the establishment figures.[48] She painted, rather than collaging, this image (which was originally approximately A3 in size, measuring 430mm × 290mm) to have greater control of the composition.[49] She has depicted the four establishment figures as gazing directly at the viewer in a knowing manner. As such, they seem to question the viewer's passivity in consuming the image. This message is reiterated in the Crass stencil graffiti, which comments on the advertisement using a model's legs to sell goods and reads *Who do they think they're fooling, you?* To the left of the picture, another piece of graffiti reads 'Whoever you vote for the government wins', while the left of frame depicts a rape scene in which a man has a woman in a headlock, which Vaucher says 'kicks it all home'.[50]

Although Vaucher's work commented on the political situation following Thatcher's election win in 1979, her weightier critique occurred in light of the Falklands War and Thatcher's re-election for a second term in 1983 (see Chapter 6). Prior to this, her focus was still on the wider theme of institutional power imbalance, which she had explored throughout the 1970s. The concern with relational abuses of power and female subordination through the institution of the family that had characterised *International Anthem 2* (1979) also informed her designs for the release of Crass' second album, *Stations of the Cross*.

Similarly to the way her painted illustrations were often presumed to be photomontage, Vaucher's collage work has often surpassed the limitations of the medium, providing an illusion of depth within a two-dimensional format. The collage that she created as an insert for *Stations of the Cross* (1979), for example, deploys a sense of interior space akin to a stage, which provides the setting for the familial drama to play out (see colour insert, Plate 6). Vaucher's image draws on surrealism in creating anti-rationalist juxtapositions and a sense of unease that seems to reflect the artist's unconscious. Her image evokes Pop Art works, most obviously the famous collage by Richard Hamilton, *Just What Is It That Makes Today's Dream Homes So Different, So Appealing* (1956), in its intention to send up markers of social status; in this case, the idealised family unit. However, Vaucher's image stresses the violence that is inherent to this situation. The grainy, monochrome photos of the band, performing in front of banners displaying the CND, anarchy and peace and Crass symbols, set these concerns within the wider political and punk orientation of Crass.

Vaucher's image focuses on the family as an entity that fosters violence, through engendering gender-specific roles and obligatory relationships. By playing on the Good Friday ritual The Stations of the Cross, its title associates the suffering this 'ideal' family undergoes to the Christian story of crucifixion. As with several of her illustrations for *International Anthem 2*, discussed in Chapter 4, this image portrays a scene that is intense and claustrophobic. This provides the context for the characters to play out the subjective tensions inherent in a bourgeois family trap with overtones of Freudian violence. Overt references include the gun in place of the father's head that is pointed at the head of his younger son, which is juxtaposed onto the mother's body, so they are meshed in their mutual identification of the subordination they share in relation to the patriarch of the house. They are jointly represented as a puppet, with the boy's head forced into painful submission by its rods. It seems as though the whole ensemble is being made to perform a nauseating dance by the joint persecutors, the patriarch/gun and the older, protégé son, a mini-man dictator who precociously points at the mother/child figure. Vaucher attributes this image to her preoccupation with freedom for the child. She comments: 'It is about the family of course. It's about the torment of the child again and not allowing the child to be. They always have to interfere.'[51]

Vaucher's critique of this exemplary family is contextualised within the history of Western adherence to idealism. The backdrop to the scene contains references to Classical representations of beauty. Reclining languidly by the stairs is Michelangelo's (1475–1564) *Dying Slave* (1513–16), which embodies values of masculinity from classical antiquity. Just above and to the left of this is Jean Auguste Dominique Ingres' (1780–1867) nude painting, *La Grande Odalisque* (1814), which romanticises and objectifies orientalised beauty. The tiny priest figure at the top of the stairs assumes a stereotypically modest guise. These representations illustrate the theme of the subordination and objectification of the Other through the lens of Western patriarchy.[52] Vaucher's critique indicates opportunities for new political and aesthetic forms to emerge from the dissolution of imperialist power. The naked female figure exiting the room to the left suggests ways to exist beyond such colonising spaces.

While *Stations ...* seems to be antithetical towards Christian morality, it can be seen to share certain themes with this meta-narrative. On the sea monster emerging in the bottom, right-hand corner, Vaucher comments, 'It's an element that's transient as it could destroy everything very easily.'[53] This figure seems to signify death, as though the striving for individualised attainment prized in the West is illusory and will ultimately be devoured, either through its own internalised violence, or through an external, ultimate leveller. Such an outlook has overtones of moral condemnation that are rooted in Christian ideas of retribution.

The puritanical note this strikes is echoed in Crass' output, notably the refrain 'In all your decadence people die!' that Libertine screams repeatedly at the end of their track, *Shaved Women* (1979).[54] This is also seen in the rules applied to living at Dial House, which differentiated itself from punk culture more widely in its restraint. The ban on drugs that had been one of the founding decisions of Dail House, for example, continued during the Crass years. Vaucher recalls,

> That is not to say that some haven't sneaked in and it isn't to be puritanical about it. It's just that even in the face of a lot of the stuff that went on during the Crass' years especially; this house was left alone by the authorities. And we were sitting targets. So we'd have been pretty stupid to have entertained anything like drugs. Plus I've never taken drugs and I have no interest in them. I find life exciting and hard enough as it is.[55]

The anti-religious stance implicit in the *Stations of the Cross* artwork was more overtly visible in the poster for the *Reality Asylum/Shaved Women* release (see Figure 5.4).

Vaucher's illustration includes the figure of a young Jesus with stigmata from the famous pre-Raphaelite oil painting *Christ in the House of His Parents* (1849–50) by John Everett Millais. Behind him the adult Christ appears on the cross, depicted with his eyes rolled back into his head. This figure is set against a stormy sky and is flanked by a man with a gun and a collapsing wooden church. In the foreground, the hill is strewn with women prostrating themselves, recreating the ritual ascent of Reek Mountain in Ireland every year by pilgrims.[56] Here, however, the figures lying on the ground are taken from a photo of the My Lai massacre in Vietnam.[57] In this image, Vaucher highlights the masochistic subservience that the church has required of women, who are made to follow a leader who is shown to be inadequate. As such the

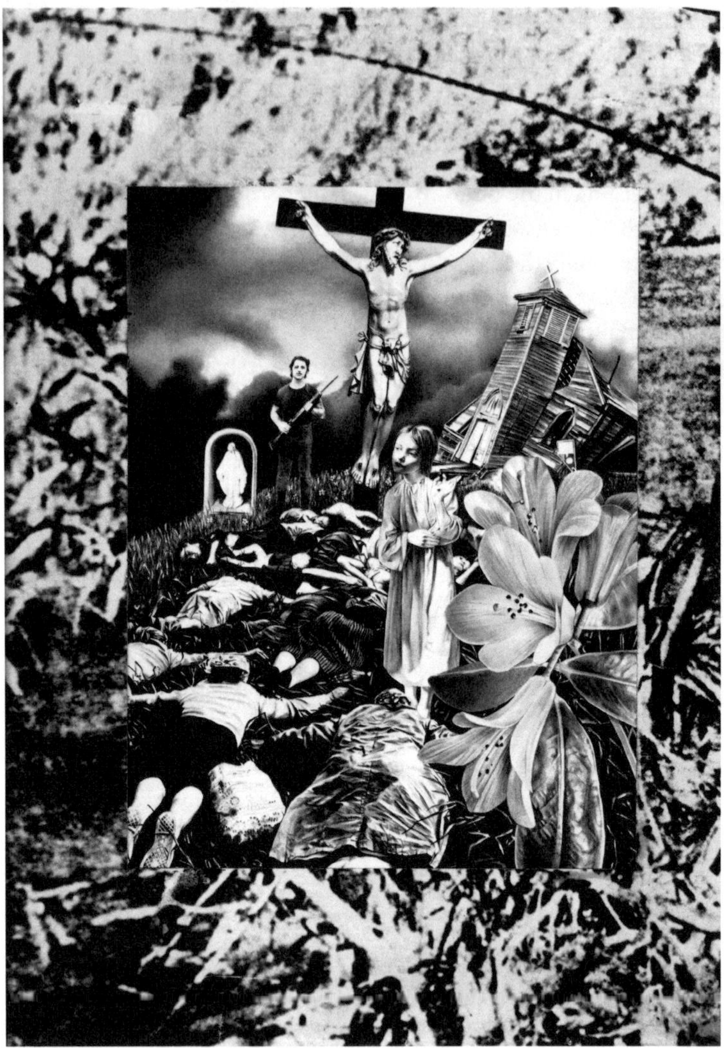

Figure 5.4 Gee Vaucher, Poster for Crass' 7" single, 'Reality Asylum', Crass Records, 1979, gouache with collaged frame, 300mm × 240mm

Church is shown to use images of the crucifixion to create a sense of guilt, thereby justifying women's suffering. This image provides a visual counterpart to the track 'Reality Asylum', which features Libertine reading out a poem by Rimbaud (taken from his book, *Reality Asylum*, 1977) that provides a searing attack on the misogyny induced by Christianity, against a backdrop of warfare and ominous sounding choir music. This fiercely anti-religious stance would

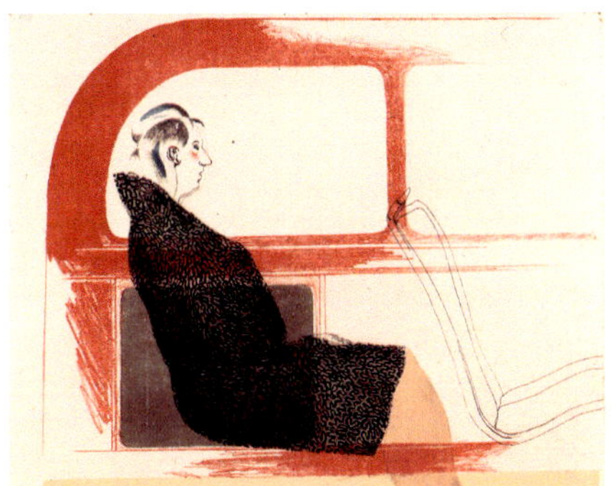 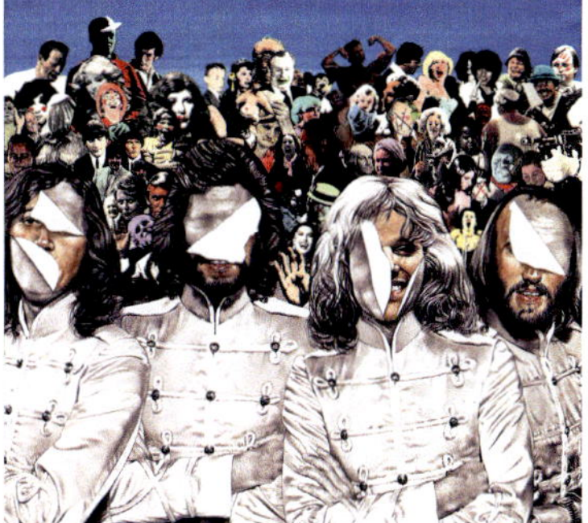

Plate 1: Gee Vaucher, *Illustration*, 1963, lithography and etching, 410mm × 260mm

Plate 2: Gee Vaucher, Bee Gees Record Review, *Rolling Stone*, 1977, watercolour, gouache and collage, 240mm × 130mm

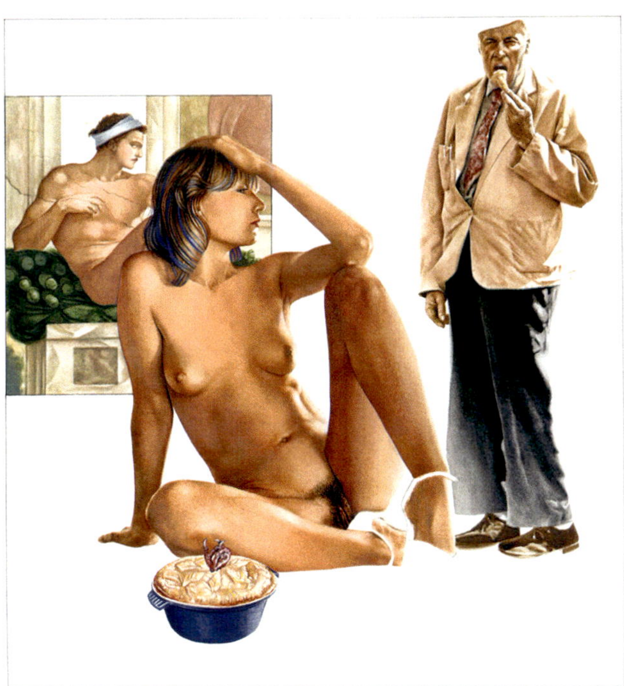

Plate 3: Gee Vaucher, Illustration for *Pent-Up*, 1975, gouache, 250mm × 240mm

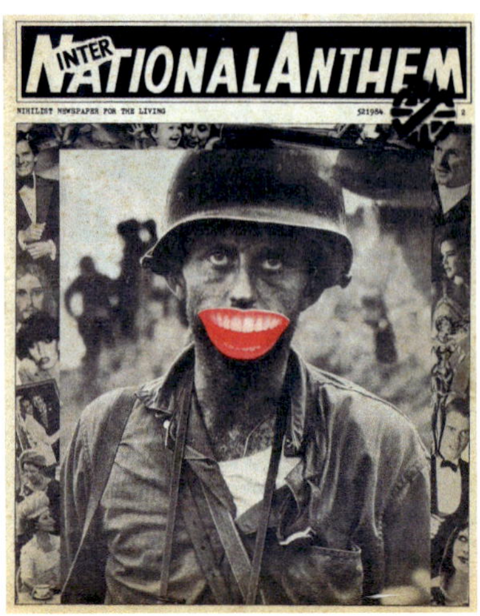

Plate 4: Gee Vaucher, Untitled Collage, *International Anthem 2: Domestic Violence,* 1979, 340mm × 270mm.

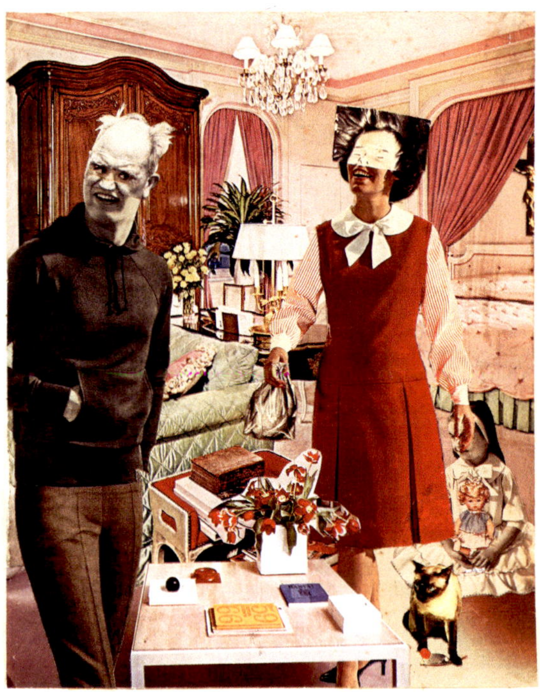

Plate 5: Gee Vaucher, Untitled Collage, *International Anthem 2: Domestic Violence,* 1979, 270mm × 250mm.

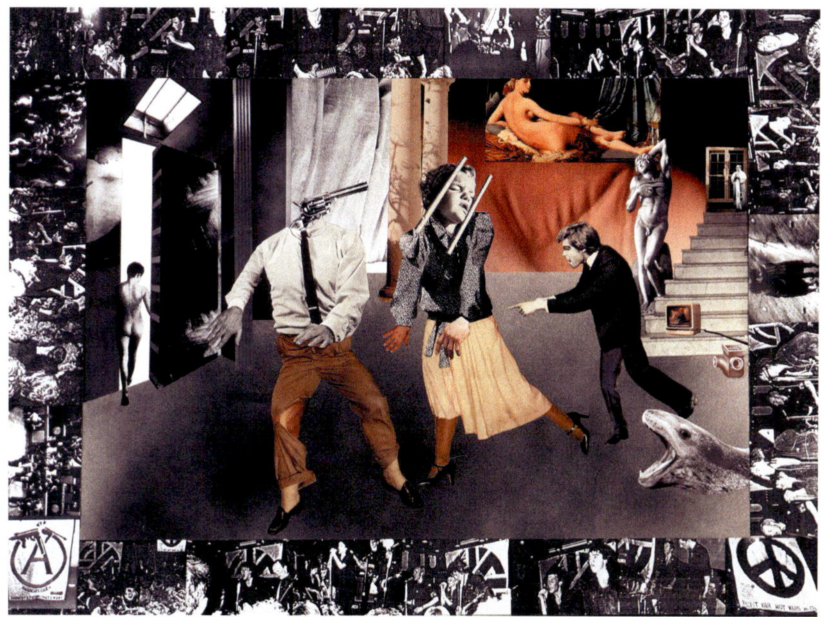

Plate 6: Gee Vaucher, fold-out poster for Crass' album, *Stations of the Cross*, 1979, collage, 820mm × 580mm.

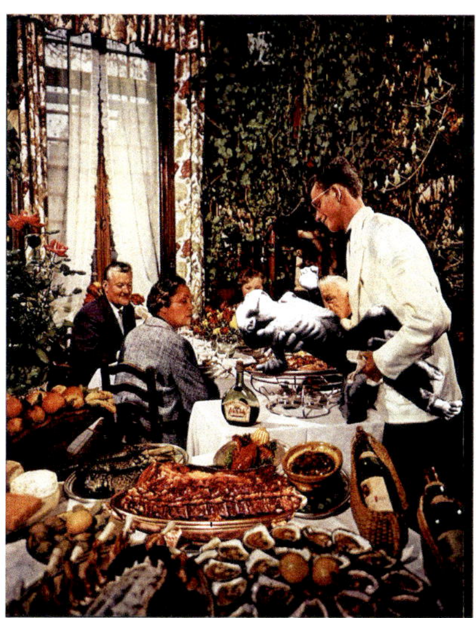

Plate 7: Gee Vaucher, Untitled Collage, *International Anthem 3: Deception and Perception*, 1980, 280mm × 210mm.

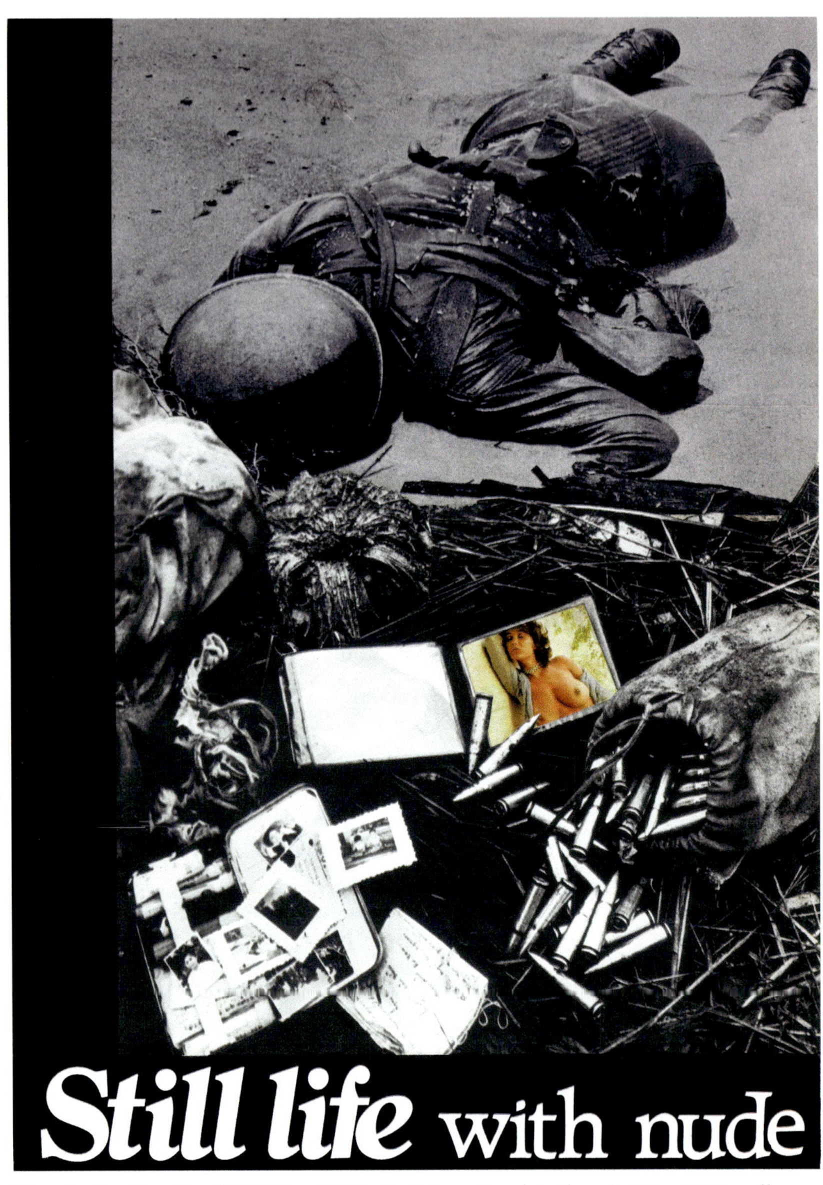

Plate 8: Gee Vaucher, Still Life with Nude, *International Anthem 5: War*, 1983, collage.

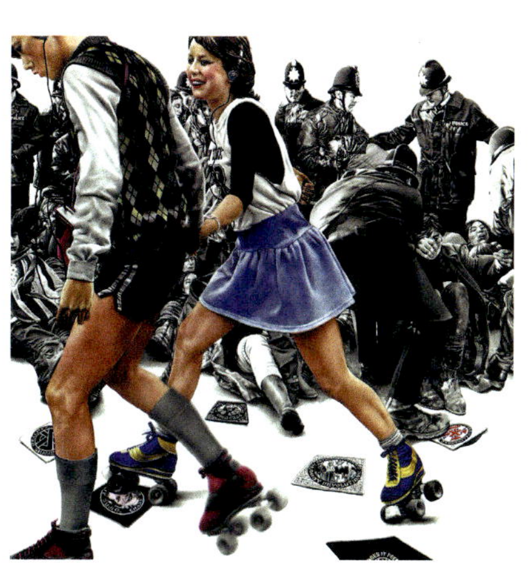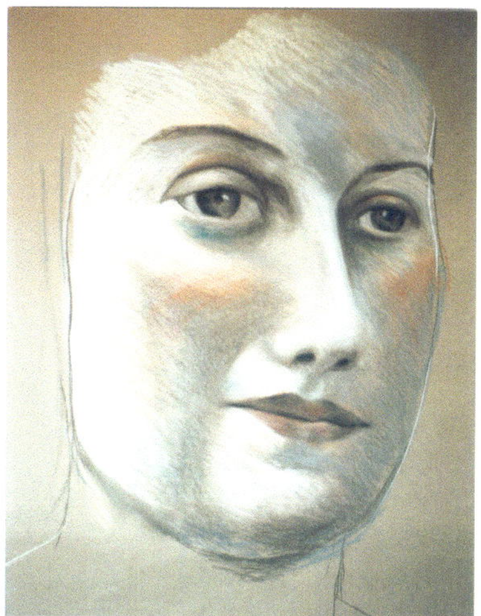

Plate 9: Gee Vaucher, Cover, Crass' album, *Best Before 1984*, 1986, gouache, 220mm × 210mm.

Plate 10: Gee Vaucher, *Hetty*, 1995, pastel, 1330mm × 1140mm.

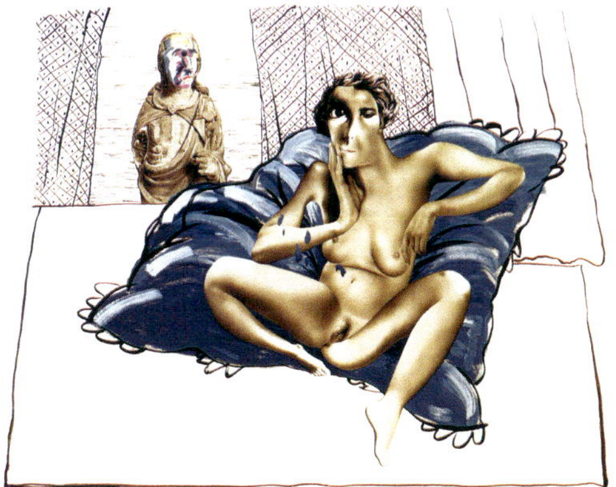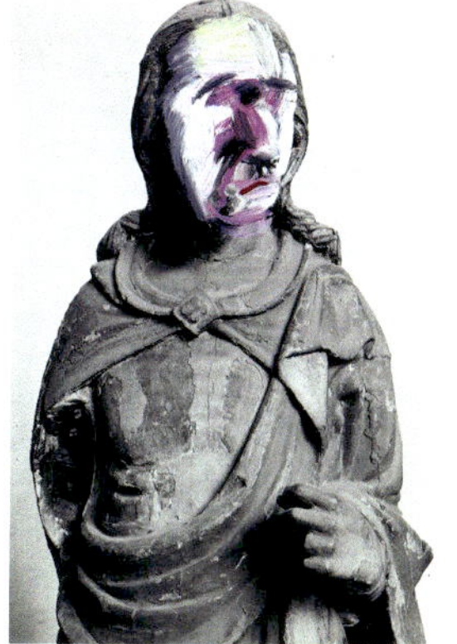

Plate 11: Gee Vaucher, *Untitled*, 1993, photographs and oil paint, 150mm × 100mm.

Plate 12: Gee Vaucher, *Untitled*, 1992, gouache, 540mm × 420mm.

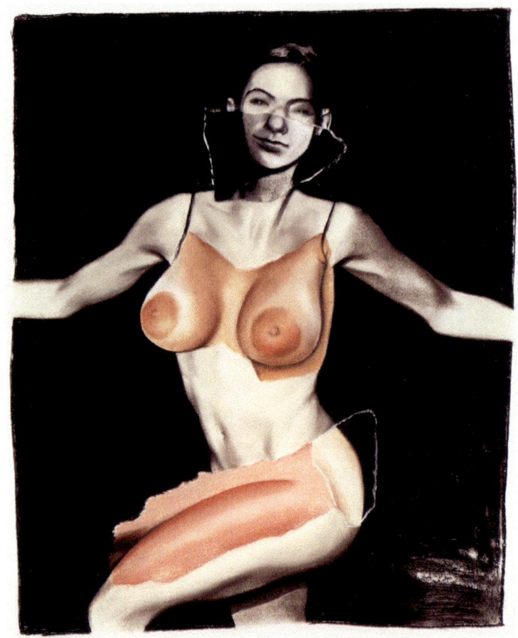

Plate 13: Gee Vaucher, *Pastel Drawing*, 1994.

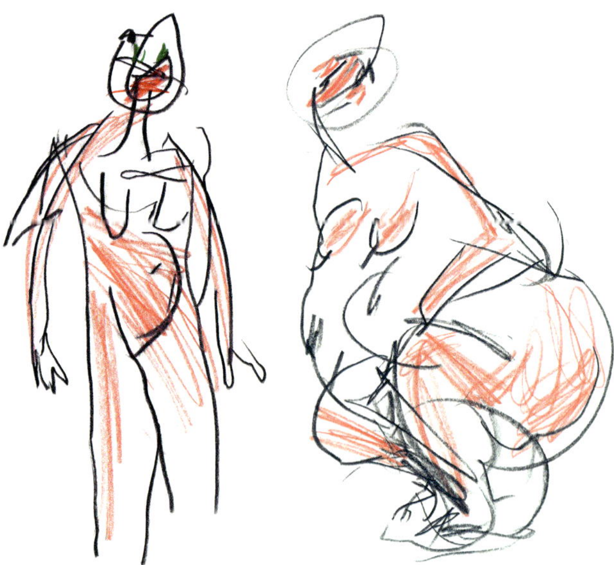

Plate 14: Gee Vaucher, *Untitled*, 1996, coloured pencil drawings, 330mm × 260mm.

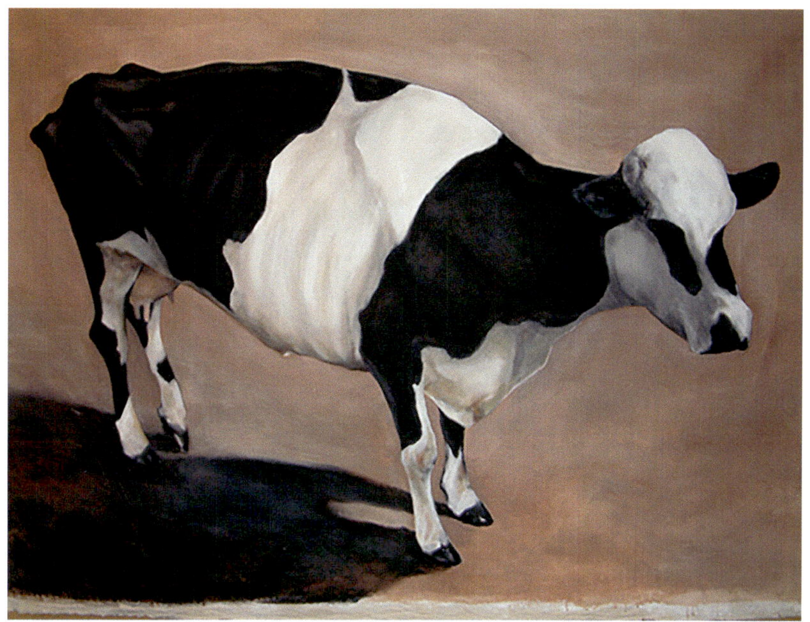

Plate 15: Gee Vaucher, *Cow*, 1997, oil paint, acrylic and wax crayon on canvas.

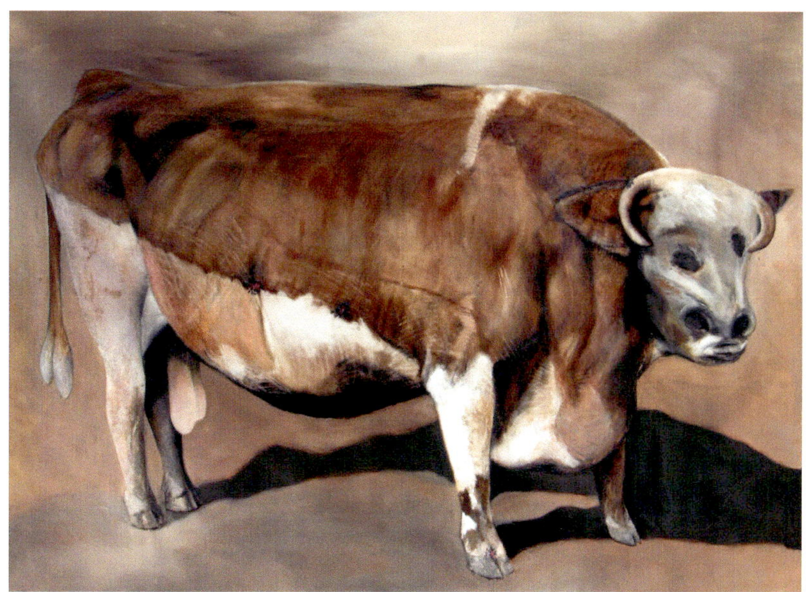

Plate 16 Gee Vaucher, *Bull*, 1997, oil paint, acrylic and wax crayon on canvas.

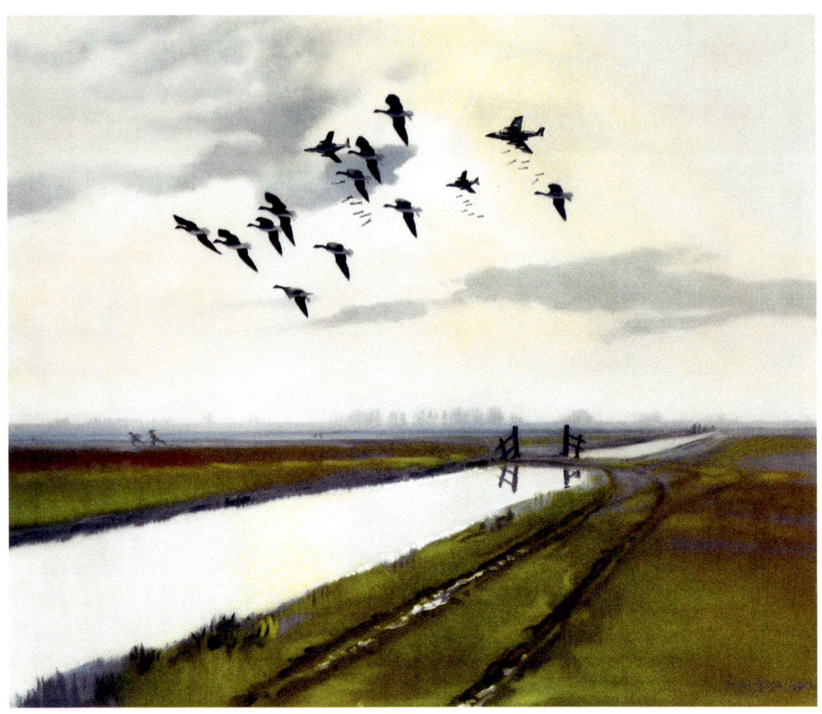

Plate 17: Gee Vaucher, *Great Scott*, 2008, colour screen-print, 550mm × 620mm.

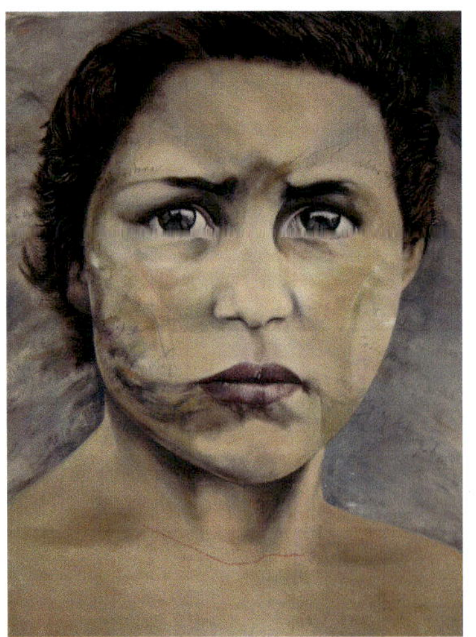

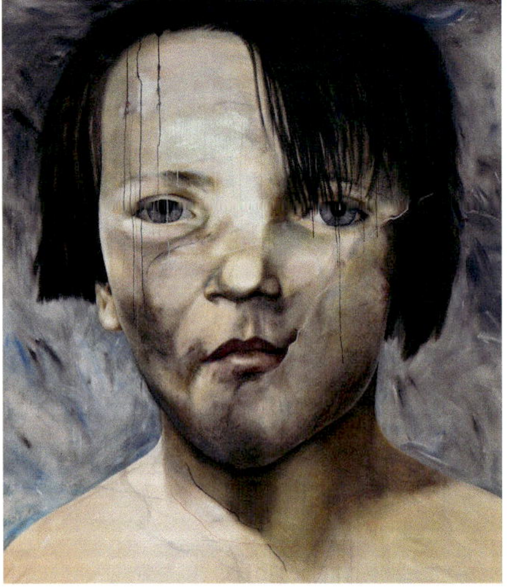

Plate 18: Gee Vaucher, *Children Who Have Seen Too Much Too Soon*, 2006–16, oil painting, 7ft square (approx.)

Plate 19: Gee Vaucher, *Children Who Have Seen Too Much Too Soon*, 2006–16, oil painting, 7ft square (approx.)

feature prominently in their output and within anarcho-punk more widely during the ensuing years.[58]

While first-wave punk had provided an emancipatory space for women, this was weighed against many factors that were misogynist, reactionary and patriarchal. Working in a heavily sexist rock industry, many female musicians struggled to make headway. Within mainstream society, women dressing in revealing or provocative clothing were often subject to attack.[59] The punk scene itself, particularly as it spread from its avant-garde, pop crossover incarnation on the Kings Road to mainstream appeal for largely male audiences, could be equally repressive. Liz Naylor, who co-edited the Manchester post-punk fanzine *City Fun* (1978–84) with Cath Caroll and later managed the UK's leading Riot Grrl band, Huggy Bear, commented, 'While there were men wrestling with questions of masculinity and feminism; there were just as many, content to leave it unreconstructed. A lot of the punk boys were just regular knobheads who happened to have spiky hair.'[60]

This perhaps goes some way to explain why, unlike their first-wave predecessors, female post-punk bands such as the Au Pairs (1978–83) and the Raincoats (1977–84, 1993–) were explicitly feminist and fostered a low-key, gender-free look. The presence of high-profile women in anarcho-punk, notably Vi Subversa (Poison Girls), Eve Libertine and Joy de Vivre (Crass), and Zillah Minx (Rubella Ballet) also ensured a female, often feminist, perspective permeated the scene. Subversa had a profound impact in this regard. A middle-aged woman and mother of two, she broke both music industry and punk conventions, and brought a unique perspective shaped by her twenty years' involvement in the peace movement, the 1960s anarchist scene and latterly the women's movement, to punk.

This new perspective was reflected in the zines, which provided space for debates on female emancipation and the subversion of traditional gender roles. However, while they grappled with issues such as sexism, the attitudes expressed within them sometimes showed how deeply such ideas were ingrained. In response to a provocative tirade on punk music in *NME* by Julie Burchill, for example, *Ripped and Torn* featured a response that read, 'Here is a three part recipe for success when your fifteen minutes of fame's run out, just as you've run out so many others: 1) Get out of town, 2) Babies, 3) Shut Up.'[61] In punk's early years, it took zines created by women, such as *Jolt* (1977) and later *Brass Lip* (1979), to prioritise female musicians and take an anti-sexist stance.[62] As such they facilitated views articulated by female punk musicians and artists that were often overlooked in the male-dominated music industry and press.[63] *Brass Lip* was sophisticated in its design compared to most punk-zines. Its layout juxtaposed graphics with text to form a stark aesthetic that correlated with its subject matter. Its focus on sexism, as well as ethnic minorities and gay liberation, was in many ways a direct attack on the values established within the counterculture of the 1960s, which predominantly championed libertarianism geared towards white, heterosexual men.[64]

Vaucher's critique both overlapped with and diverged from the feminist one articulated in punk-zines. *International Anthem* (1977–81) was anarchistic compared to other feminist punk-zines in its portrayal of female oppression as just one aspect of broader societal control. Along similar lines, Poison Girls created the fanzine *Impossible Dream* (four issues between 1979 and 1986), which featured photomontages interwoven with Poison Girls' lyrics denouncing power and writing by Andrea Dworkin, William Burroughs and the poet Janet Dube, among others. It focused on issues of militarism, sexual politics and degenerate capitalist culture and politics.

The ideas communicated in *International Anthem* and *Impossible Dream* resonated with anarcho-feminist ideas, which were gaining traction at the time.[65] Anarcho-feminists provided a perspective on anarchism orientated to women, while also reacting against the mainstream and hierarchical power structures that they believed increasingly defined feminism by the late 1970s.[66] They aimed to revive the leaderless structure that had characterised feminism's earlier second wave.[67] In this they built on the ideas of Emma Goldman, which also received renewed attention at the time (see Chapter 2). Goldman argued that women accepting State sanctioned rights and advancement in a world shaped by commercial interests amounted to collusion with the power imbalance inherent to that 'system'. While she recognised the need for equality between the sexes, she argued that women would achieve this through radical autonomy. This has clear parallels with Vaucher's personal philosophy, and the sentiment would find one of its most complete expressions in the third Crass album, *Penis Envy*.

Penis Envy (1981) featured exclusively female vocals from Eve Libertine and Joy de Vivre, as well as increasingly multi-faceted musical structures that moved it away from the overtly punk sound of Crass' first two albums. Reflecting themes that had to this point been most evident in the work of Poison Girls, the album was focused on issues such as marriage and the objectification and control of female sexuality. Libertine provided a particularly angry indictment of male sexual objectification and violence towards women in the track 'Bata Motel', which was subject to a charge of obscenity.[68]

Vaucher's striking illustrations for *Penis Envy* explore the extent to which sexuality and gender are social constructs. The album insert features an angel comprised of various collaged parts (Figure 5.5). These are assembled in a seemingly haphazard way, revealing their torn and overlapping edges, yet still

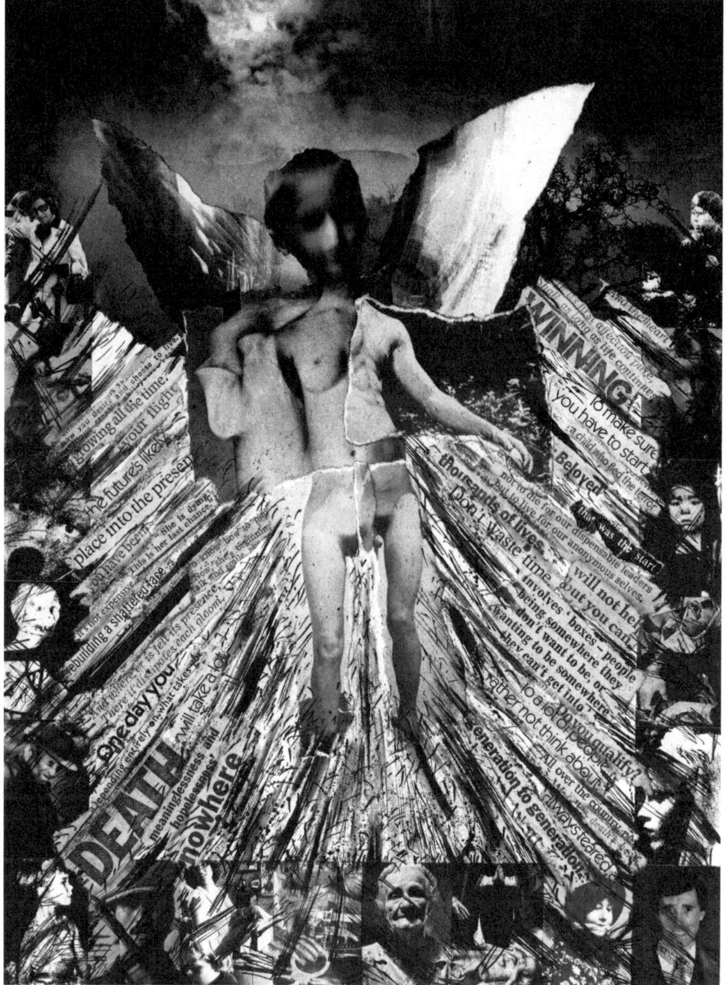

Figure 5.5 Gee Vaucher, Inside illustration for Crass' album, *Penis Envy*, Crass Records, 1981, collage and ink, 290mm × 210mm

provide an incredibly convincing whole. The eroticised body combines male and female elements, while the face is ethereal; more connected to the otherworld alluded to in the stormy sky. The strips of newspaper cuttings fan out from the angel figure like light rays. Their content combines the horrific with the mundane, thereby commenting on the mass media's portrayal of real life.

Vaucher's angel, which transgresses gender boundaries, provides a riposte to Freud's famous concept of 'penis envy' that gave the album its title. Rather than a predetermined gender identity precipitated by a crisis centred on the

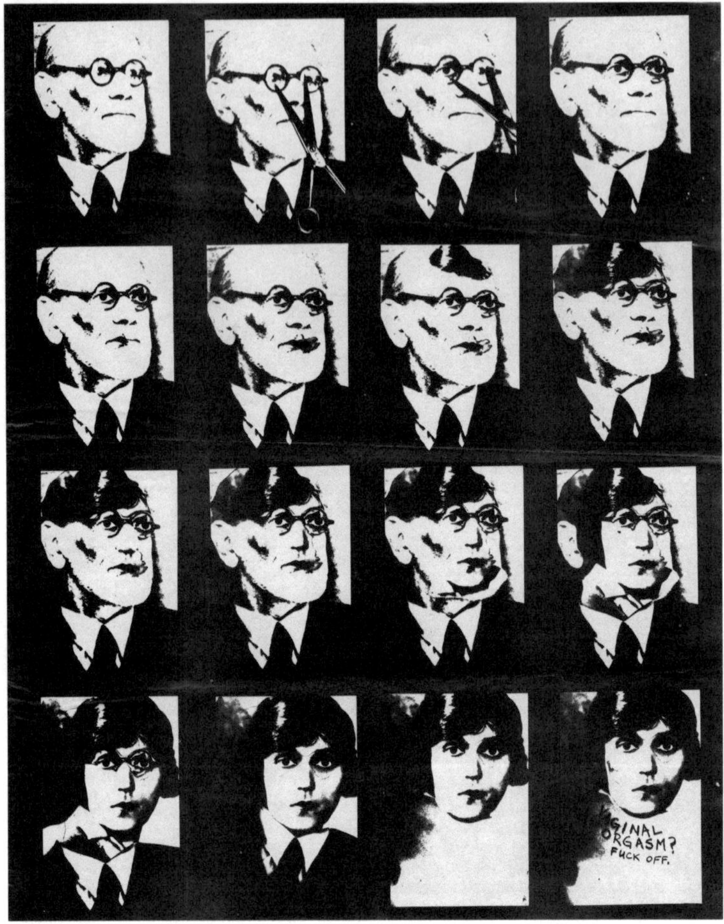

Figure 5.6   Penny Rimbaud, Illustration for *International Anthem 3: Deception and Perception*, 1980, collage

lack of a penis, her figure has a fluid identity, embodying male and female characteristics.

Along comparable lines, Penny Rimbaud created a collage (see Figure 5.6) for *International Anthem 3: Deception and Perception* (1980), which features a headshot of Freud, frame by frame mutating into that of a woman, with the slogan 'Vaginal Orgasm? FUCK OFF' in the final image. Rimbaud knocks the patriarchal basis for Freud's notion that vaginal orgasm was the natural experience for a mature woman, while clitoral orgasm was symptomatic of immaturity. The swipe at Freud is also part of Crass' wider disavowal of leaders, as the lyrics to their track 'Suck' on the album, *The Feeding of the Five Thousand* (1978) illustrates.

> Do you really believe in Buddha? Buddha sucks
> Do you really believe in Jesus. Jesus fucks.
> Is it alright really? Is it alright really?
> Is it working?
>
> Do you really believe in Marx? Marx fucks.
> Do you really believe in Thatcher? Maggie sucks.
> Is it alright really? Is it alright really?
> Is it working?
>
> Do you really believe in the system? Well, ok
> I BELIEVE IN ANARCHY IN THE UK
> Is it alright really? Is it alright really?
> Is it working?

The release of Penis Envy saw a shift in punk-zines, which began to engage more with anarcho-feminist ideas, dedicating an escalating amount of space to such concerns in the ensuing years.[69] This perspective was also reflected in the political situation on the ground. The women's protests at Greenham Common in the early 1980s, for instance, provided a space for anarchism, feminism and punk to intersect.[70] The oppositional, direct confrontation with authority that this represented would characterise a new era in which the polemic of Crass and anarcho-punk more widely became increasingly acrimonious in the wake of the Falklands War and the re-election of Margaret Thatcher.

Notes

1   Vaucher in email correspondence, May 2021.
2   Vaucher quoted in G. Berger, *The Story of Crass* (London: Omnibus Press, 2008), p. 93 (updated via email correspondence, May 2021).
3   Ignorant, *The Rest is Propaganda* (Norfolk: Dimlo Productions, 2020), p. 159. The artist Anthony Maccall recalls a charged performance by Crass in New York, while Crass member, Pete Wright, believed their presence in that scene to be 'pretty much irrelevant', in Berger, *The Story of Crass*, p. 94.
4   Vaucher in interview with Groß, 2002.
5   Vaucher in email correspondence, April 2021.
6   Ignorant, *The Rest is Propaganda*, pp. 117–118.
7   See Berger, *The Story of Crass*, pp. 28–40.
8   Vaucher in email correspondence, May 2021.

9   See Ignorant, *The Rest is Propaganda*, pp. 130–132 on the involvement of Crass' members in the London squat scene.

10 Vaucher in interview with Groß, 2002.

11 Vaucher in email correspondence, May 2021.

12 Vaucher in interview with Binns, 2013.

13 Despite being a nonplaying member of the band, she also wrote several songs, including 'G's Song' which she penned while still living in New York, 'Time Out', 'Contaminational Power' and 'Crutch of Society'. She also occasionally provided vocals on Crass' records.

14 Vaucher in interview with Reuland, in E. Reuland and J. MacPhee, *Realising the Impossible: Art Against Authority* (London: AK Press, 2007), p. 71.

15 Vaucher in interview with Groß, 2002.

16 Vaucher in interview with Groß, 2002.

17 Phil Free and his three children and Eve Libertine and her son lived there at one point.

18 Vaucher in interview with Binns, 2013.

19 CRASS JOURNAL: A record of letters, articles, postings and emails, February 2009–September 2010 concerning Penny, Gee and Allison's 'Crassical Collection'. Available at www.crassicalcollection.com/crass.pdf (accessed 20 September 2020).

20 Ignorant in interview with Binns, 2020.

21 Vaucher in interview with Groß, 2015.

22 Vaucher in interview with Groß, 2015.

23 Eve Libertine, quoted in Berger, *The Story of Crass*, p. 109.

24 Diboll, in email correspondence, December 2020. *Acts of Defiance, Anathema, Enigma, Fack, New Crimes* and *Pigs for Slaughter* were among other notable fanzines that were formed under the inspiration of Crass.

25 Diboll in conversation (phone), December 2020.

26 Vaucher in interview with Groß, 2002.

27 Vaucher in interview with Groß, 2002.

28 The most obvious example of this was the series of compilation albums, *Bullshit Detector*, released by Crass on the Crass Records label between1980–84. The LPs were comprised of music recordings, demo tapes and visual material that had been sent to the band from unknown/little known bands.

29 J. Baines, 'The Freedom of the Press Belongs to Those who Control the Press', in N. Carpentier, P. Pruulmann-Vengerfeldt, R. Kilborn, R. Olsson, H. Nieminen, E. Sundin and K. Nordenstreng (eds), *Communicative Approaches to Politics and Ethics in Europe* (Tartu: ECREA & University of Tartu Press, 2009), p. 118.

30 Rimbaud in interview (skype) with R. Binns, April 2021.

31 Crass were supported in this endeavour by their future label mates Poison Girls, who had recently re-located from Brighton to Burleigh House, a licensed squat close to Dial House.

32 S. Thompson, 'Crass Commodities', *Popular Music and Society* 27:3 (2004), p. 316.

33 Steve Ignorant elaborates further on their motivation for creating the independent record label in M. Worley, 'The End Result: An Interview with Steve Ignorant' in M. Dines and M. Worley, *The Aesthetics of our Anger: Anarcho-Punk, Politics and Music* (Colchester/New York: Minor Compositions, 2016), p. 293.

34 P. Dale, 'The Beginning of a Continuation' in *Anyone Can Do It: Traditions of Punk and the Politics of Empowerment* (PhD Thesis, 2011), p. 203 (note 17).

35 Rimbaud acknowledges this in interview in R. Bestley and A. Ogg (eds), *The Art of Punk* (London: Omnibus Press, 2012), p. 176.

36 In 'Crass Commodities', Thompson argues that Crass' success is limited to their function as an enterprise within an overarching capitalist economic framework rather than constituting anything revolutionary.

37 Crass Records produced twenty-one albums and thirty-six singles, of which twelve albums and twenty-five singles were by other bands, predominantly released between 1980 and 1984.

38 Conflict put such issues centre stage with their blatant lyrics and the visual material accompanying their record releases (see in particular their inserts and cover for 'To A Nation of Animal Lovers', 7" EP, released on Corpus Christi, 1983). As well as the focus shown in their music, Flux gave out thousands of leaflets on vivisection, anarchy and pacifism at their gigs (tract entitled Flux of Pink Indians by Hammy in *Roar*, No 7, 1983). Also see the front cover to the Subhumans' single, 'Evolution', 1983, which presents a cartoon by Nick Lant, featuring a vivisectionist in his animal laboratory. The rear cover presents a photograph of a cat surrounded by a list of cruelty free cosmetics companies.

39 Vaucher in email correspondence, May 2021.

40 See A. Larsen 'Fast, Cheap and out of Control: The Graphic Symbol in Hardcore Punk', *Punk & Post-Punk* 2:1 (2013), pp. 91–106.

41 See M. Perry 'Mark P Pisses on the lot of Em!', *Sniffin' Glue*, No. 5 (November 1976), p. 2. Also see 'Question: The Scene?' In *Sniffin' Glue,* No. 11 (July 1977), p. 5, by Steve at Rough Trade. Rough Trade was the record shop with a back room, which Perry used for a while as the office for *Sniffin' Glue*, after moving it from his small bedroom in his parents' council flat.

42 See Vaucher and Rimbaud's autobiographical accounts of their childhoods in G. Vaucher, *Crass Art and Other Pre-Post Modern Monsters* (Colchester: Firstsite, published in collaboration with Minor Compositions, 2nd Edn, 2014), p. 2 and P. Rimbaud, *Shibboleth: My Revolting Life* (Edinburgh: AK Press, 1998), pp. 17–69).

43 R. Bestley and R. Binns, 'The Evolution of an Anarcho-Punk Narrative, 1978–84', in The Subcultures Network (ed.). *Ripped, Torn and Cut: Pop, Politics and Punk Fanzines from 1976* (Manchester: Manchester University Press: 2018), p. 134.

44 Bestley and Binns, 'Anarcho-Punk narrative', p. 134.

45 Vaucher in interview with Groß, 2002.

46 Vauchern interview with Groß, 2002.

47 Vaucher in interview with Groß, 2002.

48 Vaucher, Interview with Binns, 2018.

49 Vaucher in interview with Binns, 2018.

50 Vaucher in email correspondence, May 2021.

51 Vaucher in interview with Binns, 2013.

52 The use of the term Other has been articulated by Jean-Paul Sartre in relation to The Look ('Being and Nothingness, An Essay on Phenomenological Ontology', 1943) which posits visibility as constituting an individual's subjection through another's gaze. Authors Frantz Fanon (*The Wretched of the Earth*, 1961) and Edward Said (*Orientalism*, 1978) famously utilised this term with reference to colonialism and race.

53 Vaucher in interview with Binns, 2013.

54 Vaucher has stated that she argued for the line to read 'In all *our* decadence people die'. 'We should not have been left out of the equation in the first place.' In email correspondence with Binns, 2021.

55 Vaucher in interview with Groß, 2015.

56 Vaucher in interview with Binns, 2018.

57 Vaucher in interview with Binns, 2018.

58 Bestley and Binns, 'Anarcho-Punk Narrative', pp. 142–145.

59 Viv Albertine has spoken about the abuse and violence members of the Slits were subjected to in her autobiography, *Clothes, Clothes, Clothes. Music, Music, Music. Boys, Boys, Boys* (London: Faber & Faber, 2015).

60 Liz Naylor quoted in L. O'Brien, 'The Woman Punk Made Me', in R. Sabin (ed.), *Punk Rock: So What? The Cultural Legacy of Punk* (London: Routledge,1999), p. 194.

61 D. Tony, 'Live at the Witch Trials', in *Ripped and Torn*, Issue 17 (March 1979).

62 *See* Caz Blaze's chapter, 'Invisible women: the role of women in punk fanzine creation' in *Ripped, Torn and Cut: Pop, Politics and Punk Fanzines* (Manchester: Manchester University Press: 2018), pp. 72–91.

63 Bestley and Binns, 'Anarcho-Punk Narrative', p. 139.

64 See *Brass Lip*, Issue 1 (1979), p. 19 for a critique of the macho posturing and inherent misogyny in the music produced by rock stars such as Jimi Hendrix and the Rolling Stones.

65 The first UK anarcho-feminist groups appeared in 1977, subsequently forming a national network that had disbanded by 1980. Lynne Farrow originally coined the term *Feminism as Anarchism* in her influential essay of the same name (1974). Other significant essays include *Anarchism: The Feminist Connection* by Peggy Kornegger and *Socialism, Anarchism and Feminism* by Carol Ehrlich. Both appeared in the anthology *Reinventing Anarchy: What Anarchists are Thinking These Days* (London: Routledge and Kegan & Paul, 1979).

66 See P. Kornegger, 'Anarchism: The Feminist Connection', in Black Rose Anarcho-Feminists (ed.), *Quiet Rumours, An Anarcha-Feminist Anthology* (London: Dark Star, 1980), pp. 34–36.

67 Kornegger, 'Anarchism: The Feminist Connection', pp. 33–34.

68 Although the conviction of the record for obscenity was overturned by the Court of Appeal, the ban remained for the lyrics to Bata Motel.

69 See 'The Private Shop', *Blind Faith* 1 (1981), 'Underneath They're all Angry Loveable' and 'Daily Star Bird', in *Fack*, No. 6 (1981), p. 5 and p. 18 respectively, 'Face of Fashion' in *Anathema*, No. 2, p. 11, 'The Working Woman' in *Acts of Defiance*, No. 3 (1982), p. 10, 'True Love' in *Acts of Defiance*, No. 6 (1983), p. 27. See *Incendiary 2, Special Rock n Roll Impotence Extravaganza* (1985), p. 10, on the theme of prostitution and an interview with the band Lost Cherries in *Wake Up*, No. 4, Dave (1984), p. 5, on the meaning of their stance against sexism and organised religion.

70 See L. Robinson, 'Anarcho-Feminism and Greenham Common: Always More than Either, Or', in G. Bull and M. Dines (eds), *And All Around Was Darkness* (Portsmouth: Itchy Monkey Press, 2016), pp. 47–57.

6

Post-punk, hardcore and the dissolution of the dream

While Crass brought a distinct vision of anarchism, pacifism and feminism into punk through their output in the early years, as the 1980s progressed they became increasingly focused on the authoritarianism, divisive politics and neo-liberal economics of the Thatcher government. Thatcher provided the locus for opposition from various quarters due to her extreme political-economic stance, harsh posturing and high visibility. While the Left in general was focused on opposition to the Tory regime, the anarchist perspective differed in that it saw Thatcherism as one instance of power abuse within a hierarchical structure of government that was itself fundamentally flawed. These concerns are evident in Vaucher's portrayal of the hypocrisy and corruption of world leaders of varying political denominations in the fold-out poster accompanying the Crass single, 'Nagasaki Nightmare' (see Figure 6.1).

The image portrays the world leaders doing deals at the expense of the poor, powerless and disenfranchised. While Ronald Reagan and the Soviet leader Leonid Brezhnev are the most dominant figures, also prominent to the left is Margaret Thatcher, replete in a ball gown, depicted dancing with Chairman Mao. Pakistani President, Muhammad Zia-ul-Haq (1978–88) is behind them, while the Canadian Prime Minister, Pierre Trudeau (1968–79 and again from 1980–84) is positioned behind Reagan. To the far right of the image are Fidel Castro and Indira Ghandi.[1] To the left of Thatcher in the foreground stands a Japanese woman with a bandaged head and a child, while a charred corpse

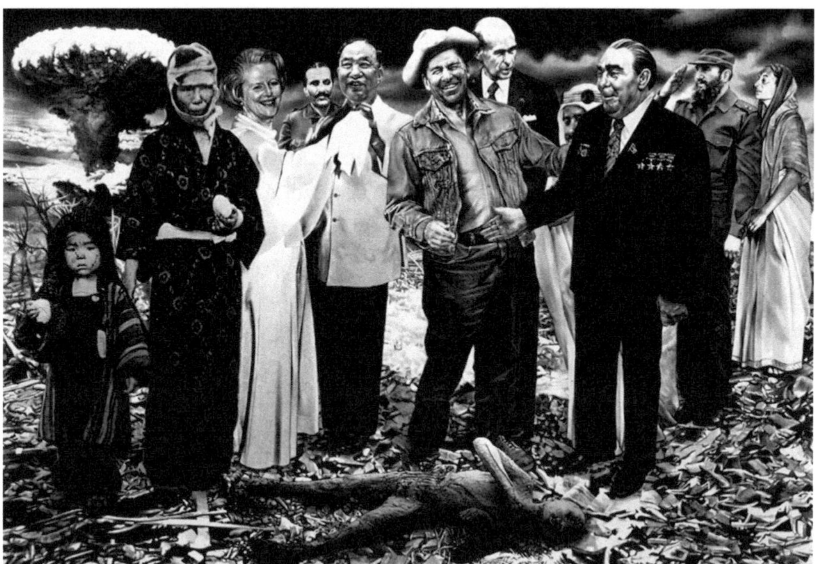

Figure 6.1   Gee Vaucher, Illustration for the Crass 7" single, 'Nagasaki Nightmare'/'Big A, Little A', Crass Records, 1980, gouache and collage, 320mm × 210mm

lies at the feet of the world leaders. These figures are the innocent victims of the US atomic bombing of the Japanese city of Nagasaki during the Second World War.

Vaucher has described the profound effect of growing up in the aftermath of Hiroshima and Nagasaki. The threat of nuclear war that overhung the 1950s had returned by 1980, with Britain acting as a third power amenable to siting US missile bases on its shores. The fold-out for this single had as its centrepiece a map that showed the extent of nuclear power and weaponry throughout the UK. In its strong moral purpose, its use as a political weapon and the appropriation of mass media imagery to reveal a concealed truth behind the image, Vaucher's work at this time mirrored that of her contemporary Peter Kennard. Their work had been symptomatic of radical art production during the 1970s (see Chapter 3). By the early 1980s, they both focused on subjects of poverty, war and injustice, with a distinct antipathy to the dominant ideas of Thatcherism.[2] The precedent provided by the pioneering Berlin Dadaist artist, John Heartfield, in creating work concerned with communicating a message with a clear social and/or political purpose is most clearly manifest in their work during this period. However, while Heartfield and Kennard worked within the medium of photomontage, Vaucher continued to incorporate painting into her representations. On this illustration Vaucher notes, 'The Nagasaki victims are collaged photos, they're the real people and the ground is real and all the rest is painted.'[3]

Heartfield's chief objective had been to utilise new media such as photography to serve a socially progressive purpose. As such, his approach fulfilled philosopher Walter Benjamin's call for the re-functioning (*Umfunktionierung*) of this new media, as outlined in his essay, *The Author as Producer* (1934). Heartfield shared Benjamin's Marxist allegiance, while Kennard's left-wing orientation is reflected in his decision to work closely with organisations including CND, The Labour Party and the Greater London Council (GLC) during the 1980s, following his previous involvement in the movement against the Vietnam War. The correlation between his design language in this period and that used as agitprop by the earlier peace movement is striking.[4]

While Vaucher was not aligned with left-wing politics, she shares both a critique of institutional power and humanitarian ideals such as equality and justice with these artists. Crass, Poison Girls and anarcho-punk more widely, were broadly supportive of CND in the early years. Vaucher recalls CND being at a low ebb at this point, operating out of a tiny office on John Street near the British Museum (London). Rimbaud and Libertine had visited to offer help getting the message to younger people, and Crass handed out CND leaflets at their gigs.[5] They also held benefit gigs for CND among a host of other causes. However, as CND grew once more into an increasingly mainstream mass movement, a gulf became apparent between them and the anarchist leaning, minority, youth subculture of anarcho-punk.[6]

Vaucher's humanitarian concerns permeated the content of her third *International Anthem* (1980), which included articles on war and religion, and newsreel photos of the horrific after-effects of nuclear attacks. Common assumptions about the sanctity of the newborn baby were overturned by material that decried birth as violence; an extension of ownership of individuals by parents, family and society. The emerging globalised economy and the exploitative outcomes of this for Third World countries provided another focus. The collage in Plate 7 (see colour insert) for example, shows a starving child being offered as a menu option to wealthy, complacent Western diners.

This and subsequent *International Anthems* (*4: Northern Ireland*, 1981 and *5: War*, 1983) articulate an increasingly hostile antipathy towards the Thatcher administration. The untitled illustration in Figure 6.2 depicts the British Prime Minister applying lipstick, using the blood of a corpse as a mirror. Vaucher here uses her painting technique to distort and exaggerate the expression on Thatcher's face, bestowing her with a silliness that contrasted with the sternness of her public image. The impression given is that Thatcher

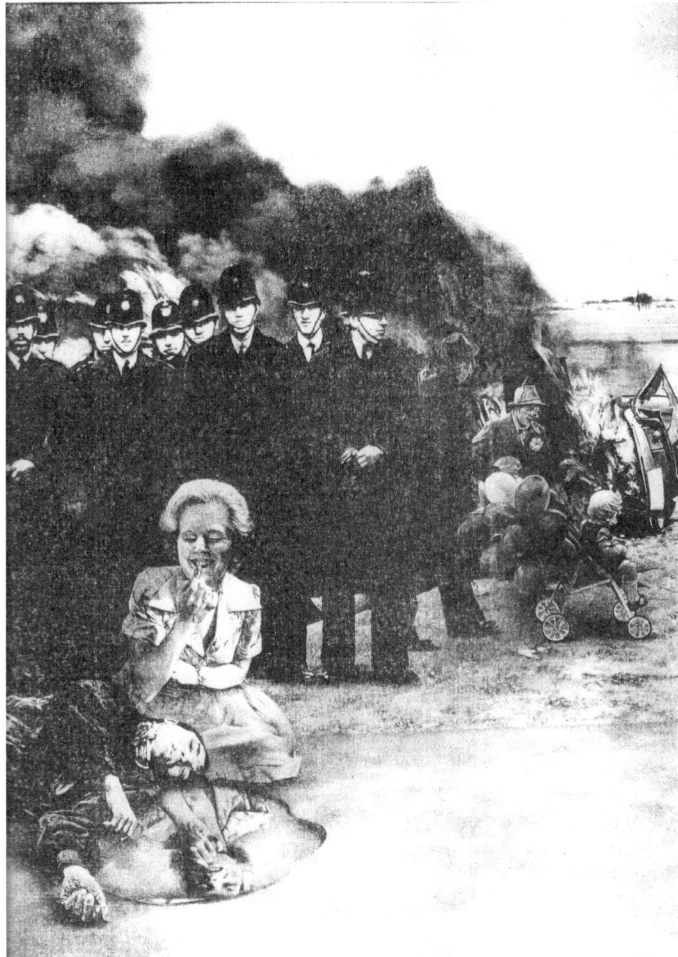

Figure 6.2   Gee Vaucher, Illustration for *International Anthem 3: Deception and Perception*, 1980, gouache

is gloating over the death of the Latin American woman. This image was created in the context of Thatcher's support for the USA's funding of troops, in particular death squads, in Latin America. She would also form a close, mutually supportive relationship with the brutal Chilean dictator Augusto Pinochet, something that led to fierce criticism in left-wing and alternative media, including anarcho-punk-zines.[7] Vaucher, however, denies an affiliation between the Latin American corpse figure and political events in those countries; stressing its emphasis was on the deteriorating situation in Britain.[8] There is the line of police, who stand guard in the aftermath of an incendiary attack, while an old man struggles by, pushing a child in a buggy festooned with balloons. This declinist, politicised critique of a Britain going to ruin became a recurring theme in anarcho-punk graphics more widely.[9]

The creative licence Vaucher used to create visual distortions is exemplified in her hybrid illustration of the Queen and Pope (Figure 6.3), which appeared in *International Anthem 4: Northern Ireland* (1981).

She describes her painting process for this image, for which she worked from an assortment of photographs, as follows. 'To do something like this, I

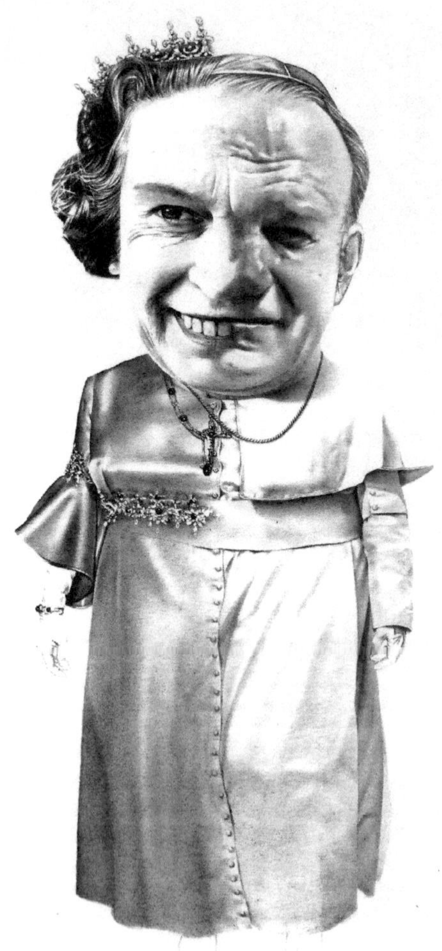

Figure 6.3   Gee Vaucher, Illustration for *International Anthem 4: Northern Ireland*, 1981, gouache

would have to find the right images needed. I looked for a dress that was very similar to the robe worn by the Pope; plain, silky, shiny, close enough to merge the two images. Obviously she didn't have that cross on. I painted it to merge with her jewels.'[10]

This image was produced prior to the flexibility afforded by computers. She further comments on the importance of the physicality of the process.

> I certainly wouldn't use Photoshop, because it wouldn't work for me. The original has got depth. If you see the original, it's definitely hand painted, it's got a presence. It's got a quality. I would say there's no sterility to it, you get the lumps and bumps that go with a handmade object. Maybe it's your own hand, when you've been working, that has made the card slightly darker. You've forgotten to put a bit of paper there and keep it clean, but that's all part of the process, the reality. There's a tea stain on one piece; can't remember which.[11]

This image provides commentary on the competing interests that have ruled Ireland for centuries. Through unifying the Queen and Pope in a grotesque caricature, she seems to imply that despite their divergence, they fulfil a comparably oppressive societal role in that country. The punk scene in Northern Ireland represented a rare respite from the sectarianism that engulfed the region at the time, and Crass reflected this in a statement they released on the back cover of the single 'Bad News', by Hit Parade (Crass Records, 1983). 'Our Concern for the H block prisoners is humanitarian and *not* sectarian and is the same concern that we feel for all those who suffer the direct effects of violent oppression.' These ideas were reflected in the setting up of Warzone, a hugely influential anarcho-punk collective that founded the nonhierarchical community centre, Giros, in the mid-1980s.[12]

International Anthem 4 was conceived as an attempt to portray a real picture of the historical background to the Troubles, to counter disinformation and the resultant paranoia generated by the media in the UK. Vaucher produced several illustrations and nearly 200 pages of writing before being overwhelmed by the enormity of the subject. This, together with financial issues and time pressures, meant it was never completed, though she released all the images and unedited writings in a collected edition of the newspaper in 2018.[13]

The time pressures that contributed to the abandonment of *International Anthem 4* were primarily a result of the demands she and Rimbaud were under through their work with Crass. Earlier collectives such as EXIT had played to a niche crowd, but Crass gave the older members of the band the ability to reach a youth audience in its thousands. The new form of anarchism they espoused arose out of the unique socio-historic circumstances of the time, in which neo-liberalism was emerging as the dominant ideology, leading sub-cultural groups to abandon the mainstream altogether. It is, however, worth noting that anarchists with more political than subcultural leanings have criticised punk, including anarcho-punk, for essentially offering a superficial understanding and practice of its ideas.[14] It is also worth noting that Crass were not consciously following an anarchist belief system. Vaucher commented, 'The term anarchists wasn't something we applied to ourselves, but we adopted it gradually as people thrust it on us and we re-evaluated what the word meant.'[15] So in part, Crass' direction was formed through dialogue with their audiences; the movement they helped to create.

Conversely, a lot has been said retrospectively about whether Crass con-stituted an inversion of Thatcherite individualism.[16] Their mantra, 'There is no Authority but Yourself', is sometimes equated with individualistic materialism and the disregard for wider society associated with the Thatcher–Reagan era. However, the focus on the individual as a precursor to forming communities of like-minded people, with an intention for social change, owes more to the radical art, culture and politics of the counterculture. It is also easy to ascribe maxims such as this to an overarching anarchist ideology, when in fact they have a more parochial meaning. In the context of young punks faced with pressures to conform, the phrase can perhaps more accurately be interpreted as an exhortation to stand up for yourself and not be pushed around.

Rimbaud cites a karmic yoga belief that individuals should all help one another as the key to their philosophy. He credits his outlook to the influence of individualist existentialism rather than anarchist philosophy, and also asserts that Dial House was founded along the lines of principles set out by psychologist R. D. Laing (who was also an existentialist). He comments, 'Having lived at Dial House with two fellow artists for two or three years, I tired of the per-sonalised nature of our existence together and decided to remove all the locks from the doors. The immediate result was that the two other residents moved out, leaving me alone, but not for long. Within months the place became the hub of activity that it has remained to this day.'[17]

Vaucher describes her personal interpretation of anarchism as follows:

> For me this meant looking inward and pulling myself apart. Thinking, why do I have these ideas? How much am I indoctrinated by my family, the State, school? What did I accept or reject along the way? Is who I am now my choice, or is it merely the acceptance of social requirements. To me anarchism is the turning over of oneself and having the courage to look within.[18]

This introspection can provide an impetus for initiating change in the external world. Vaucher notes, 'For me this leads to creative ways of doing things, which involves ultimate respect for everyone and everything. That also means that I'm no more important than the next just because I may have fame as an artist.'[19] In terms of how Crass might have influenced others in this direction, she notes,

> I would say that the overriding similarity between people's stories is that they did it their way. They understood what they needed from Crass and ran with it. They pursued what was in their heart. We have heard those stories from a policeman to publisher, nurse to gardener. Who cares? They're doing it with the same morality they first ran with, doing it with honesty. It's important. There's no reason why you can't go into the police force and do it with love, do you know what I mean? Why should you label everybody in that profession pigs? [20]

While Crass' anarchist stance represented a rejection of political systems, a lot of what Crass did was inherently political, and the anti-militarism that had featured in their work from the outset became more prominent as the 1980s progressed. Vaucher's design for *Your Country Needs You* (the poster included with *The Feeding of the 5000 (The Second Sitting)* (1981)) took its title from the famous army recruitment poster for the First World War, which featured Lord Kitchener (the British Secretary of State for War) pointing at the viewer. Instead, Vaucher juxtaposed this statement with an iconic photograph taken by Ghislain Bellorget in Vietnam (1968) that featured the withered hand of a war casualty skewered on a barbed wire fence (see Figure 6.4). Posters featuring the design were also flyposted among heavy-duty sex posters in London's red-light district, Soho.

A similar process can be seen with Vaucher's image *Welcome Home* (1982), a fold-out poster accompanying the Crass single, 'How Does it Feel (to be the Mother of a Thousand Dead)?' (see Figure 6.5). The title references Margaret Thatcher's decision to take Britain to war over the Falkland Islands, an episode that marked a turning point in Crass' response to her leadership. The poster features a propagandist representation of a bomber pilot returning home to embrace his ecstatic wife and baby. His face, however, has been sabotaged to reveal a grinning skull. This encroachment of brutal violence ruptures the idealistic veneer the image would otherwise hold.

Vaucher used shock to disarm the viewer, but this was with the intention of engaging with serious subject matter, chiefly social and political injustice. Again, this resonated with work by anti-war Dada artists over half a century earlier, and as with Peter Kennard's work for CND and artists of a comparable ilk, it owes a clear debt to the radical material produced by free press agencies set up by 1960s and 1970s protest movements – this *Know your Enemy* anti-Vietnam war poster from 1966, for example (see Figure 6.6).

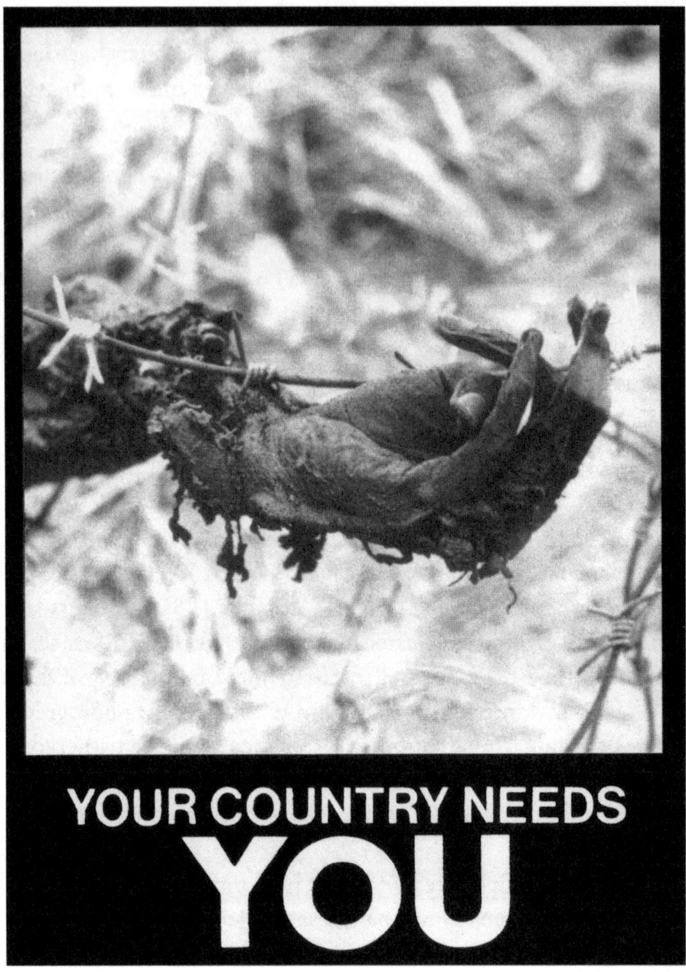

Figure 6.4   Gee Vaucher, Fold-out poster, Crass album, *Feeding of the 5000 (Second Sitting)*, Crass Records, 1981

In both cases, the propagandist terms, 'Welcome Home' and 'Know Your Enemy' (1966), were used ironically to destabilise the original meaning of the image, while conversely the image completely undermines the received meaning of the text. *Welcome Home* was already not quite convincing as a propagandist representation. The female figure's rapturous reception of the soldier appears too carefree for an occasion that is surely more emotionally loaded. Vaucher makes this hesitation on the part of the viewer more explicit by adding the mutilated face and corpse stare of the soldier, thereby sending up the original image and exposing the disturbing reality it conceals.

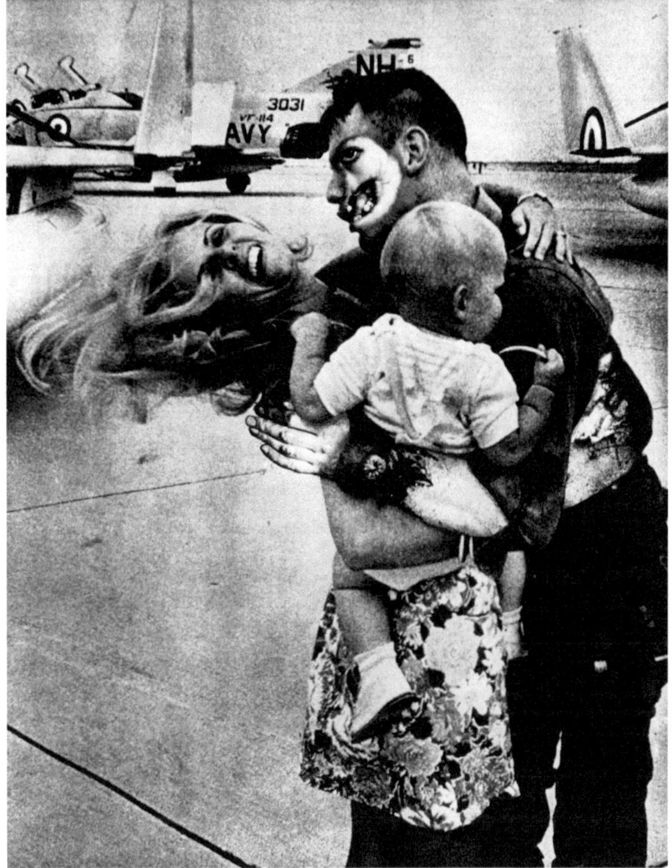

Figure 6.5 Gee Vaucher, Fold-out poster, Crass 7" single, 'How Does it Feel?'/'The Immortal Death', Crass Records, 1982, collage

Crass were increasingly coming to the attention of the authorities, and the release of 'How Does it Feel …' prompted the Tory MP Timothy Eggar to attempt to get the single banned under the Obscene Publications Act. The lyrics to their track, 'Sheep Farming in the Falklands', released on a 7" single the following year, referred to a political hoax perpetrated by Crass, known as 'Thatchergate'. Reminiscent of Orson Welles' War of the Worlds stunt (1938), Thatchergate involved Pete Wright cutting and splicing together material that he'd recorded from the TV. George McKay describes it as follows:

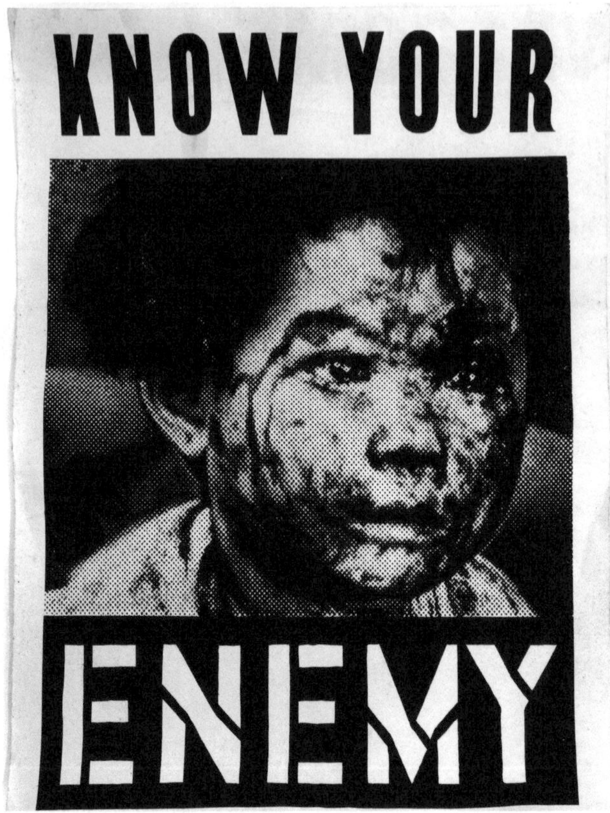

Figure 6.6   Anon, *Know your Enemy*, 1970

These were edits of a recording purportedly of a telephone conversation between Ronald Reagan and Margaret Thatcher. On the tape Thatcher admits responsibility for the sinking of the Argentinian ship *Belgrano* during the war, and Reagan threatens to use nuclear weapons in Europe in order to defend the United States. Information not in the public domain was used, supplied to Crass by a sailor who was in the Falklands – it included the accusation that HMS Sheffield (which was hit by an Exocet missile) was effectively sacrificed by navy commanders in order to protect a nearby aircraft carrier on which was Prince Andrew.[21]

The tape was leaked to the press, which led to the US State Department labelling it as Soviet KGB propaganda. It also aroused concern among the UK's Secret Intelligence Service, MI6. Eventually, in 1984, The *Observer* revealed Crass to be the perpetrators, thereby making a mockery of the State response.

Also in 1983, Crass released their fifth album, *Yes Sir I Will*. The front cover featured a representation of the figure of Christ on the cross (see Figure 6.7). The crucified man, with a gaping, rotten wound that stretches from his mouth and a war medal pinned to his bare chest, returns the look of the viewer, making this searing indictment of religion and martyrdom deeply uncomfortable to look at.

The visual, lyrical and musical content of *Yes Sir I Will* is vitriolic, providing an embittered critique of the political situation. The album included Vaucher's

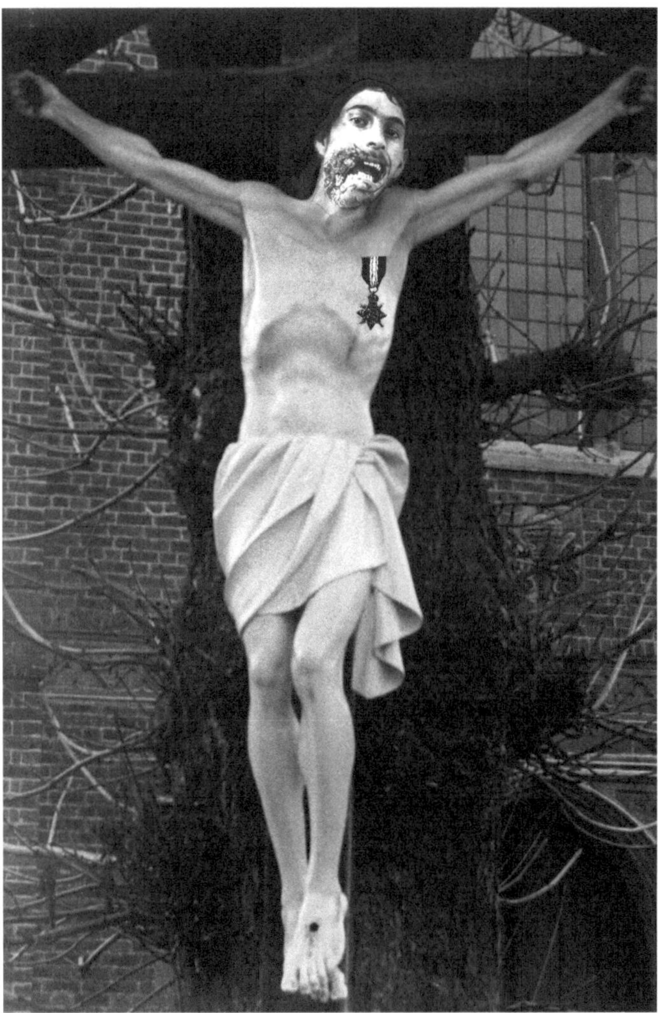

Figure 6.7   Cover, Crass album, *Yes Sir I Will*, 1983, collage, 320mm × 250mm

Poor, but Loyal image, which took a seemingly innocuous photograph of a patriotic street scene and construed it as deeply ironic. Instead of proud troops returning home, an official drags the battered corpse of a young soldier through the expectant throng. The album's fold-out poster featured a photograph of a disfigured soldier from the Falklands War, Simon Weston, meeting Prince Charles (see Figure 6.8). The image and its accompanying caption were taken from The *Sun* newspaper and re-presented, without any necessity for détournement.[22] Simply reprinting it within the context of a Crass album provided it with its inverted meaning.

The increased emphasis on anti-militarism in Vaucher's work was reflected in her fifth *International Anthem* (1983). Her collage, *Still Life with Nude* (see Plate 8, colour insert) comments on the futility of war, as well as the de-humanisation of women that occurs in such desensitised masculinist environments. This is illustrated via the pin-up, which stands out in colour within the otherwise monochrome image. Vaucher's critique chimes with the words of Emma Goldman, who was a vehement proponent of political pacifism. Goldman's anarchist-feminist critique was directed at how the state's institutions were inherently *male* and oppressed *women* specifically, a sentiment echoed

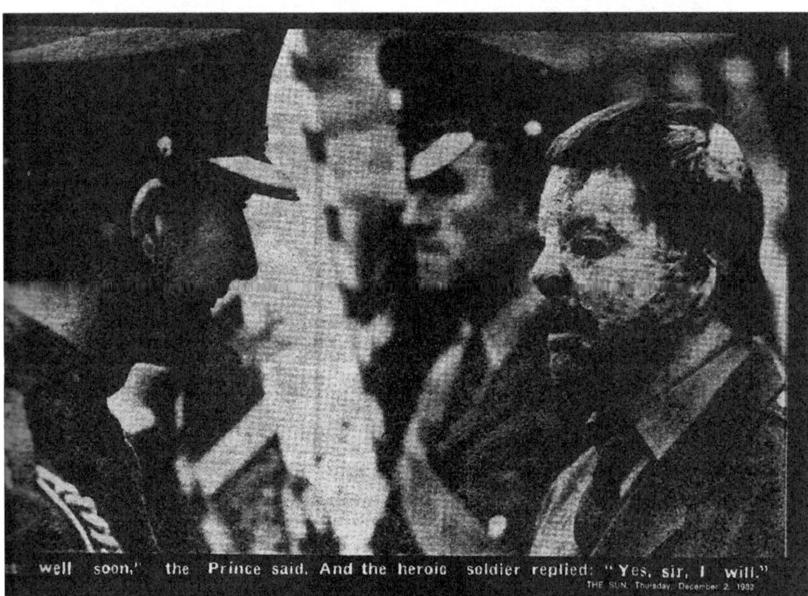

Figure 6.8   Gee Vaucher, Fold-out poster, Crass' album, *Yes Sir I Will*, Crass Records, 1983

in Anarcho-feminism, which construed institutional power (the military, the church and legal family) as inherently masculine. At Goldman's trial in July 1917 for conspiring to impede the draft, she said, 'It is organised violence at the top which creates individual violence at the bottom.'[23] On the suppression of women to facilitate state violence she argued,

> The insatiable monster, war, robs women of all that is dear and precious to her. It exacts her brothers, lovers and sons and in return gives her a life of loneliness and despair. Yet the greatest supporter and worshipper of war is woman. She it is who installs the love of conquest and power into her children; she it is who whispers the glories of war into the ear of her little ones … Yes, it is woman who pays the highest price to that insatiable monster war.[24]

Vaucher has commented that she needed to be in the right frame of mind when engaging with the disturbing material that she used in her work. She observed,

> This work doesn't even touch the tragedy of their situations … Can you imagine actually experiencing it? You can't, because you would have to cut off … You would be faced with a live or die scenario. The closest I've been to this kind of danger is in Northern Ireland; guns and various armies on the street and you don't know what is going to blow or when. But I can't say that I've really ever been in that extreme situation where something needs to come into play for you to survive and in a good mental state. And I have had my doubts that many people that have gone through that extreme experience actually do survive in a good mental state. I really don't think so. So, yes, it is very heavy; it is meant to be, but it's still nowhere near the actual experience.[25]

On the impact of her work, she adds,

> I don't know if it works or not. I mean, I don't know if it makes people shut off because they don't want to see anymore and fails because of that … I hope it has a deeper effect; rather than making people feel upset and negative, does it make people more positive? Does it make them happy? I like to think so in the sense that they say, 'why do we allow this to happen? What can I do in my world, for my community to help?'[26]

The Thatcher era saw people increasingly disempowered as politics became more removed from everyday life. One of many ways that this was apparent was in the expansion of State authoritarianism, as demonstrated in the increased surveillance of and hostility towards political protest or challenge.[27] The sense of an increasingly distant and unresponsive government fuelled an aesthetic focused on all the wrongs and barbarities committed by politicians and the State. The anarcho-punk-zines' visual representations on themes such as this were particularly explicit, and the image of Thatcher appeared with increasing frequency.[28]

Vaucher's insert for the Crass single 'You're Already Dead' (1984) comments on the 'Special Relationship' between Thatcher and Reagan (see Figure 6.10). The figure of Thatcher is shrunk to that of a baby, being nursed by Ronald Reagan, who is portrayed as a founding American mother with the talons of a bird of prey, shitting on the world.[29]

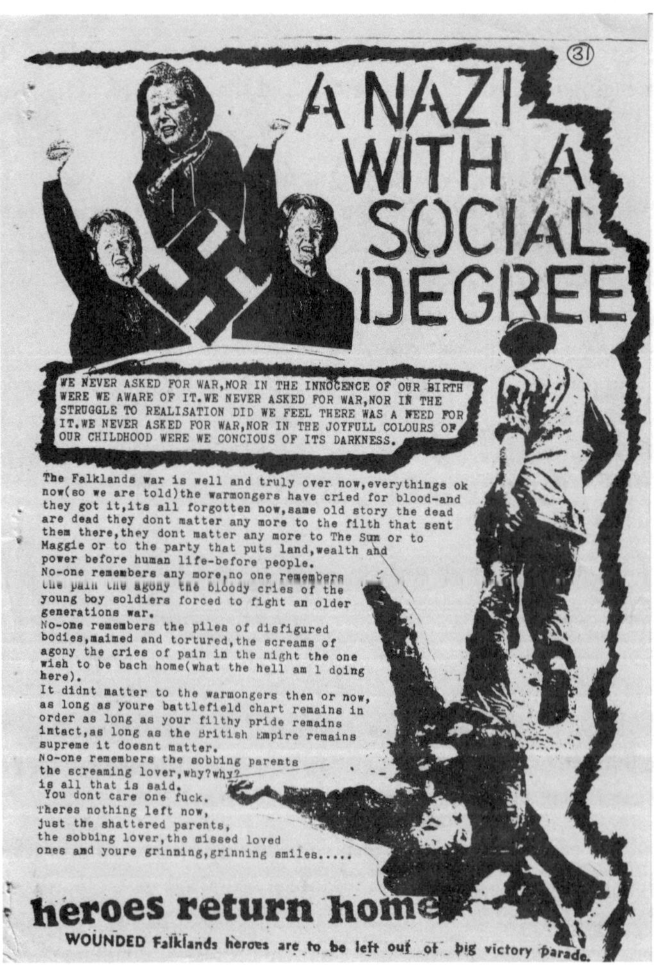

Figure 6.9 *Acts of Defiance, No 6, 1983*

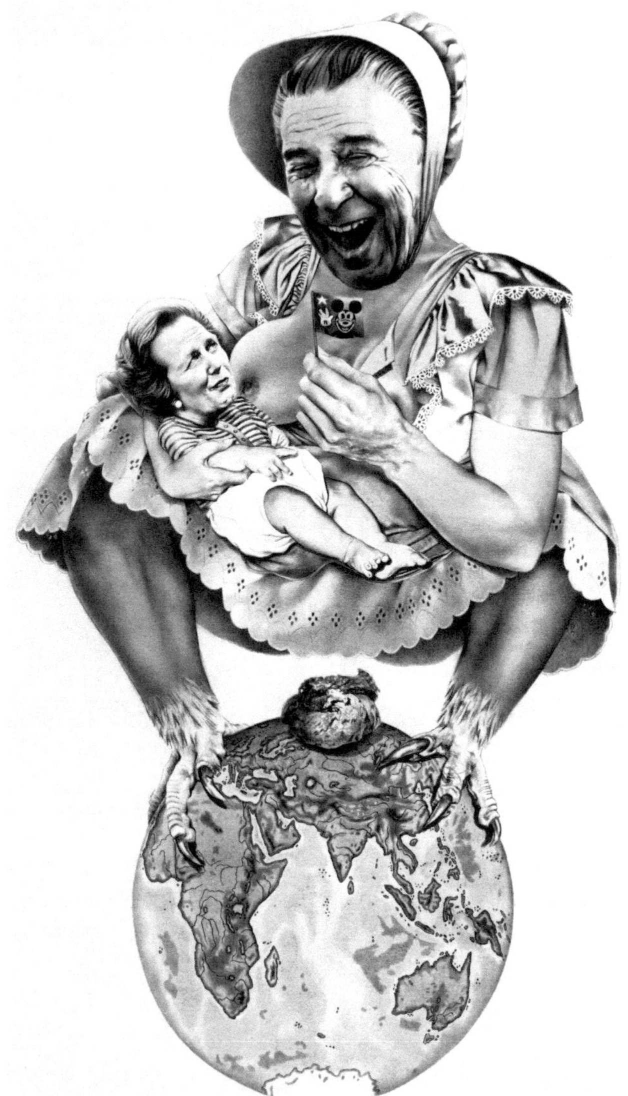

Figure 6.10   Gee Vaucher, Insert, Crass' 7" single, 'You're Already Dead', Crass Records, 1984, gouache

Vaucher's preoccupations with worldwide inequality and the exploitation of the Third World (see *International Anthem 3* in particular) also became a prominent focus in the scene more widely. Anarcho-punk graphics were beset with dystopian images of starving children and the dead and wounded victims of war and other atrocities.[30]

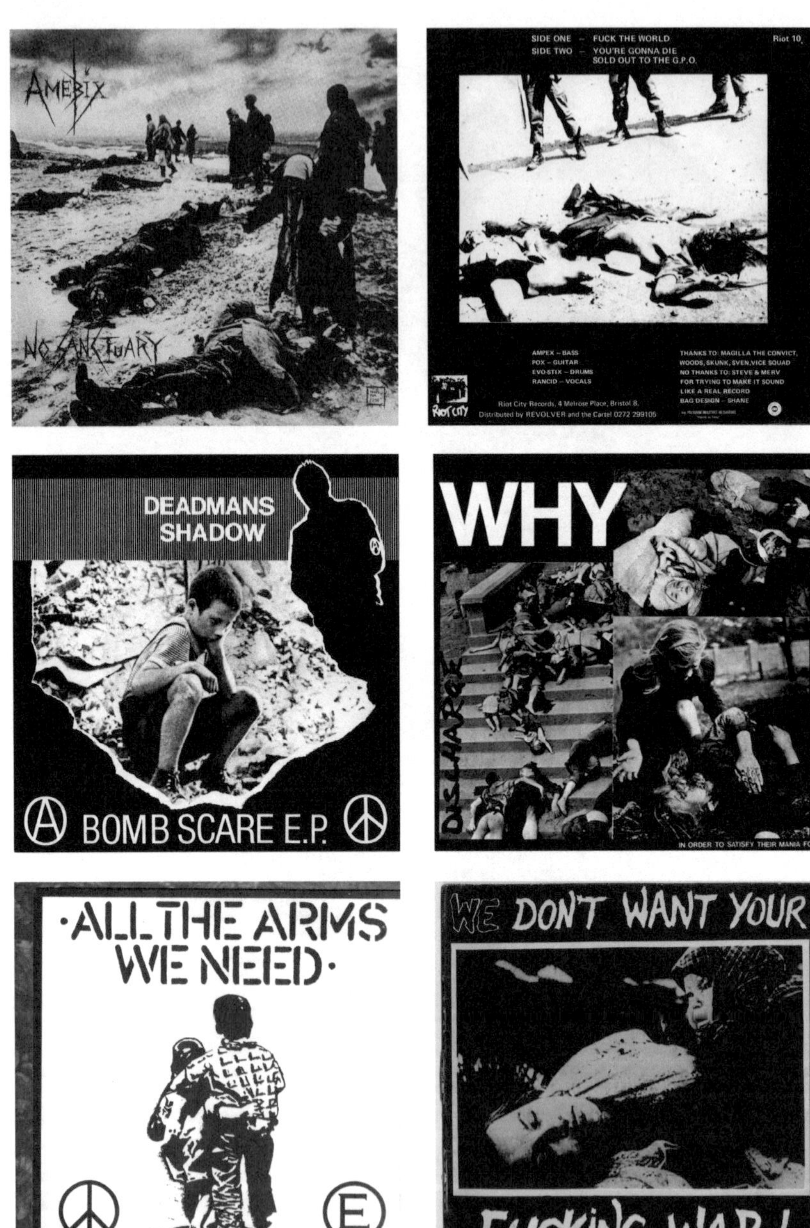

Figure 6.11   Various punk and anarcho-punk record sleeves, 1982–84

Punk had inspired those without formal training or expertise to become cultural creators and arbiters. By the late 1970s, a host of musicians, artists, writers and various other creatives had answered its DiY call. Within anarcho-punk in the UK, there was Blinko (Rudimentary Peni), Squeeler (Icons of Filth), Nick Lant (Subhumans) and Dr Inadequate Phuck, aka Richard Chubb/Gubby (Zounds). The guitarist for Crass, Andy (N.A.) Palmer produced amorphous artwork for a range of anarcho-punk record releases, including *The Eye* by KUKL (Crass Records, 1984) and *The Fucking Cunts Treat Us Like Pricks* by Flux of Pink Indians (Spiderleg Records, 1984). Sometimes, as with Vaucher, the designs alluded to an underlying ideology or political outlook. Otherwise, the work of artists such as Squeeler and Blinko communicated a more introspective and haunted sense of angst, akin to expressionism. Either way, despite their low profile, these artists provided original and high-quality designs that had a strong impact within the punk scene they operated in.

Despite the nihilism that was associated with first-wave punk, it was upbeat by contrast with the sombreness that pervaded the later post-punk, anarcho-punk and hardcore genres. The insert to Subhumans EP, *Rats*, for example reflects many of these abiding themes (see Figure 6.12). Reportage photographs of global inequity, here embodied in the starving mother and child, sit alongside the political protest for peace at Greenham Common and the corresponding authoritarian police presence. There is also the very Vaucher-like inclusion of an idealised family from a lifestyle magazine whose members are oblivious to the scenes of protest, misery, exploitation and annihilation occurring around them.

While Vaucher's work with Crass had a formative influence on the aesthetic and ideological direction of anarcho-punk, it also played a role in the emergence of hardcore (on both sides of the Atlantic). The front cover of the only album produced by US hardcore band Crucifix (1980–85), for example, echoes her use of reportage photography in their reuse of an image by the renowned war photographer, Don McCullin (see Figure 6.13). The stencil lettering on the rear cover is also a well-established Crass trope, reminiscent of the inside cover of *Feeding the 5000* (see Figure 5.2). The insert, featuring reportage photographs of starving African children juxtaposed with Reagan, Ku Klux Klan members and corpses, is similarly evocative of Vaucher's Crass work from an American perspective.

Her output has particular resonances with the work of Winston Smith for the iconic West Coast hardcore band Dead Kennedys. Dead Kennedys (1978–86) emerged from the former heartland of the counterculture, San Francisco, to pick up the gauntlet thrown down by first-wave punk in the UK. Their caustic take on American politics and culture was witty and satirical,

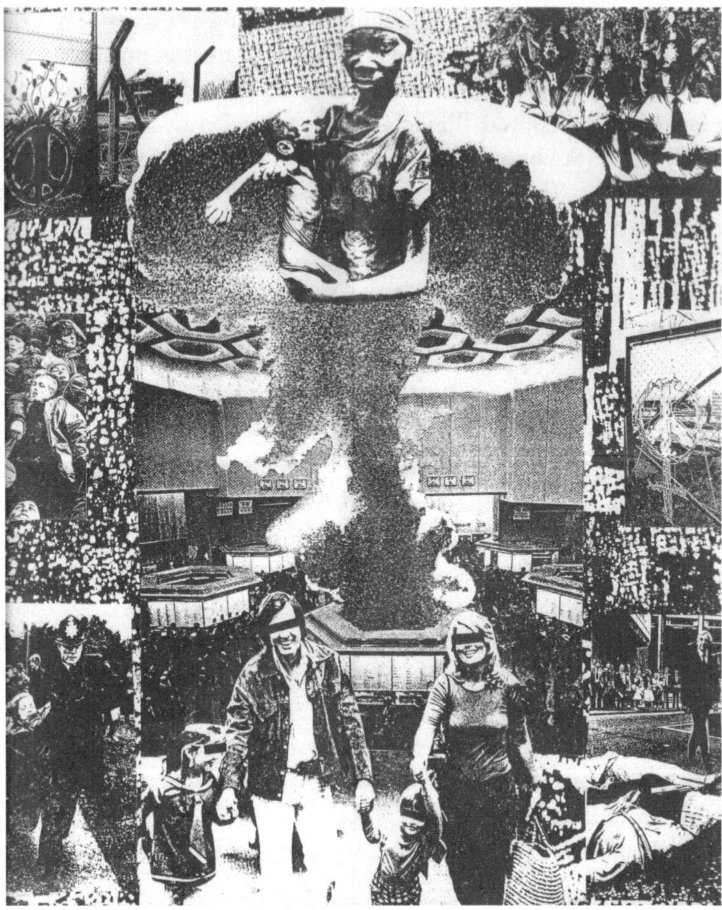

Figure 6.12   Insert, Subhumans 7" EP, *Rats*, Bluurg Records (Fish 10), 1984

while their music was both visceral and technically brilliant. They were cynical about the liberal, ostensibly left-wing media and music establishment in the US, which was centred on San Francisco at the time. They perceived it to be permeated with ageing hippies whose original political ideals had matured into behaviour that was egocentric and exploitative.[31] However, like Crass, they simultaneously wanted to take on the experimentation, DiY ethos and questioning of authority that characterised hippie communities during the 1960s. On many levels, they therefore represented continuity with the true spirit of the counterculture, rather than a rejection of it.[32] Their lead singer and songwriter, Jello Biafra, has discussed how the band was influenced by Crass, despite his opinion that a lot of bands released on the Crass label were

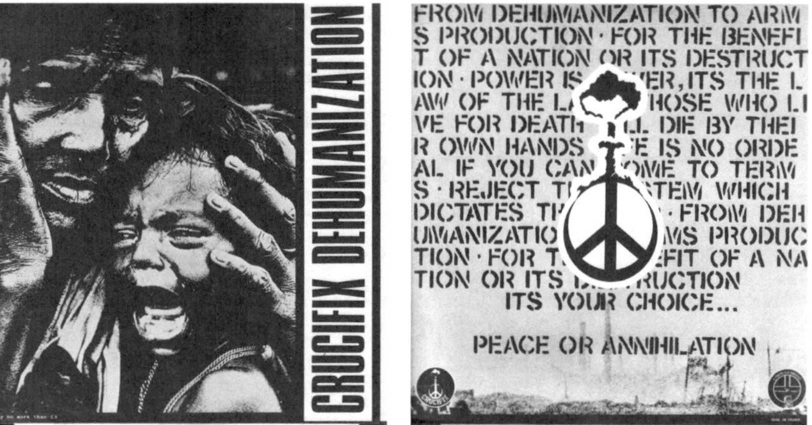

Figure 6.13   Front and rear covers, Crucifix LP, *Dehumanisation*, 1983

'mush.'[33] While Dead Kennedys would go on to have a higher profile, Crass and the anarcho-scene in the UK provided an invaluable precedent for their endeavours.

Building on the approach of Crass, their releases featured a host of pull-outs, posters and pamphlets featuring politically inflected artwork. Much of this was produced by West Coast artist and illustrator Winston Smith, while Jello Biafra created some work either himself or in collaboration with Smith. Biafra shared the political outlook and satirical humour of Vaucher and Smith, but his collages lacked their vision, skill or sophistication. While crediting Vaucher's work as inspiring, Biafra overlooked the prevalent humour in her output, commenting, 'I wanted to do some special art after seeing the foldout artwork that Crass was coming up with. I thought, wow, imagine if Crass was funny!'[34]

Several of the images Smith used for Dead Kennedys record releases (and others on their Alternative Tentacles label) originated in the magazine *Fallout* (1978–85), which he had self-published in partnership with the artist Jayed Scotti (who later joined the punk rock band, Feederz). *Fallout* included political commentary, spoof flyers and advertisements together with satirical collage and illustration work. The magazine's aesthetic was monochrome and gritty. Unlike Vaucher's work for *International Anthem*, but akin to punk fanzines more widely, the work in *Fallout* clearly displays the cut 'n' paste process used in its construction.

The experimentation facilitated by this independent format allowed Smith to develop the clever and iconic music graphics that now seem inextricably tied to the music and message of Dead Kennedys, in much the same way that

Vaucher used *International Anthem* to develop the ideas and visual language she would use with Crass.

The cover to the *Let Them Eat Jellybeans* compilation album, for example, evolved from a collage in *Fallout* on the wider topic of corporate dominance, societal greed and inequity (see Figures 6.14 and 6.15). Similarly, the iconic cover for Dead Kennedy's *In God We Trust* 12" developed from his image *Idol*, which had been printed in Fallout in 1977.

Smith was from the same generation as Vaucher and influenced by comparable ideas stemming from the counterculture. Indeed, they later became

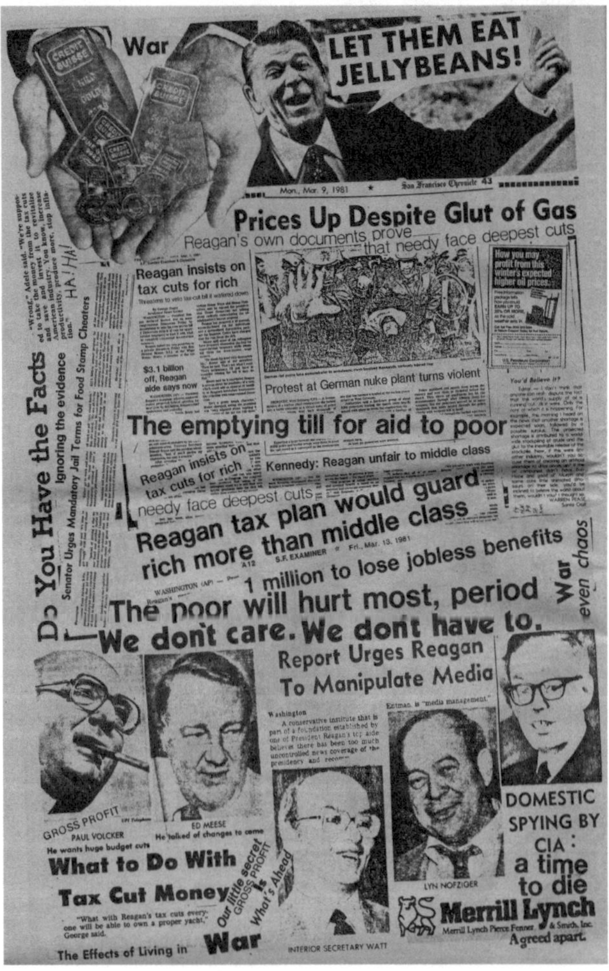

Figure 6.14 Winston Smith, Fallout Productions and Biafra, *Fallout*, No. 4, 1981

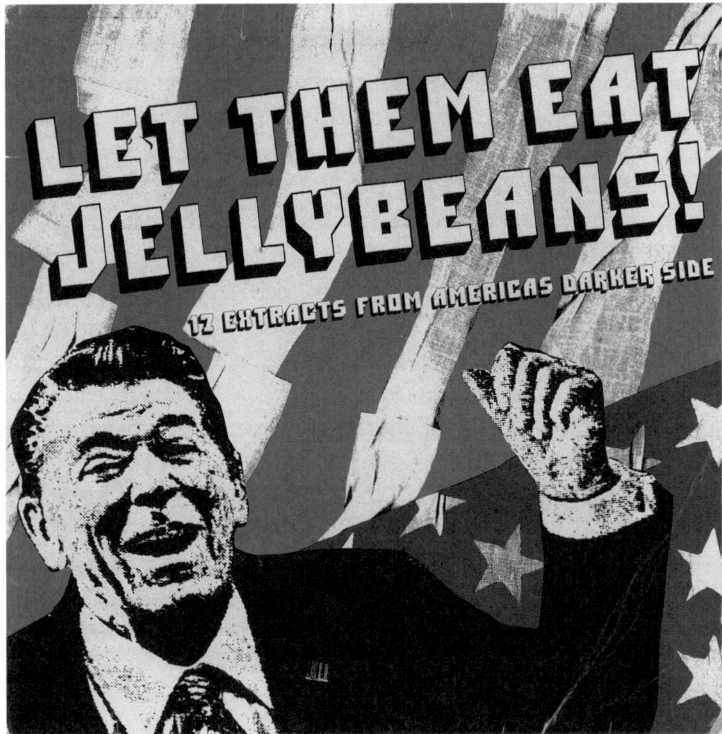

Figure 6.15 Winston Smith, Fallout Productions and Biafra, *Let Them Eat Jellybeans*, compilation LP, Alternative Tentacles, 1981

friends when Smith made contact with Vaucher shortly after Crass disbanded.[35] Both artists critiqued religious and State oppression as well as the role of the family in installing top-down social norms. Both also commented on global inequality and exploitation, while much of the artwork accompanying Dead Kennedy's releases was directed specifically at the foreign policy of the States under Reagan. A pessimistic outlook permeates their work for these bands, as reflected in their preoccupation with State power, warmongering and the prospect of nuclear holocaust, as well as rising social inequality and injustice. Dead Kennedys single, 'Kill the Poor' (1980), for example, depicts the prospect of nuclear annihilation as a method of social cleansing; thereby satirising the disposability with which government viewed certain sections of society.

Smith also resuscitated the iconography associated with 1950s consumerism. As with Vaucher, this echoed the work of critical Pop Artists such as Richard Hamilton, albeit through a darker lens. Dead Kennedys sought to expose the corruption, injustice and violence at the heart of the American dream. This related to Reagan's attempts to revive 1950s conservative social values as a reactionary component of his neo-liberal economic policies.

Smith's collages are quite Orwellian, showing the interiors of State institutions of confinement, imprisonment and surveillance. This fits with the artist's decision to take on the name of the protagonist in George Orwell's famous book, *Nineteen Eighty-Four* (1948), as a direct response to the changing face of American society that he perceived on returning to the States in 1976, after studying art in Italy for seven years. By contrast with the work produced by Vaucher for Crass, his emphasis seems very 'male'. Absent is the focus on the subordination and exploitation of women within patriarchal society. In its place is an existential fear of the State's machinery of control. While the use of pin-ups by the underground press in the 1960s was often tongue in cheek, the intention was also to titillate. By contrast, Smith's recycled depictions of women in idealised family portrayals or pin-ups satirises 1950s culture in the context of Reagan's neo-conservatism. They are self-consciously two dimensional, reflecting the hollowness behind the fantasy. Vaucher's approach differs from that of Smith and other designers of hardcore graphics in her desire to imbue her subjects with personality and agency (see Chapter 3).

As well as its influence on the genres of anarcho- and hardcore punk, Vaucher's aesthetic also had parallels with that seen in the concurrent post-punk scene. While in general the genre was more cerebral and less confrontational than the work of Crass, it frequently featured images of urban decay, as well as politicised imagery drawn from reportage photography.[36] One key comparator is the British graphic designer Mike Coles (b. 1951), who was the director, producer and visual artist for the independent label, Malicious Damage (1979–). Like Vaucher and Smith, Coles had an autonomous approach towards design production.[37] He created record sleeves, posters and flyers for Red Beat and Ski Patrol while he later produced designs for the Orb, Youth, Transit Kings, The Pop Group and Shriekback. Of particular relevance to Vaucher are the photomontage and collage works that he created for post-punk band Killing Joke in the early 1980s. His designs contained elements common to punk, including the use of a stark, monochrome palette, often juxtaposed with red or other flat primary colours. The doom and gloom permeating post-punk and indie music was echoed in this work, which depicted urban environments, often featuring the tower block as a motif. This trope features on the iconic cover of Killing Joke's eponymous first album (1980) (see Figure 6.17). As with the Crucifix album above (see Figure 6.13), Coles built the cover around a well-known photograph by war photographer Don McCullin, which depicts Irish youth escaping British troops by leaping over a wall in Derry. Coles increased the contrast to an extreme degree through photocopying,

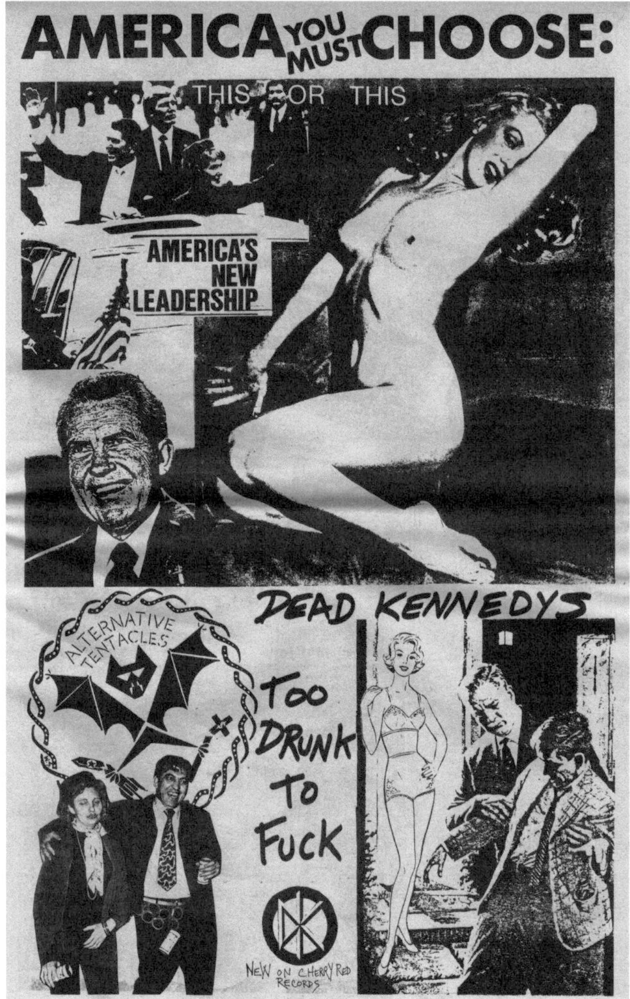

Figure 6.16   Winston Smith, Fallout Productions and Biafra, *Fallout*, No. 4, 1981

leaving the figures silhouetted, while the band's name is daubed on the wall in white paint.[38]

Stark photographic elements were often juxtaposed with imagery taken from glossy magazines from the 1950s. While this again evokes Pop Art, in Coles' work there are more sinister undertones, with the appearance of scary clowns, the grinning, inane figure of Mr Punch or the red eyes that punctuate the facade of aspirational looking figures. Similarly to Vaucher, Coles incorporated newsreel footage of the victims of political violence and war – soldiers

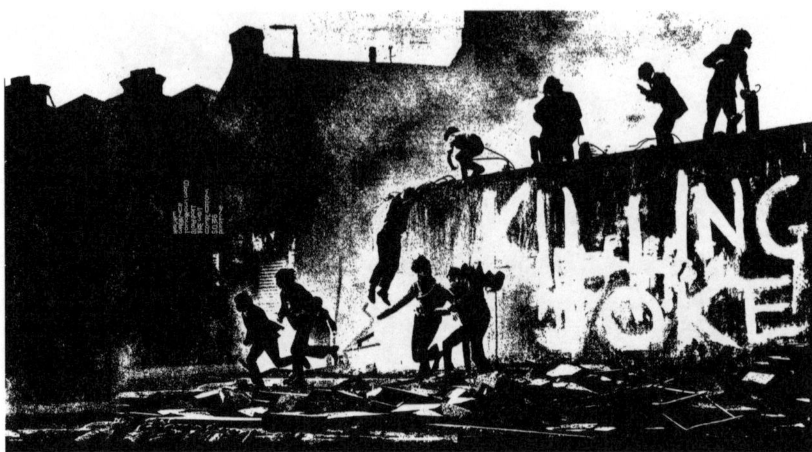

Figure 6.17   Mike Coles, Album cover, *Killing Joke*, Killing Joke, Malicious Damage, 1980

dead in the trenches, for example. This was often combined with references to mass culture in ways that made it appear inane or grotesque; the cover of Killing Joke's 'Wardance' 7", for example, featured Fred Astaire tap dancing on a mass grave in killing fields, set against a blood-red sky. Again like Vaucher, Coles deployed the use of irony in his appropriation of images featuring, for example, a Benedictine monk making his way through a crowd of Seig Heiling Nazis for a Killing Joke poster (Malicious Damage, 1980). This image already existed as a photograph depicting the ease this church figure felt in such company. Coles would later use the image on the cover of a compilation album, but for the poster, the only intervention he made was to add the band's name. This echoes the re-purposing of images for anti-propagandist purposes seen in Crass' designs.

While Vaucher's religious representations seem unconnected to her Methodist upbringing, the Catholic iconography that Coles grew up with features heavily in his work. Christ on the cross, the Virgin Mary and candles are scattered throughout. Glamour and pin-up culture also feature, again in the context of its 1950s heyday, which together with disparate elements and a gaudy colour palette create a dynamic assemblage verging on kitsch. It appears as a form of punk psychedelia, featuring visual disorientation and optical illusions. Coles' use of the pin-up seems symptomatic of darker recesses of the mind with uncanny, sinister and erotic undertones. Coles and Smith were symptomatic of post-punk and hardcore graphics more generally (as well as the overwhelming musical output from the scene) in that they lacked a focus on issues of female subordination within their wider concerns regarding institutional power. In this context, Vaucher's work is vital in representing a female perspective and take within a punk idiom that is meant to be libertarian and yet is heavily male dominated.

Crass had provided the spur for heated debates and re-interpretations of issues and themes centred on their pacifist take on anarchism, as reflected in anarcho-punk music and graphics and the content of anarcho-punk-zines. However, this retreated into some quite doctrinaire and unoriginal regurgitations of Crass' ideas and Vaucher's aesthetic as the scene became more stagnant in the mid-1980s.[39] By then, Crass were also close to burnout. Vaucher recalls their exhausting schedule, 'It would take me a while to do the work and then we were off on tour. So, it was never ending. We'd come back off tour and there'd be another record in the making.'[40]

Crass are widely believed to have prophesied their eventual dissolution in 1984 from the start. Their records were catalogued in declining order: 621984, 521984, 421984 etc, suffixed with the date 1984. While there is some disagreement among its members on this,[41] by that time, Crass' existence was seemingly coming to a conclusion anyway. In the aftermath of the Falklands War and the associated propaganda campaign, Thatcher's administration achieved a demoralising second election win.[42] Disagreements about their line on pacifism had also intensified, contributing to the band's split.[43] This occurred in the context of Crass' involvement with the Stop the City demonstrations (1983–84), which, despite modelling a successful form of autonomous activism, saw an authoritarian clampdown by the police as the protests progressed.[44] Ignorant recalls,

> There had been discussions and increasingly heavy ones and disagreements among band members about what direction we should take. And some people were up for a more confrontational approach, while others were more into the pacifist line. Not guns and shooting people. More, how do you fuck up the telephone system kind of thing. There were lots of big discussions and I think that everyone was getting very tired of it.[45]

The bitterness of the concurrent Miners' Strike also coloured the scene, and indeed it was on their way to play a benefit gig for striking miners in Aberdare in Wales (1984) that it became apparent that Crass were going to split. Andy Palmer was the first one to declare his intention to leave, followed by Eve Libertine and then the others. Vaucher states, 'The band stopped when Andy said he would. Crass could not continue without everyone continuing together.'[46]

Reflecting on their breakup, Ignorant observed, 'I think that when we got home, there was this collective sigh of relief, coupled with what the fuck do we do now?' adding, 'Once we'd made the decision to stop, we could all see just how tired, dark and miserable we had all become. We'd put ourselves in this dark room and we couldn't see the light anymore. And suddenly this door opened and there was colour.'[47]

The year 1984 concluded an intense period of politically charged work for Crass, the end of which also signalled the beginning of a new chapter. The members of Crass would increasingly follow divergent paths, while after a brief respite Vaucher would re-emerge to find her voice as a solo artist.

Notes

1   The identities of all figures were confirmed by Vaucher in interview, 2013.

2   Other well-known, satirical works that critiqued Thatcher during this time included the poster, *Gone with the Wind: The Most Explosive Love Story Ever* (designed by John Houston and Bob Light for the *Socialist Worker* paper, 1980), and Cath Tate's *Prevent Street Crime* postcard (1982).

3   Vaucher in interview with Binns, 2013.

4   See, for instance, Kennard's *Never Again* poster (1983) created in response to the threat of nuclear power, which strongly evokes the original CND poster, *Stop Nuclear Suicide* (1963) by FHK Henri.

5   Steve Ignorant describes members of Crass visiting the CND shop in Kings Cross to collect information to copy and distribute via their gigs and events in M. Worley, 'The End Result: An Interview with Steve Ignorant', in M. Dines and M. Worley (eds), *The Aesthetic of our Anger: Anarcho-Punk, Politics and Music* (Colchester/New York: Minor Compositions, 2016), pp. 294–295.

6   Rebecca Binns discusses how this rift progressed over time in R. Binns, '"It's your world too, you can do what you want": The Role of Subcultural Activism in Stop the City Protests (1983–1984) and its Implications for Political Protest in Britain', *Contemporary British History*, forthcoming.

7   See, for instance, 'America's Back Yard = El Salvador, Guatamala, Honduras and Nicaragua. Death Squads = killing, rape and torture', in *Time Bomb*, Issue 1 (1984), p. 5. On Thatcher's support for repressive regimes in South Africa, Ireland and Latin America (specifically Chile), see 'Repression', in *Acts of Defiance*, Issue 6 (1983), p. 9.

8   Vaucher in interview with Binns, 2018.

9   See Steve's (Wilf) poster insert for The Mob's 7" single, No Doves Fly Here (Crass Records, 1981) and the front cover for Liberty's album, *The People Who Care are Angry* (Mortahate, 1986) among a host of others.

10   Vaucher in interview with Binns, 2018.

11   Vaucher in interview with Binns, 2018.

12   See Francis' Stewart's writing on this subject in F. Stewart, *Punk Rock is my Religion: Straight Edge Punk and 'Religious' Identity* (Abingdon: Routledge, 2017) and F. Stewart,

'Our Own Place: Giro's and Punk', *Freckle, Northern Ireland*, Issue 6 (2017), pp. 92–95.

13 G. Vaucher, *Crass Art and Other Pre Postmodernist Monsters 1961–1997* (London: Existencil Press, 2nd edn, 2014), p. 58.

14 See A. Gordon, 'They Can Stuff Their Punk Credentials 'cause it's Them That Take the Cash: 1980s Anarcho-Punk-Ethical Difference and Division', in M. Dines and M. Worley (eds) *The Aesthetic of our Anger: Anarcho-Punk Politics and Music* (Minor Compositions: Colchester, 2016) pp. 227–251, which highlights divergences among traditional anarchists, various strands of punks and 'new age travellers' within that scene. See also J. Donaghey, 'Bakunin Brand Vodka: An Exploration into Anarchist-punk and Punk-anarchism', *Anarchist Developments in Cultural Studies*, 1 (2013), pp. 138–170. Also see Murray Bookchin's well known polemic, *Social Anarchism or Lifestyle Anarchism. An Unbridgeable Chasm* (Edinburgh: AK Press, 1995) and a critical response to it in an article by Lawrence Davis, 'Social Anarchism or Lifestyle Anarchism: An Unhelpful Dichotomy', *Anarchist Studies*, 18:1 (2010), pp. 62–82.

15 Vaucher in interview with Binns, 2013.

16 See Simon Reynolds; referred to in T. Vague, *The Great British Mistake, 1977–92: A Fourteen and a Half Years' Struggle Against Lies, Stupidity and Cowardice: A Reckoning with the Destroyers of the Punk Rock Movement* (Edinburgh: AK Press, 1994), p. 31. Ex-Crass member, Pete Wright, has levelled a similar accusation at Crass. See his letter to Mark Hodkinson of Pomona Sounds that forms part of the Crassical Collection letters at www.crassicalcollection.com/crass.pdf (accessed July 2018). For the contrary position, see R. Cross, 'There is no Authority but Yourself. The Individual and the Collective in British Anarcho-Punk', *Music and Politics*, IV:2 (2010), pp. 1–20.

17 Rimbaud in interview with Binns, 2018, updated via email correspondence, June 2021.

18 Vaucher in interview with Binns, 2018.

19 Vaucher in interview with Binns, 2018.

20 Vaucher in interview with Binns, 2018.

21 G. McKay, 'CRASS 621984 ANOUK4U2', in G. McKay, *Senseless Acts of Beauty: Cultures of Resistance Since the 1960s* (London/New York: Verso, 1996), p. 81.

22 Simon Weston was injured when the Sir Galahad was struck by an Argentine missile in June 1982, during the Falklands Conflict. He was widely commended in the British press, largely due to this image on the front cover of The *Sun*.

23 Emma Goldman quoted in P. Marshall, *Demanding the Impossible: A History of Anarchism* (London: Harper Perennial, 2007), p. 404.

24 E. Goldman, *Anarchism and Other Essays* (Auckland: Floating Press, 2008), p. 202. First published by Mother Earth Publishing Association, New York, 1910.

25 Vaucher in interview with Groß, 2002.

26 Vaucher in interview with Groß, 2002.

27 The Police and Criminal Evidence Act, 1984 extended police powers of arrest, detention and interrogation, as well as rights to search individuals and premises.

Thatcher's strategy to break the unions and undermine people's ability to protest was exemplified in the series of weapons, including the introduction of strike ballots, outlawing of flying pickets and the surveillance of protestors, introduced to suppress the Miner's Strike (1984–85).

28 See R. Bestley and R. Binns, 'The Evolution of an Anarcho-Punk Narrative, 1978–84', in Subcultures Network (ed.), *Ripped, Torn and Cut: Pop, Politics and Punk Fanzines* (Manchester: Manchester University Press, 2018), p. 140.

29 Bestley and Binns, 'Anarcho-Punk Narrative', p. 140.

30 See inserts to Flux of Pink Indians 7" single, Strive to Survive, Spiderleg Records, 1982, and the System/Virginia T 7" EP, The Warfare, Spiderleg Records, 1982.

31 For further exposition on this, see A. Ogg, *Dead Kennedys: Fresh Fruit for Rotting Vegetables, The Early Years* (Oakland: PM Press, 2014) p. 17.

32 In *Dead Kennedys*, Ogg (p. 12) includes a quote from the band's guitarist, East Bay Ray, to this effect.

33 Biafra quoted in Ogg, *Dead Kennedys*, p. 69.

34 Biafra quoted in Ogg, *Dead Kennedys*, p. 137.

35 Vaucher in interview with Binns, 2021.

36 See, for instance, the album cover The Pop Group, For How Much Longer do we Tolerate Mass Murder, Rough Trade, 1980.

37 See Mike Coles' own account of the years he spent homeless and/or doing odd jobs rather than towing the line in conventional employment and of his battle against the Catholic indoctrination of his youth in R. Bestley, "'I wonder who chose the colour scheme, it's very nice…": Mike Coles, Malicious Damage and Forty Years in the Wilderness', *Punk and Post-punk*, 5:3 (2016), pp. 311–328.

38 McCullin's original photograph appeared in *The Sunday Times Magazine* on 16 December 1971.

39 See Bestley and Binns, 'Anarcho-Punk Narrative', p. 138.

40 Vaucher in interview with Binns, 2013.

41 Whereas Vaucher, Rimbaud and De Vivre have all confirmed that Crass prophesied their dissolution in 1984, Phil Free believes the countdown to this year was just a literary reference, rather than concrete plan, in G. Berger, *The Story of Crass* (Oakland: PM Press, 2009), p. 258. Ignorant agrees, saying, 'When I asked Penny what would happen if Crass wanted to continue beyond 1984, his response was "we'll just go into minus figures, or something like that. We'll work it out". So there really wasn't this idea that we were going to stop in 1984.' Ignorant in interview with Binns, 2020.

42 Thatcher won the election in 1983; however, this was with a reduced percentage of votes cast, as the opposition was split between Labour and the SDP.

43 Ignorant in interview with Binns, 2020.

44 See the film on the Stop the City protests, directed by Crass members Mike Duffield and Andy Palmer, 'Stop the City 83–84', 1984. www.youtube.com/watch?v=ByS9wv8mOFo&t=1s (accessed 14 May 2021).
Also see P. Rimbaud, 'Stop the City: 1 2 3 4, We'll be Back Some Day with More', *Punk Lives* 10 (1984), pp. 19–22; R. Cross, 'Stop the City Showed Another Possibility',

in M. Dines and M. Worley (eds), *The Aesthetic of our Anger: Anarcho Punk, Politics and Music* (Colchester: Minor Compositions, 2016), pp. 117–157; and Binns, "'It's your world too, you can do what you want'".

45   Ignorant in interview with Binns, 2020.

46   Vaucher in email correspondence, June 2021.

47   Ignorant in interview with Binns, 2020.

7

Post Crass introspection: postmodernism and the anti-rationalist avant-garde

The intense six-year period that Crass lived and functioned at Dial House had seen them undertake a relentless schedule of writing, recording, self-releasing and touring, made all the more onerous without the support of a major label. They provided extensive support to a DiY network of zinesters, bands and record labels, were involved in political pranks that led to them being placed under surveillance by the authorities and became involved in direct action, including the Stop the City protests (1983–84). Crass were also involved in ongoing spats with the press and rival strands within punk, as well as battles with far-right and far-left activists.[1] Factionalism also set in at The Autonomy Centre (1981–82), an anarchist social venue in Wapping that Crass helped to finance and set up with Poison Girls from the proceeds of their joint single 'Persons Unknown'/'Bloody Revolutions'. The advent of identity politics and politicised subcultural rivalries in the early 1980s also proved particularly divisive in Vaucher's view. She observed, 'The timing was right, disparate "alternative" groups were saying exactly that, "we are right, you are wrong" and separating themselves from each other. I thought, for Christ's sake, we're supposed to be coming together.'[2]

The weighty tone of Crass, which had been reiterated in anarcho-punk and politically left-leaning milieus more widely, was something its members sought ways to counteract following their disbandment in 1984. This was the motivation behind the release of the *Acts of Love* album (Crass Records,

1984), which featured a selection of Vaucher's illustrations, originally created to accompany a series of poems by Rimbaud in 1972–73. The recordings comprised fifty of these poems sung by Eve Libertine to a score of classical and synth music.

The illustration in Figure 7.1 is reflective of the tone of the album, and had been produced to accompany poem no. 17:

> Where have we smiled like this before?
> Clasped each others' hands?
> Was it you that cried, choking,
> When first the blackbirds sang?
> My worst moments are destroyed in the gleam of your eye.

Given that both the poems and illustrations originated in Dial House's pre-Crass era, it is perhaps unsurprising that they reflect a positive, even romantic vision more in sync with the free festival scene than the dark latter days of Crass, and indeed the album was dedicated to their old friend Wally Hope.

Rimbaud also created the designs for a final, distinctly avant-garde 12" released under the name of Crass, *Ten Notes on a Summer's Day: The Swansong* (Crass Records, 1986). Vaucher notes, '*Ten Notes* … was very much a personal project for which, quite apart from the music, Penny did most of the artwork

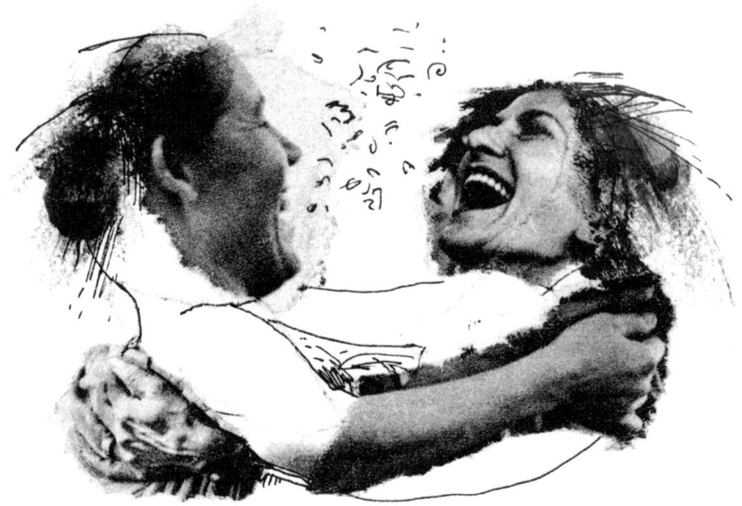

Figure 7.1 Gee Vaucher, Illustration, *Acts of Love*, 1972, collage and ink, 123mm × 100mm

and I was only involved in getting the album cover print ready.'[3] Again moving away from the oppositional nature of the band, the album insert featured interlocking text that read variously 'Lovers All' or 'Love Over all'. It included an announcement of the band's termination on its sleeve.

Crass then released a compilation album, *Best Before 1984* (Crass Records, 1986). Vaucher photographed some kids skating up and down outside, which she used for her painted illustration on the front cover (see Plate 9, colour insert). Their carefree appearance (the girl wears a ra-ra skirt and baseball top, while the boy wears a diamond tank top) and their treatment in vivid colour contrasts with the Crass-like monochrome image of British police breaking up a protest, while a load of discarded Crass records are scattered on the ground. Vaucher comments, 'It's a hint of us moving on because they're actually skating over all that Crass stuff. That's all gone. The colour represents the youth really; what's ahead.'[4]

Vaucher continued to produce artwork for a range of record releases post Crass, including the cover to *Friendly as a Hand Grenade* LP by Tackhead (World Records, 1989) and the poster accompanying *Wasteland* LP by Radical Dance Faction (Earth Zone, 1991). Steve Ignorant would go on to perform with several other bands post Crass. He'd been in a relationship with Vaucher during the Crass years, but despite this being over, their friendship and collaboration continued during this period, and indeed has been sustained to the present day. Vaucher produced artwork for a number of his projects, including the front cover to 'Goodbye to All That'/'Child of our Times', a 7" single by Schwartzeneggar (Rugger Bugger Records, 1992), and the front and rear cover, inner sleeve and label for *Live in the US* LP by Stratford Mercenaries (self-released, 1997). Later she would design the front cover to the *Who We Touch* album by the Charlatans (Frinck Recordings, 2010) as well as a selection of record sleeves for the jazz Babel Label.

While the aftermath of Crass signalled new directions – away from the weightier aspects of their work, further afield in Britain at the time, the situation was grim. The devastating conclusion of the Miners' Strike (1984–85) was followed by the police ambush of the Peace Convoy on its way to Stonehenge (the free festival that was initially conceived and organised from Dial House), in The Battle of the Beanfield (1985).[5] The convoy was made up of travellers and their families, who opted for self-sufficiency and life on the road, living in their vehicles or makeshift structures, such as benders and tipis. They lived communally and valued sharing, rather than struggling to pay the rent/mortgage and striving for attainment through conventional work. Vaucher observed, 'Thatcher didn't like that very much at all; because these people could avoid the census and other means of monitoring. So, the government was extremely heavy and violent towards them.'[6] Acknowledging the role Crass played in encouraging this movement, she adds, 'A lot of the travellers used to follow us around and they were encouraged by us to find different ways of living. A lot of those people who decided to take that new path, to think outside the box, were people that we knew from the Crass period; from gigs and so on. They joined forces with older, more experienced people from the Stonehenge group before.'[7]

The late 1980s was a relatively low-key period for Vaucher, who felt exhausted after the intensity of the Crass years. Her mother was terminally ill, and Vaucher moved back to Dagenham for two years (1987–89) to care for her at her home. This was an all-consuming undertaking, which left her unable to produce any artwork. She notes, 'My creativity went into making mum laugh, cooking nice food and all the rest of it, until we finally said goodbye.'[8] She also took on organising the funeral and 'laying out' her mum. The band all pitched in, with Rimbaud building the coffin, Steve Ignorant doing the carving and her brothers doing the polishing. She notes, 'I lined it with material chosen by mum (she was practical and cool to the end). The funeral was taken by Penny where various friends spoke, and Joy and the rest of the band made the food for the gathering afterwards. In a way it reflected the spirit of my mother, so, although very sad, we rejoiced her life to the end.'[9]

She reflects on the timing, in winter, just before Christmas, which meant 'she could lie in State for a week at Dial House. She had lots of visitors, which was nice. All her children and grandchildren could visit.'[10]

A few years after this episode, Vaucher resumed her creative practice; and one of her works in this new period was *Hetty* (1995) (see Plate 10, colour insert), a large portrait in pastels of her mother as a young woman.

Despite her involvement in radical art collectives, most of Vaucher's pre-1990s output can loosely be described as illustration. This new period would see her returning to mediums she hadn't engaged with since art school. In the twenty-first century this would extend to installation and sculpture, but as she began on this journey it was largely focused on drawings and paintings, which often incorporated collage.

One early work contains some interesting references to the previous decade, while also pointing to the change of emphasis that would characterise her work in the 1990s.

The dream-like ensemble of her untitled pen and ink work (see Figure 7.2) from 1998, was inspired by Picasso's etching *Minotauromachy (La Minotauromachie)* from 1935. In place of Picasso's Minotaur is a similarly mythological creature emerging from the sea, wearing a human mask. The children in Vaucher's illustration provide a contemporary reference with their

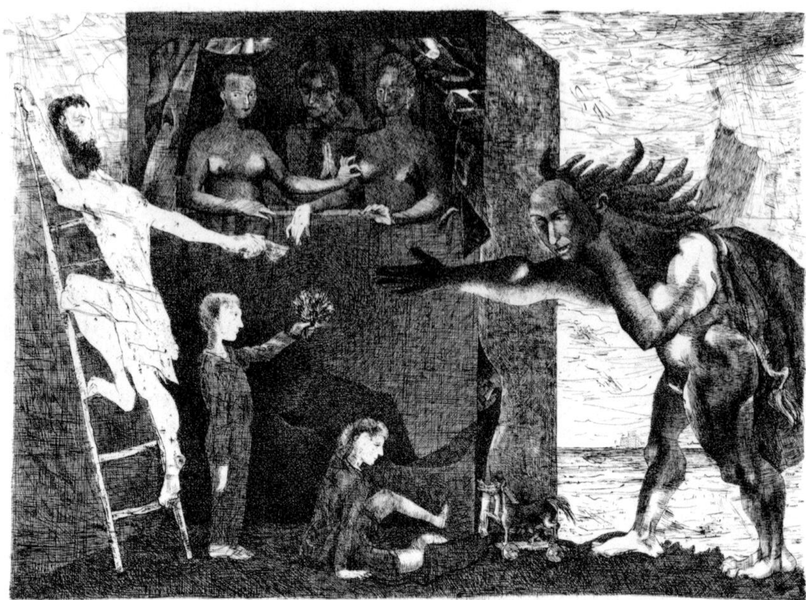

Figure 7.2   Gee Vaucher, *Untitled*, 1991, pen and ink, 530mm × 390mm

new-age traveller haircuts. One of them presents a peace offering to the beast, evoking the girl holding the candle and flowers in Picasso's image. In place of Picasso's languid figures in the puppet theatre are characters drawn from the sixteenth-century painting *Gabrielle d'Estrées and one of her sisters*. This featured the mistress of King Henry IV of France in a bath with her sister, who is pinching her nipple, apparently to indicate her pregnancy.[11] Vaucher, however, has re-interpreted their expressions so that the pincher seems to register surprise. She says that the third figure in the shadows is 'Gee, who is peeping out through the curtain in homage to Picasso'.[12] In its incorporation of real life, art historical and quasi-mythical elements, and its strong symbolist connotations, the image is a far cry from any of the work she did for Crass.

This is not to say that her preoccupations changed completely. While on the face of it her work in this period lost the didacticism of her earlier output and took a more introspective turn, clear continuities are still evident. There is an ongoing interest in the dynamics of human interaction and how this responds to, is shaped by and/or circumvents powerful forces. The focus is less overtly political, instead exploring the nature of existence with great insight – and often humour. The subject is overwhelmingly human, and often physiological, while many of her works featured partial abstractions of the human form. A series of gouache paintings from 1992, for example, combine different

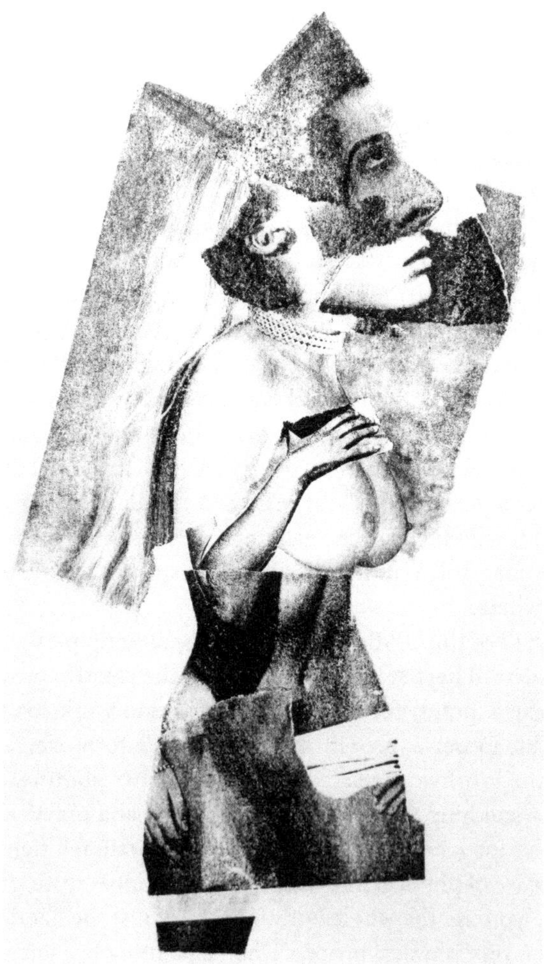

Figure 7.3   Gee Vaucher, *Bride*, 1992, transfer print, 320mm x 390mm

body parts and facial features in Picasso-like assemblages (see Plate 11, colour insert). However, despite their discordant, at times exaggerated, elements, they resist a total deconstruction of the human form.

The background of the image features a character from another early work from this period (see Plate 12, colour insert). This picture was part of a series in which Vaucher painted over photographs of statues from Classical Antiquity. Her expressionistic gestures undermine the status of the originals as definitive statements on high art. In this respect, her approach evokes that of the Situationist Asper Jorn (1914–73), who used loose, often childlike paint strokes in his modifications to original artworks.[13] This is also a distinguishing feature in the work of the artist, Banksy. His *Paint Pot Angel* (2009) bears an uncanny resemblance to Vaucher's approach here.

Despite working in new mediums, collage continued to be an overriding feature of Vaucher's work. As with the presence of the classical statue in the gouache painting, she would often recycle her own work, Xeroxing it and ripping up the copies for use in new creations, observing, 'They're all progressions.'[14]

In 1994–95, she produced a series of pastels (which included the image of her mother in Plate 10) that built on the aesthetic of her earlier gouache works. Interestingly, collage functions in this series in much the same way as it did in her earlier output. These pastel drawings give the appearance of having assembled together separate elements in order to play with form. They break down the different components of the body and face. As in her works throughout the period, the figures are predominantly female, but they frequently combine old and young faces, and male and female body parts into single figures. Again, as with the gouache paintings, they resist complete deconstruction of the human form, rather combining disparate elements to create a recognisable whole.

The first half of the 1990s had been a loosening up period for Vaucher, when she immersed herself in the substance of the creative process, without having to make a point, form a critique or create work for instructional purposes.[15] This looser approach also enabled her to move away from the meticulous, fine brushwork that was required for her photorealistic painted illustrations, something that was also necessitated at a practical level as her eyesight was no longer up to it, and she says 'her brain felt tight!'[16] She also enjoyed the sense of physical immersion that went into creating larger works, commenting, 'you use the whole body, instead of just the hand at the end of your arm. It's a very physical process when a painting is bigger than the eye can take in at close range'[17] Even with smaller works, she recalls beginning to use her whole arm in contrast to just her hand and wrist.

This freeing up process is evident in a series of acrylic paintings on canvas, depicting amorphous bodies that almost burst from the boundaries of the picture plane, and a set of pencil drawings (see Plate 14, colour insert) that are similarly expressionistic (both from 1996). The aesthetic of these would feed into two more controlled series that she embarked on later that year.

Much Ado About Something: A Play of Metaphors (1996–) embraced this new-found freedom, while returning to a theme that Vaucher had explored in Crass and *International Anthem*, namely the twisted manifestations of the psyche that can result from strict religious upbringings. During a stay at an artist's residency, Braziers Hall, in 1996, Vaucher created an installation piece in a disused Victorian Sunday school in the surrounding woodlands. She came across an assortment of abandoned and neglected objects on the hall stage and imagined it as the setting for a Victorian schoolmaster's sermons on hell and damnation. While the images she produced in response all engage with this theme, they provide a poignant and obtuse play on language and meaning that contrasts dramatically with the direct and powerful graphic communication that characterised her earlier explorations of the subject. The inversion of the title of the famous Shakespeare play also points to her intention with the work, which she describes as a black comedy (concerned with human suffering) as opposed to one concerned with polite witticisms.

The images combined expressionistic sketches with snippets cut out from the story and exercise books she'd found on the stage. The resulting collages follow the biblical narrative of the Stations of the Cross, which depicts the events leading up to Christ's crucifixion, placing the characters in a 'play' that in her words '… has been running for over two thousand years'.[18] Her earlier illustration work for children's books, magazines and indeed Crass stood her in good stead in this endeavour, which she approached almost as a brief.

This was not, of course, the first time Vaucher had responded creatively to the Stations of the Cross, but unlike her artwork for the *Stations of the Crass* album (see Plate 6, colour insert), which only referred elliptically to the original narrative, here she engaged with it head on. The first illustration, entitled *Suffer the Little Child* (Figure 7.4), provides Vaucher's response to the first Station, in which Pontius Pilate condemns Jesus to die. The title is taken directly from a bible story in which his disciples tried to turn away some children who had been brought to him to be cured (Mathew 19:14, King James Version). The collage ostensibly reflects the original intention of this statement, to show how Jesus valued and accepted children. However, the caption could also be seen to allude to negative aspects of childhood religious conditioning, with its emphasis on suffering as a pathway to salvation, as promoted by the Church and fostered through the martyrdom of Jesus. 'Then again,' she notes, 'if you look closely at the collaged child, he is poor, who is caring?'[19] In alluding to the series as a 'play of metaphors', Vaucher sends up the status of the biblical story as truth; instead viewing our 'hero', Christ, and the supporting cast as players in a plot she says is 'as good as it is incomprehensible'.[20]

While, through this work, Vaucher continues the questioning and undermining of grand narratives that was fundamental to her work with Crass, her response to religion here is more complex and subtle. The illustrations and accompanying captions are not overtly critical, but still undermine the purpose of the original language as defined within the structures in which it was created.[21] In this, her approach resonates with R. D. Laing's imperative

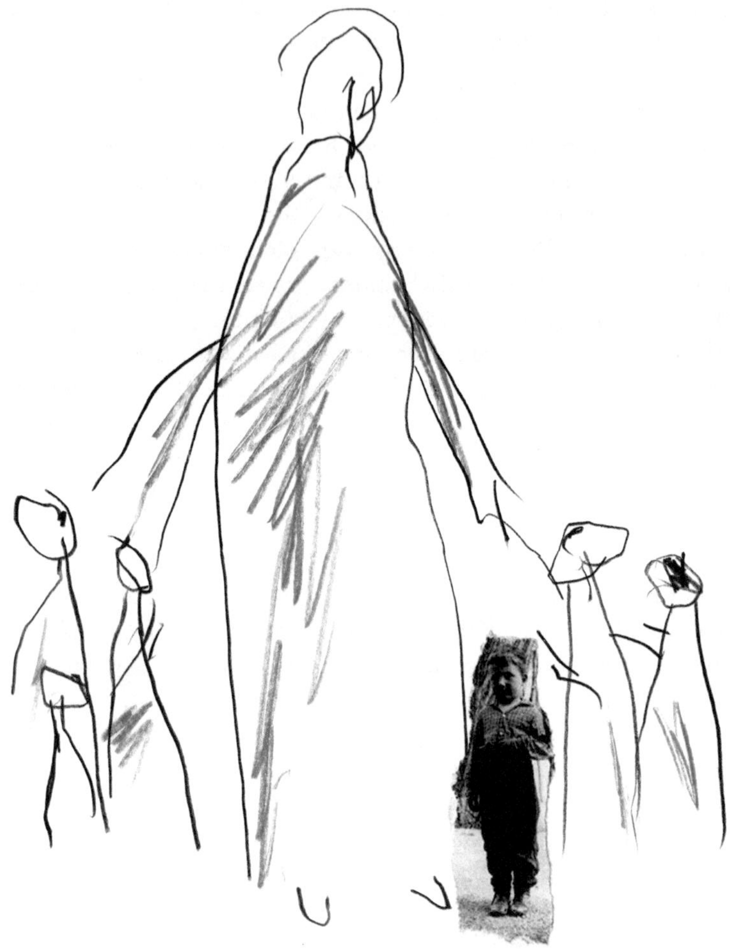

Figure 7.4   Gee Vaucher, 1st Station of the Cross – Suffer Little Children from *Much Ado About Something: A Play of Metaphors*, 1996

to deconstruct the internal monologue that results from an individual's early conditioning. The series reflects his use of the subjective reality of a patient, to break with the internalised voices derived from individuals and institutions that shape a child's reality.

While Laing's ideas can be seen in some of Vaucher's earlier work, in 1997 she overtly turned her attention to exploring his theories. The 2010s would see her embark on a vast seven-book series inspired by Laing's book of poetry, *Knots* (1970). In 1997, however, she produced an initial series of unpublished sketches on the subject (see Figure 7.5). Similarly to *Much Ado*

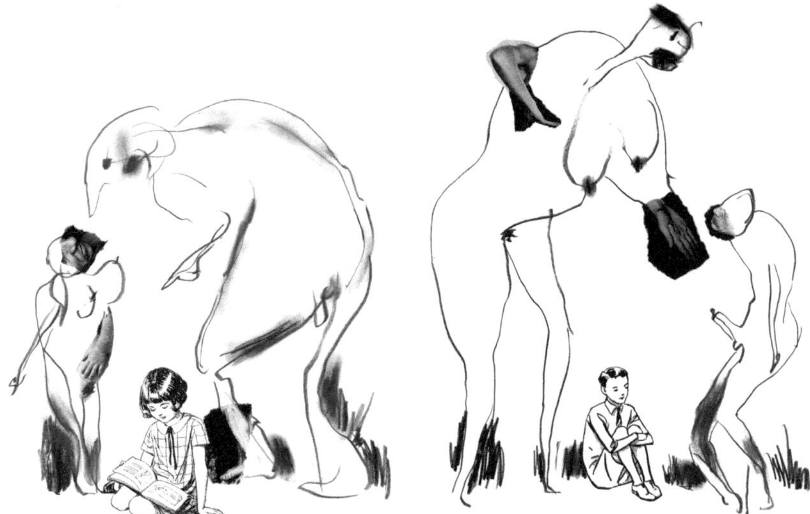

Figure 7.5   Gee Vaucher, unpublished series for R. D. Laing's *Knots*, 1997, pencil and collage, 380mm x 340mm

…, the images are surreal, but in a darker sense. Aesthetically, they build on the style of her earlier, colour pencil drawings from 1996 (see Plate 14, colour insert), using similarly fluid sketches to form domineering parental figures. These are collaged with figures of children, seemingly cut out from instructional children's books published during the post-war decades. Here, the disquieting aspects to familial relationships that Laing observed are viscerally brought to life.

Laing's succession of lucid and succinct observations on the (dysfunctional) functioning of families, and subsequent relational patterns, provided the intellectual stimulus for the series. Stemming from the psychiatrist's observations of his patients, *Knots* outlined the ties that bind, constrain and/or induce anxiety within the individual, denying them their own reality and validity. Similar themes, concerning repressive societal mores, are evident in Vaucher's series of transfer prints, *Icons* (created 1997–), which focuses on the sensuality of children (Figure 7.6).

These striking images are comprised of melded adult and child features taken from various sources including snapshots, bits of sculpture and dolls. This series critiques the enduring Victorian notion of 'purity' foisted on children. Vaucher sees this as contributing to the oppressive, contradictory, hypocritical and at times warped, environments in which many children are raised. She comments,

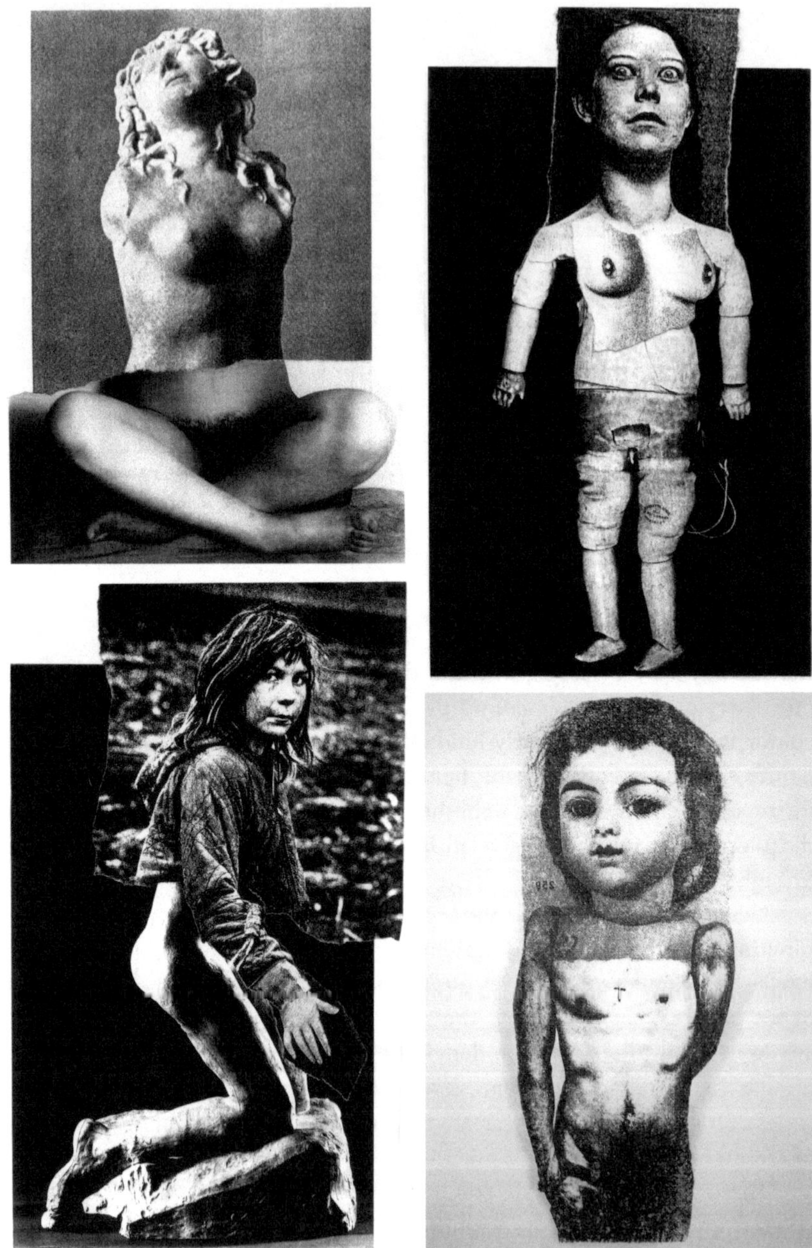

Figure 7.6   Gee Vaucher, *Icons*, 1997–ongoing, transfer prints

> I started this series when the UK was in the middle of continual news about
> child pornography etc, heavy stuff … a lot of news referring to little girls
> being dressed up like Barbie dolls, inviting that sort of thing; articles and
> conversations going on about the child as if they were just potential sex
> objects. I felt that a lot of people were afraid to see that a child, their child,
> was very sensual. There is a great difference for me between the words sexual
> and sensual. Children are very sensual beings and they can do things that we
> might find, as adults, sexual. I think we make a grave mistake in viewing
> children through our adult experience only. We forget the innocence of
> sensuality. It's a child's right to find out about their bodies, to observe each
> other. I suppose that series came out of that really. The first time I showed it
> (at The Phoenix in Exeter) I had a written comment in the visitor's book that
> said the series of prints were 'obscene and sick'. [22]

Vaucher started working on her *Icons* series in 1997 – the same year that New
Labour was elected, and the *Sensation* exhibition, at the Royal Academy,
showcased a collection of contemporary art, predominantly works by Young
British Artists (YBAs) owned by the advertising giant, businessman and art
collector Charles Saatchi. *Sensation* represented the culmination of the inexo-
rable rise of the YBAs to a pre-eminent position in the art world over the
preceding decade.

Vaucher's comment regarding the offence taken to *Icons* is interesting in
the context of the controversy provoked by some of the artworks in the *Sensation*
exhibition. Many, such as Emin's bed and Hirst's shark, were already famous,
but it was the painting, *Myra* (created by Marcus Harvey in 1995), that provoked
the most outraged response. The artwork used a mosaic of children's handprints
to form a gigantic reproduction of the famous police photo of the Moors
Murderer, Myra Hindley. Similarly to Vaucher's *Icons* series, Harvey's artwork
focused on how our relationship to children is engendered through social
forces – here the mass media. Beyond this, however, the difference between
the two is marked. Vaucher is concerned with the tendency for such forces
to project onto children an adult-construed and false notion of innocence.
By contrast, beyond a misguided attempt at commenting on the innocence
of children, Harvey's work declined to comment with any conviction on the
deeply harrowing themes it raised. As with the work of the YBAs more widely,
rather than critiquing the mass media, the painting satisfies itself with representing its worst subject matter, simply re-purposing it for consumption by an
elite gallery-going, as opposed to tabloid, audience. [23]

Harvey had himself been a punk in his teenage years, and the use of
controversial subject matter derived from the mass media as the basis for

artwork has a clear precedent in the genre. Vaucher's punk designs could likewise be seen to exploit real world events and themes, using mass media images of starvation, war victims and pornography to provoke a reaction in the viewer. Indeed, Vaucher had herself engaged with the same photo of Hindley when creating the visuals to accompany live performances of the Crass song, 'Mother Earth' (on *Stations of the Crass*, LP, 1979). The track provided a searing indictment of the hypocrisy the band saw in public reactions to the murders. Vaucher's visuals focused on the tabloid response, juxtaposing the famous mugshots of Hindley and Ian Brady with newspaper cuttings that simultaneously demonised and glamourised the pair. These were intercut with salacious headlines and sexualised imagery drawn from the same papers. This exposed the double standards implicit in the tabloid response, while suggesting the hysteria that results from such coverage is an outlet for deeply rooted violent and misogynist tendencies in society at large. Within the politically informed punk scene familiar with Crass, this statement had a clear purpose and critical intent, something missing from much of the YBAs' work. It's also noteworthy that, in keeping with the Berlin Dadaists, Vaucher and other punk/post-punk artists producing work in the 1980s were 'punching up'; taking those responsible for war, oppression and inequity as their target. By contrast, *Myra* appeared to be punching down in the disregard shown by the artist and art institution for the feelings of the victims' families and associated issues that it raised.[24] This was compounded as the controversy of the work raised its profile, contributing to the vast inflation of its value. Marcus' agent had bought the work and sold it to Saatchi for £11,000 prior to *Sensation*. After the exhibition, Saatchi sold it on to US commodities trader Frank Gallipoli for an estimated £100,000.

This is a fraction of the sums Saatchi received for many of the other exhibits, but it points to the success of the YBAs in harnessing the shifting art landscape that had been ushered in by eighteen years of Tory funding cuts. The radical artists of the 1970s had benefitted from State patronage that supported left-leaning, public and communal artists and art collectives, but from 1979 onwards this was deliberately undermined by the new regime in order to make the art world serve business interests. The YBAs were the first art movement to successfully respond to this, and even their early shows, housed in warehouse spaces in the face of gallery disinterest, were sponsored by property developers.[25] Through its embrace of individualism and the encroachment of big business into arts and culture, the movement overall was a world away from the radical autonomy of the preceding decades that shaped Vaucher as a young artist.

This difference in landscape is clearly illustrated by the contrast between *Sensation* and COUM Transmission's notorious exhibition, *Prostitution*, hosted at the ICA just over twenty years earlier (1976). The exhibition came at a point when COUM were transforming into the pioneering Industrial band Throbbing Gristle, mirroring in some ways Rimbaud and Vaucher's transition from EXIT to Crass, and the show was very much engineered by the artists to align themselves with the nascent energy of punk.[26] Nonetheless, the exhibition was distinguished by its serious intent (and success) in disturbing conventional morality. Among a host of transgressive and challenging works, Cosey Fanni Tutti's (b. 1951) collages, which incorporated pornographic images of herself from men's magazines, provoked an uproar that was symptomatic of the repressive, often hypocritical morality of that era; famously prompting the Conservative MP Nicholas Fairburn to term her and COUM 'the wreckers of civilisation'. Through her work, Cosey was challenging conservative opinion while simultaneously taking a swipe at the tendency within the women's movement and left-wing circles to view sex workers as invariably victims of male oppression. The YBAs, by contrast, did little to challenge the mores of society. Rather they appropriated punk shock tactics for commercial gain, for both themselves and the powerful art world and commercial interests that supported them.

In this respect, they drew on the precedent provided by Andy Warhol, who moved from an earlier, more ambivalent position to a more naked embrace of the world of commerce and high society over the course of his working life. In such a commercial context, anything posited as controversial/subversive was so in an 'ironic' sense; part of a sophisticated cultural game, whereby references were made to radical ideas while denying any associated meaning, and posturing rebellion was sanctioned by 'the system' of powerful art institutions and commerce. Through this act of collusion, such gestures of opposition served to strengthen, rather than subvert, the status quo.

As such, the YBAs were symptomatic of the malaise that had encumbered the concept of post-modernism by the 1990s. In 1992, the author Sadie Plant argued that the radical ideas of the Situationists, which had permeated the terrain in which Vaucher lived and worked during her young adult years, were harnessed, devoid of their original critical intention, to form the basis for a post-modern paradigm that denied meaning, difference or opposition beyond an all-pervasive consumerist culture.[27] The Situationist concept of the spectacle had been interpreted in the work of Jean Baudrillard (1929–2007) to be all-consuming, meaning that oppositional stances were rendered meaningless as they were themselves part of the spectacle.[28] Similarly, following his split from *Socialisme ou Barbarie*, Jean-François Lyotard (1924–98) argued that the Marxist basis from which to constitute a moral critique (based on the struggle of the oppressed) had been undermined.[29] Seemingly reflecting this, the work of the YBAs denied the validity of an outside space from which to constitute a moral, political or critical position.

By contrast, Vaucher's work in this period can be seen to hark back to the original tenets of post-modernism. Rather than a rejection of meaning, post-modernism had been intended to provide new ways of creating meaning in a world where the grand narratives of the twentieth century had ceased to provide answers. Her large-scale paintings, *Cow* and *Bull* (1997) (see Plates 15 and 16, colour insert), exemplify the way in which, despite abandoning a straightforwardly oppositional stance, she continued to engage with themes that had preoccupied her throughout her life.

These giant paintings, rendered on canvas, articulate her concern about how humans abuse their power in the way they relate to animals. She has painted the figures with great care and attention, so the viewer gets a full sense of their presence. The weightiness of the bull contrasts with the fragility of the cow, but their eyes are obscured. As curator Stevphen Shukaitis commented, 'We are denied a connection with these very large portraits because that mirrors how we treat animals destructively, and by extension, each other harmfully.'[30]

Vaucher uses animals in her art to highlight the Othering process humans undergo in owning, subjugating and exploiting them, while often also lampooning our anthropomorphic tendencies. This provides a telling contrast to Damian Hirst's commodification of dead animals in the production of his most recognisable works. His first installation of this kind, *A Thousand Years* (1990), featured a rotting cow's head being consumed by maggots and flies, all situated in a glass case (bought by Charles Saatchi). It was designed to produce an extreme reaction in the viewer, and helped to energise an art world that was flagging at the time. His shark poised in a tank of formaldehyde, *The Physical Impossibility of Death in the Mind of Someone Living* (1990), reinforced this approach as the dominant trademark of the Hirst brand. While such works provoke a reaction (including disgust) in the viewer, and despite the grandiloquent titling that alludes to themes of mortality, they nonetheless communicate very little about their supposed subject matter.

While in one sense the resistance of the YBAs to providing a fixed interpretation for their work could be seen as liberating, and more complex and sophisticated than some of the more didactic work of their predecessors, it can also be seen as a cop out. In the words of the Marxist art historian, Julian Stallabrass, in his excoriating critique of the YBAs, 'to refuse to offer neatly packaged solutions, to recognise complexity and ambiguity, does not have to entail refusing to say anything at all.'[31] Vaucher's work at the time – be it engaging with religion, animal rights, psychology or the rights of the child – seems to prove his point. This obtuseness is perhaps most clearly manifested

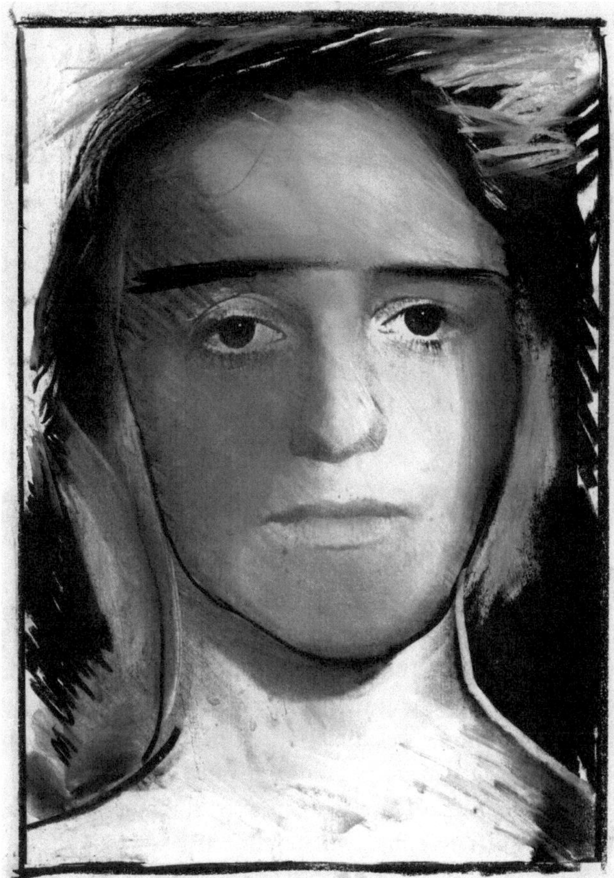

Figure 7.7   Gee Vaucher, *Self-portrait*, 1994, pastels, 310mm × 230mm

in her self-portraits from this time, a practice she occasionally returned to for the first time since art school.

These self-portraits convey something of her inner world, while resisting any fixed definitions. This is consistent with her natural reticence. As Rimbaud has commented, 'I have known Gee Vaucher for over fifty years, but perhaps could better define our relationship by stating that I have not known her for over fifty years.'[32] Her series of three collages, *See No Evil, Speak No Evil* (1997) feature the artist's face alternately completely masked in a stony texture, or masked with the exception of the eyes or the mouth (see Figure 7.8). This series uses the Japanese proverb to perhaps imply that she sees herself as a truth seer and teller. However, in the first collage, she indicates her reluctance to speak of what she sees. The second shows her speaking of things she can't

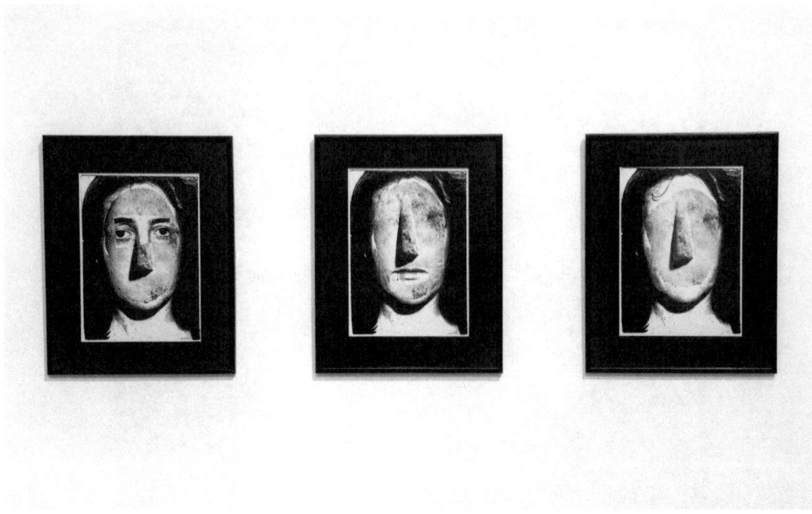

Figure 7.8   Gee Vaucher, *See No Evil, Speak No Evil*, 1997, 3 × collage, 420mm × 530mm

see or hear. Whether this is due to her being unable or unwilling, the viewer is not sure. In the third, she is completely removed from the world, appearing as a statue that is slowly being eroded. In fact, the collaged features were assembled from photos of Cycladic sculptures. The series is reminiscent of her *Icons* series, completed at around the same time, in its grainy, monochrome aesthetic and combination of a stony texture with the human form.

Vaucher's self-portraits chime with a modernist concept of the inner self, from where meaning emerges, as opposed to the post-modern denial of such positioning. Again, there is a marked contrast here to the ways in which the YBAs appeared in their work. The post-modern era was meant to have ushered in a time of liberation, where the signs and signifiers in a text took precedent over authorial intent, and the consumer became the producer. Showing how far it had diverged from this original intent, however, the 1990s was an era obsessed with celebrity and the cult of personality. The YBAs embraced this as currency, and often even high art magazines would feature pictures of the artist rather than pictures of their work. The work also often included the artist themselves. One of many high-profile illustrations is Sam Taylor-Wood's, *Fuck, Suck, Spank, Wank* (1993); a photo of the artist wearing a T-shirt featuring this statement, posing assertively, with her trousers around her ankles; as such gesturing towards third-wave feminism's reclaiming of women's sexuality. Similarly, Sarah Lucas' *Self-portrait with Fried Eggs* (1996) features the artist reclined in a chair, in jeans and a t-shirt, her legs spread apart in a self-consciously masculine pose, with two fried eggs placed over her breasts. Both images are notable for their lack of any interior meaning, conforming to the post-modern denial of any distinction between image and inner self. They are also unambiguous in the image the artist is attempting to convey about themselves and reflect the YBA's preoccupation with brand recognition. 'Deathy, edgy' Hirst, or 'confessional, confrontational' Emin; their public image was seemingly as important as their art, especially from a marketing perspective.

While this approach was a world away from Vaucher's, who remained a deeply private person, this period did see her begin to put herself forward as a solo artist. Although she began to exhibit her work in the 1980s (featuring in four shows), this escalated to nineteen exhibitions (four solo and fifteen group), both internationally and in the UK, in the 1990s. It was also at this time that Vaucher took a decisive step in the historicisation of her work with the publication of her book, *Crass Art and Other Pre Post-Modernist Monsters* (1999). It was self-produced and self-published (via Exitstencil Press) and featured opening notes by Peter Kennard and fellow Essex artist turned punk icon, Ian Dury.

At the time of release, Vaucher was still mostly known for her work with Crass, although even in this context many people didn't know that she had produced the bulk of their artwork – or indeed that she was a woman. As she notes sardonically, 'assumptions run deep'.[33] Staking a claim to the material she produced for the band could in itself be seen as a statement of intent. Alongside the Crass material, the book included a wide cross-section of her work to date, along with contextualising notes. Much of it, including extracts from *Pent Up, Homage to Catatonia* and unpublished *International Anthems*, was thereby made available to audiences for the first time.

The title of the book is notable for its conscious positioning of her work as 'Pre Post-modern'. Her work in the 1970s and 1980s on the surface fits this definition, given its clear similarities to that of early twentieth-century modernist avant-garde artists. This is most evidenced by the discernible intent of much of this work, often associated as it was with a critique of power. Even then, however, in its rejection of 'isms', it could be seen to reflect the positive interpretation of post-modernism based in 1970s radicalism, which characterised her work in the 1990s.

It is worth noting that Vaucher's autonomy from the art world has given her the freedom to work outside the dominant funding structures of the day, whatever they may be. The work emanating from Dial House in the 1970s hadn't ever been reliant on government funding, and as such was free to look beyond the left-wing remit that had underpinned much of the output by radical artists in that period. Similarly, as the art world became subservient to the interests of global capital and the neo-liberal project, she had the freedom to first work in opposition to it and then, when she returned to art practice in the 1990s, to work outside its strictures. This approach would come into its own in the twenty-first century, when her work, which often engaged once more with overtly political themes, reached new and wider audiences engaged in a search for meaning and authenticity in the wake of the Iraq War and the 2008 stock market crash.

Notes

1 See R. Bestley and R. Binns, 'The Evolution of an Anarcho-Punk Narrative, 1978–84', in Subcultures Network (ed.), *Ripped, Torn and Cut: Pop, Politics and Punk Fanzines* (Manchester: Manchester University Press, 2018), pp. 134–135 and R. Binns, 'It's Up to You: Class, Status and Punk Politics in Rock Against Racism', in I. Peddie (ed.), *The Bloomsbury Handbook of Popular Music and Social Class* (London/New York: Bloomsbury Academic, 2020), p. 91.
2 Vaucher in Interview with Binns, 2017.
3 Vaucher in email correspondence, June 2021.
4 Vaucher in interview with Binns, 2021. Crass also released the albums, *Christ the Bootleg* (Allied Records, 1989) and *You'll Ruin it for Everyone*, comprised of tracks recorded live at a Crass gig in Perth, Scotland, 1981, released by Pomona Records in 1993 with the band's permission (and re-released in 2001). *Crass Demos, 1977–79*, which provided an unofficial compilation of their demos was released on Not on Label (Crass) in 2007.
5 See A. Worthington (ed.), *The Battle of the Beanfield* (Totton: Hobbs, 2nd reprint. 2013). Tony Bunyan discusses The Battle of Orgreave (18 June 1984), as the pivotal event of the Miners' Strike, in the context of the wider para-militarisation of the police force in Britain in the 1980s. See T. Bunyan, 'From Saltley to Orgreave via Brixton', *Journal of Law and Society* 12:3 (1985), pp. 293–303.
6 Vaucher in interview with Groß, 2002.
7 Vaucher in interview with Groß, 2002.
8 Vaucher in interview with Binns, 2021.
9 Vaucher in interview with Groß, 2015, quoted in Y. Etgar, 'Domestic Violence', in S. Shukaitis (ed.), *Gee Vaucher: Introspective* (Colchester: Firstsite, published in collaboration with Minor Compositions, 2016), p. 139, updated via email correspondence, June 2021.
10 Vaucher in interview with Binns, 2021.
11 Anon, Gabrielle d'Estrées and one of her sisters, Musée Historique Environment Urbain. Available at www.mheu.org/en/timeline/gabrielle-estrees.htm (accessed 21 June 2021).
12 Vaucher in email correspondence, June 2021.
13 See C. K. Madsen (ed.), G. Grindon, A. Heil, M. Sanders and J. Thage, *Art Strikes Back-from Jorn to Banksy* (Silkeborg, Denmark: Museum Jorn, 2019), which features

Situationist inspired art, drawing a lineage from Asper Jorn to Banksy, and including work by a number of artists including Gee Vaucher.

14   Vaucher in interview with Binns, 2021.

15   Vaucher in interview with Binns, 2021.

16   Vaucher quoted in P. Allmer and J. Sears, 'Pin-Up/Cut-Up: Woman in Gee Vaucher's Assemblages', in S. Shukaitis (ed.), *Gee Vaucher: Introspective* (Colchester: Firstsite, published in collaboration with Minor Compositions, 2016), p. 52. Updated via email correspondence, June 2021.

17   Vaucher in interview with Binns, 2021.

18   G. Vaucher, *Much Ado About Something: A Play of Metaphors* (Essex: Existencil Press, 2011), Intro.

19   Vaucher in email correspondence, June 2021.

20   G. Vaucher, Much Ado About Something. Available at www.exitstencilpress.com/product-page/much-ado-about-something (accessed 1 June 2020).

21   Vaucher published all fourteen stations and accompanying notes in her booklet, Vaucher, *Much Ado About Something.*

22   Vaucher in interview with Binns, 2018.

23   Julian Stallabrass highlights how the YBAs frequently drew on mass culture, including tabloids, in a bid to make themselves and their work appear accessible, ultimately concluding that this constituted a marketing strategy in a hyper-capitalist mould. See J. Stallabrass, *High Art Lite: The Rise and Fall of Young British Art* (London: Verso, 2006).

24   See Stallabrass, *High Art Lite,* pp. 214–215.

25   The inaugural exhibition Frieze (1988) was sponsored by London Docklands Development Corporation, alongside the development company, Olympia and York.

26   Ian Trowell, in email correspondence, July 2021. Trowell is currently writing a book, *An Endless Discontent: Throbbing Gristle, Punk and Provocation* (working title) is due for publication in 2023 (Bristol: Intellect Books).

27   S. Plant, *The Most Radical Gesture: The Situationist International in a Postmodern Age* (London: Routledge, 1992).

28   Whereas Baudrillard's position in *Le Systeme des Objects* (1968) closely paralleled Debord's ideas outlined in *Society of the Spectacle,* which just preceded it, in his later work, Baudrillard broke with any structural analysis by advocating for a world without underlying meaning as an end in itself.

29   J. F. Lyotard, 'On Theory: An Interview' (Driftworks: New York, Semiotext (e), 1984), p. 29, quoted in S. Plant, *The Most Radical Gesture: The Situationist International in a Postmodern Age* (London: Routledge, 1992), p. 113.

30   Shukaitis in interview with Binns, 2016.

31   Stallabrass, *High Art Lite,* p. 155.

32   P. Rimbaud, 'A Very Private Person', in S. Shukaitis (ed.), *Gee Vaucher: Introspective* (Colchester: Firstsite, published in collaboration with Minor Compositions, 2016), p. 30.

33   Vaucher in email correspondence, June 2021.

8

Beyond the art world: political agitation and public intervention in the new millennium

Following Vaucher's hiatus from Crass, during which she turned away from the 'sensationalism' that she saw dominating the art world, her work took a more outward-looking turn as the new century dawned. This coincided with a shift in attitude within the British art world, away from spectacular art that denied discernible meaning, towards work that attempted to once again engage with society. Jeremy Deller's (b. 1966) *Battle of Orgreave* (2002), for example, re-enacted the momentous fight between striking miners and police (1984) using a combination of actors and people who were involved in the original event. Nils Norman's (b. 1966) art envisioned alternatives to homogenised urban planning in the 2000s. His interest was in anarchist pedagogies, student-led learning and alternative education. The emphasis on the collective voice, through communal living, activism and anti-authoritarianism in his work reflects the debt to the radical utopianism of the 1960s and 1970s.

Major public institutions, such as the Tate, began to challenge the Saatchi-dominated narrative that defined the 1990s, exploring work with a wider range of subject matter and basis for its validity.[1] However, it's worth noting that often the work promoted by galleries was political in a more circumspect than radical sense. For example, work by former YBAs such as Gillian Wearing, who dealt with issues of inclusivity and agency in her multi-media documentation of everyday life, and Liam Gillick, whose work observed the ideological apparatus underpinning globalised neo-liberalism, was more concerned with considering how we negotiate the terrain in which we find ourselves, than critiquing or changing the social structures that created it.

Gillick's work in this period also reveals the increasing influence of the European art movements of the 1990s in the UK from the 2000s onwards. In contrast to the YBAs, these had sought to break down the division between artists/art institutions and their audiences. The French curator, Nicolas Bourriaud, sought to capture the ethos of this movement in his book *Relational Aesthetics* (1998), which advocated the production of meaning in art through social exchange. Bourriaud, however, argued that it was necessary for this plurality to occur in the commercial sphere, making any progressive intentions subservient to its associated hierarchies and contingencies.

This merging of ethical concerns with free market economics reflected the ideals of the New Labour administration in the UK, but Vaucher also noted a grassroots embrace of a new set of values, such as the rise of vegetarianism/veganism, concerns about healthy eating and the devaluing of conventional work models. However, she also perceived the world to be 'out of balance, as it seems it has always been. How have we got to a situation where so few people call the tune for so many? The division between rich and poor has become more and more extreme at the expense of an ever increasing number of people … First imperialism; now globalisation wears a very ugly and corrupt head.'[2] This perspective was reflected in key texts published at the time. In *Empire*, Michael Hardt and Antonio Negri argued that rather than providing opportunities for freedom, the globalised information age transposed what was previously Western, nation-state supremacy onto the worldwide stage, with more oppressive outcomes.[3]

Vaucher also expressed concerns about the impending environmental crisis, observing, 'We have to pull back and consider "how are we, as humans, going to survive? How will the next generation cope with the crap that we are leaving behind?"'[4] This message, which would become foregrounded through Extinction Rebellion (2018–), also evoked the 'social ecology' articulated by the anarchist Murray Bookchin (1921–2006) whose ideas had contributed to the countercultural zeitgeist of the late 1960s and 1970s.[5]

These concerns were in sync with the growing anti-globalisation movement that had developed during the Blair administration. Following large-scale rallies in the UK and across Europe opposing G8 conferences, the 'Carnival against Capitalism' (1998), it found its most recognised manifestation in the 1999 Seattle World Trade Organisation protests. This movement was itself inspired by the Stop the City demonstrations that Crass had been involved in, and ran counter to the dominant narrative of the time, in which, especially in the UK, dissent was subsumed and co-opted by New Labour. All this was to change, however, following the seismic shift initiated by the events of 9/11.

The willingness of the Blair government to support the US in its plan to invade Iraq, its fabrication of evidence to support such an action, and its blatant disregard for public opinion opposing such a war, laid bare many of the flaws of the New Labour project. While the members of Crass had never bought into this, the advent of the war brought them together once again. For Vaucher, this was a return to collaborative work for the first time since the 1980s, as Penny Rimbaud, Eve Libertine, Joy de Vivre, Steve Ignorant, Andy Palmer and Pete Wright came together under the name The Crass Collective, staging an event at the Queen Elizabeth Hall protesting the impending Iraq War (2002). The event also featured associates such as Ian MacKaye of DC hardcore bands Minor Threat and Fugazi, the Jordanian–British founder of Graeae Theatre Company, Nabil Shaban, and The English Chamber Choir. It was coloured by the performance of Pete Wright, who under the name of Judas 2, hired an actress to act as a heckler, in an attempt to expose what he perceived to be the failings of Crass as a political entity: their inability to change the world. By extension, Wright was implying that the concert itself was a pointless endeavour. The other members had intended the protest to bring about a sense of togetherness with the audience, and Vaucher has said she was more than upset at what she perceived to be Wright's 'arrogant and underhand attempt to sabotage everyone's positive intentions. We already knew that such a concert could never be enough against the forces of war, but we felt it was important to try and make more voices heard.'[6]

The year 2002 also saw Crass members take part in an afternoon of performance and Crass film screenings at the National Film Theatre, as part of its *Never Mind the Jubilee* Season, which commemorated the Queen's 50th year on the throne and the 25th anniversary of punk. The films, created by Vaucher and also featuring material by Mick Duffield, were screened in a large room where their collaging of loud, disturbing sounds and brutal imagery, featuring nuclear explosions, Nazi soldiers, concentration camp inmates and war victims had a profound effect on its audience.[7] Graphic designer Dominic Thackray, who reviewed the Crass films in an article for the BFI website, recalled, 'It was meant to be compered by the comedian Rob Newman, but he bottled out of the Q&A with Gee. He was traumatised! Steve [Ignorant] got some beers from the green room and handed them out to the audience and the Q&A became a lot more relaxed, informal and funny.'[8]

Vaucher also provided artwork and films as backdrops to gigs and performances by The Crass Collective, who changed their name to Crass Agenda in 2003. They became a fixture at the Vortex Jazz Club, and fronted a campaign against its closure when the building, on Stoke Newington Church Street (Hackney, London), was acquired by property developers. The club subsequently moved to Dalston (further south in Hackney) in 2005.

The development pressures faced by the Vortex were associated with the endemic gentrification that has accelerated in London and its environs from the late 1990s. During this period, the former members of Crass who remained at Dial House had themselves faced the prospect of eviction, with the ancient building and its impressive gardens threatened with redevelopment. Rimbaud and Vaucher, with support from the local community, fought off a slew of development proposals that would have also enveloped surrounding land used for recreation by the whole village. In light of this, the developers auctioned off the land in 2002. Having rejected, or at least not sought, property ownership in the past, as part of their wider anarchistic principles, they found themselves with ownership as the only viable option. Having little in the way of cash reserves, an extensive fundraising effort was made.

This threat to Dial House was the inspiration behind Rimbaud's re-working of the Dylan Thomas' play *Under Milk Wood*, which the Crass Collective performed at the Vortex in 2005. In his version, property developers move into the mythical Welsh village, with the little fishing port transformed into a lido, the pub being 'yuppified', and the people being thrown out of their home to make way for a new estate. Rimbaud comments, 'the main protagonist is totally based on the guy who was working on behalf of Peer Group International, trying to get us out. So it was very direct.'[9]

Since 2005, the collective has continued to perform under the name Last Amendment, making regular appearances with a wide range of musicians and performers. Their latest incarnation is as 'L'Académie des Vanités. They have continued to the present day, with Rimbaud and Libertine performing well into their seventies. Accompanied by Vaucher's striking visuals, their performances are at least as powerful as anything they produced in their younger years.

The aftermath of the Iraq War also saw Vaucher re-engage with themes of pacifism and anti-militarism in her artwork, though this later output embraced a wider set of mediums and often reveals a more subtle and varied aesthetic to her overtly polemical work with Crass. One prominent example is the immersive installation, *The Sound of Stones in the Glasshouse* (2006); a collaboration with the artist, Christian Brett.

Vaucher elaborated on Brett's original conception of a stand-alone structure, with the name of every country where the USA has instigated or taken part in a war etched into the glass panels, by adding a set of wall panels and projecting films inside the glass edifice. Each panel documents the track record of one American president, listing the wars they were involved in alongside

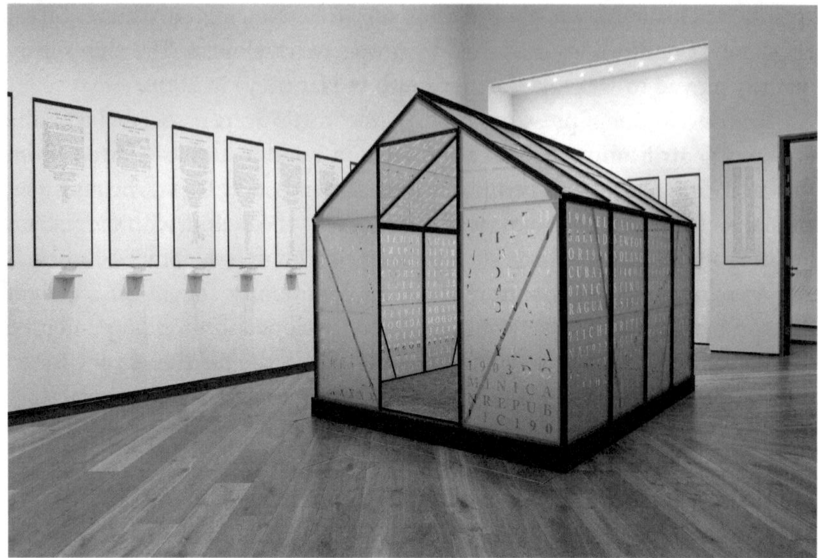

Figure 8.1 Gee Vaucher and Christian Brett, *The Sound of Stones in the Glasshouse*, installed at 96 Gillespie Gallery, London, 2006

damning or ironic quotes taken from their speeches, ending starkly by listing the number of people killed on their watch. In the first installation at 96 Gillespie Gallery (London), she placed grass seed in bowls beneath each wall panel and people were encouraged to throw some in the greenhouse, which had been filled with soil. Over time the grass grew, and people were invited, on the closing night, to take away a piece of the 'turf' and plant it somewhere else. The installation went through various updates for subsequent exhibitions before becoming a centrepiece for her major retrospective at Firstsite (Colchester, 2016).

The Sound of Stones ... reflects Vaucher's willingness to engage with high art techniques and adopt a more conceptual means of communication concerning the theme of pacifism. However, the same period saw Vaucher also revive her practice of making political interventions in the public sphere. The flyposting and graffiti campaigns she'd engaged in with Crass had strong correlations and connections with the contemporaneous street art scene. While the scene had its roots in the 1970s and 1980s, it made a profound incursion into the public discursive space and art world during the 2000s; its preoccupations with the increasing encroachment of corporations and State surveillance of public and personal realms having particular resonance to the times.

Vaucher has been a friend and creative collaborator of Banksy's since he got in touch with her by phone in the 2000s, when he was already renowned as a graffiti artist in the UK. She notes, 'Working in isolation, I very often don't know what's going on in the art word and when he rang and said this is Banksy, I said, "Sorry, I don't know anyone called Banksy".'[10] Since then, he has been a stalwart supporter of Vaucher's art, having been blown away by it in his youth. He comments,

> As a teenager I got into punk and the art that came with it, but by its nature most of the stuff was pretty naive or messy. It wasn't until I saw Gee Vaucher's Crass poster depicting the Queen, Pope, Justice and Thatcher as punks [see Figure 5.3] that something in me caught fire. It was the sheer virtuosity. This was 'real' art – but for the left. Somehow that picture made me feel our side could win.[11]

Certain aspects of her aesthetic and political philosophy can be seen in his work. The Parisian street artist, Blek le Rat, is widely credited as the inspiration for Banksy's use of stencils. However, there are also clear echoes of Crass' distinct stencil lettering (itself inspired by the graffiti they noted on the New York subways) that featured on their spray-painted slogans, and their record covers and inserts.

The overlapping themes in the work of both artists are marked: both of them critique war, militarism, State power and globalised capitalism, while advocating people's freedom from the interests of coercive forces. Both also emphasise the loss of autonomy and inequities incurred by children on the blunt end of these forces. Both use satirical humour and provide timely comment with political relevance in their work. Following the same path as Vaucher, Banksy draws on the legacy of the Situationist-inspired slogans that appeared on walls during Paris '68, along with early graffiti art and punk. As with these rebellious antecedents, their work has the potential to intervene in the circulation of messages intended to reinforce the ideology of a capitalist society. In keeping with Debord's pronouncements on how 'the Spectacle'[12] commodifies culture, inducing reification and the mediation of people's experience and relationships towards capitalist interests, their work functions to hijack, appropriate and subvert these visual codes and symbols, thereby providing new meaning.

Vaucher's street art is an extension of her DiY ethos, her anti-establishment orientation and her desire for art to reach an audience beyond the confines of the art world and impact on social change. Banksy's maxim, 'I like to think I have the guts to stand up anonymously in a western democracy and call for things no one else believes in – like peace and justice and freedom,'[13] reiterates Vaucher's outlook. While it was at odds with the dominant ideology in the art market in the 1990s, it was symptomatic of the emerging zeitgeist of the new, politically engaged era.

Vaucher's desire to subsume her individual identity in order to communicate political ideas effectively is seen in several, public realm projects that she was involved with in the 2000s. She had contributed works to Banksy's Santa's Ghetto Christmas pop up store in 2002, 2004 and 2005, and when the concept was taken to Palestine in 2007, Vaucher was one of twenty artists who went along. The event held in Bethlehem to raise awareness of the situation in Palestine and to raise money for specific projects there, has become best known for the wall art its participants produced. However, Vaucher spent most of her time talking to people and helping the other artists rather than graffitiing the wall. She reflected, 'I'm not a public artist, I found it hard to contribute to the wall.'[14] The Israeli Government had begun construction of the wall in 2000 to cut off access from Gaza to Israeli-occupied territory, which has led to it being referred to by Banksy (among numerous others) as the 'biggest open air prison in the world'.[15] The wall is considered illegal by the United Nations, but from Vaucher's position it points to a wider problem. 'No barriers anywhere; that is another answer', she states, reflecting her alignment with the No Borders movement. She continues, 'Certainly not that wall, and certainly not Israel's attitude and total disrespect, debasement and robbery of the Palestinian people. But that's a big subject.'[16]

This reference to the complexity of the situation is telling. While her preoccupation with Palestine and opposition to the Iraq War mirrors the tone of left-wing movements in this period, her approach reveals clear differences. Much of the opposition to the Iraq War was co-ordinated by the Stop the War Coalition, which grew out of the Socialist Workers Party, in much the same way that Rock Against Racism had in the 1970s. In the 2000s Vaucher supported their position, and the coalition sponsored the *Pax Britannica* exhibition at the Aquarium Gallery in 2008, that featured her work alongside that of Banksy, Guardian cartoonist Steve Bell and others. The Stop the War Coalition's focus was on Western Imperialism and its perceived pro-Israeli agenda. This would later prove problematic in the wake of the Arab Spring, where Western governments' hesitant alignment with anti-Assad forces in Syria meant they adopted what was seen as a pro-Assad stance, despite his regime's well-documented atrocities and crimes against humanity.[17] Vaucher's support of Syrian refugee causes in this latter period, the majority of whom were fleeing persecution by Assad, reveals the flexibility in her position, unencumbered as it is by an overarching ideology. Her focus is on common people and power imbalance, wherever it may manifest, something also reflected in her 2008 collage, *Israeli Soldiers* (Figure 8.2).

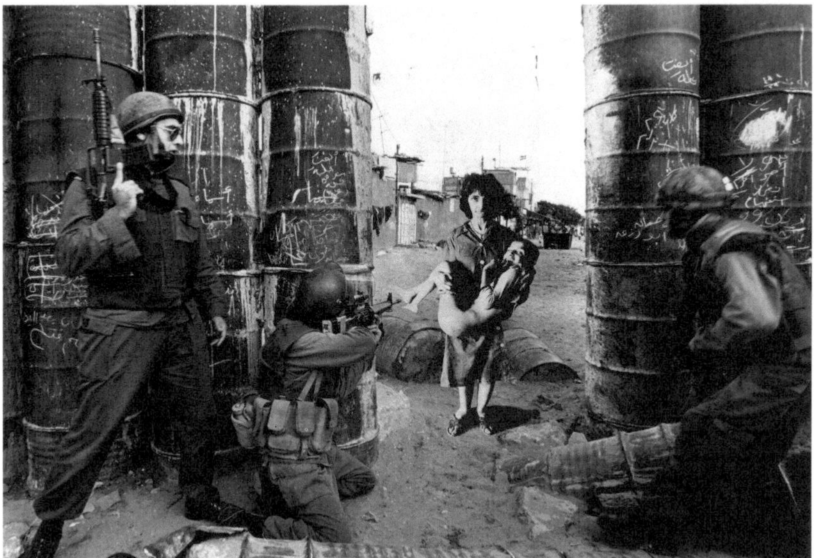

Figure 8.2   Gee Vaucher, *Israeli Soldiers*, collage, 2008

The year 2008 saw further engagement with the situation in Palestine, when she and several other artists were commissioned by the London Nakba Project to respond to the 60th anniversary of the creation of the State of Israel. This gave her the opportunity to explore digital art production. She commented, 'I seem to remember each artist had three huge billboards each in different parts of London. The first idea I had only showed one tank behind the old man, but the billboards demanded landscape rather than portrait orientation, so I added more tanks [see Figures 8.3 and 8.4]. I don't really do collage on screen, but this was a perfect occasion where Photoshop came into its own.'[18]

The image has strong visual similarities to the iconic image of a student standing in front of tanks in Tiananmen Square, instead featuring an old man hunched over a walking stick walking away from the tanks. It alludes to the disparity of might in the forces at odds in Palestine, and the effect this has on the rights of often fragile or defenceless civilians. This work functions as agit-prop, in much the same way as her political work with Crass (1977–84). However, by making such large-scale public realm interventions, it had the potential to reach a far wider audience, outside of this earlier niche punk milieu.

The pacifist themes that re-emerged in her political work in the 2000s are reflected elsewhere in her output during this period. Her paintings on top of found prints, *Great Scott* (2009) (see Plate 17, colour insert) and *Flying*

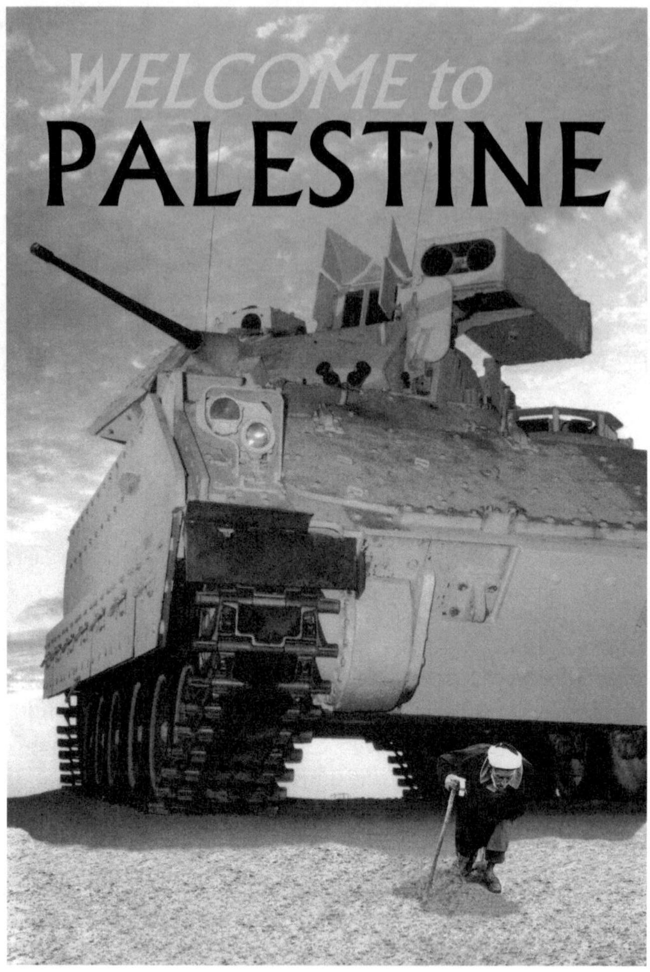

Figure 8.3   Gee Vaucher, *Al-Nakbah*, collage, 2008

High (2016), subtly alter the existing landscapes by nestling warplanes in amongst migrating flocks of birds, while *All at Sea* (2021) inserts a dinghy carrying fleeing refugees into an idealised seascape.

The period had also seen the re-emergence of her contemporary Peter Kennard, who also contributed to the Bethlehem and Nakba projects, and exhibited at the Pax Britannica exhibition. His *Photo Op* collage (2007), produced in collaboration with Cat Phillips, featured a jubilant Tony Blair taking a selfie in front of an Iraq war scene, and arguably became a defining image of the era. It was an earlier work of his, however, that provided a precedent for *Great Scott* and *Flying High*. In *Haywain with Cruise Missiles* (1980) Kennard

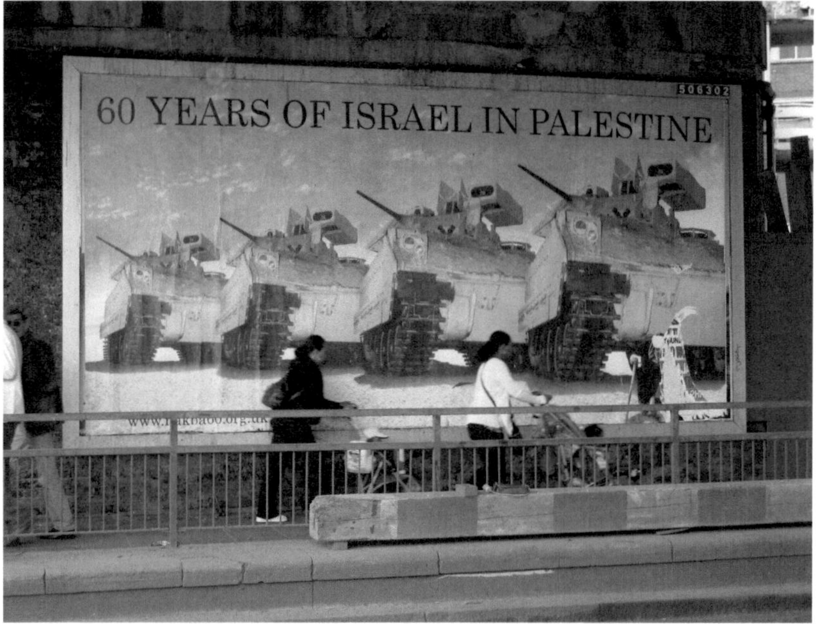

Figure 8.4   Gee Vaucher, *60 Years of Israel in Palestine*, collage, 2008

had used photomontage to insert nuclear warheads into the cart (haywain) depicted in the iconic Constable painting. A whole subgenre of Banksy's work also features sabotaged oil paintings; his *Show me the Monet* (2005) – in which upturned, discarded shopping trollies and a traffic cone are added to the waterlily pond of Monet's masterpiece – being perhaps the most famous. Both works undermine the art historical status of the original work and disrupt how they have come to embody idealised portrayals of the past, by providing politicised comment on a contemporary issue.[19]

While the originals for *Great Scott, Flying High* and *All at Sea* were charity shop finds, Vaucher used a comparable act of détournement to establish a dialogue with works of high art status, notably in her collage, *Pietà* (2010), which attacks the futility of violence (see Figure 8.5). She here inserts the photo of a dead man, which she has positioned in place of Christ, into a photo of the original sculpture by Michelangelo (1498–99). The male figure wears twentieth-century utilitarian dress that contrasts with the refined drapery used to depict figures in Renaissance art. In place of the Christian icon of martyrdom, this figure is universal. Vaucher here undermines the authority of both Renaissance masterpiece and biblical story to insert her own comment on human suffering. She explains,

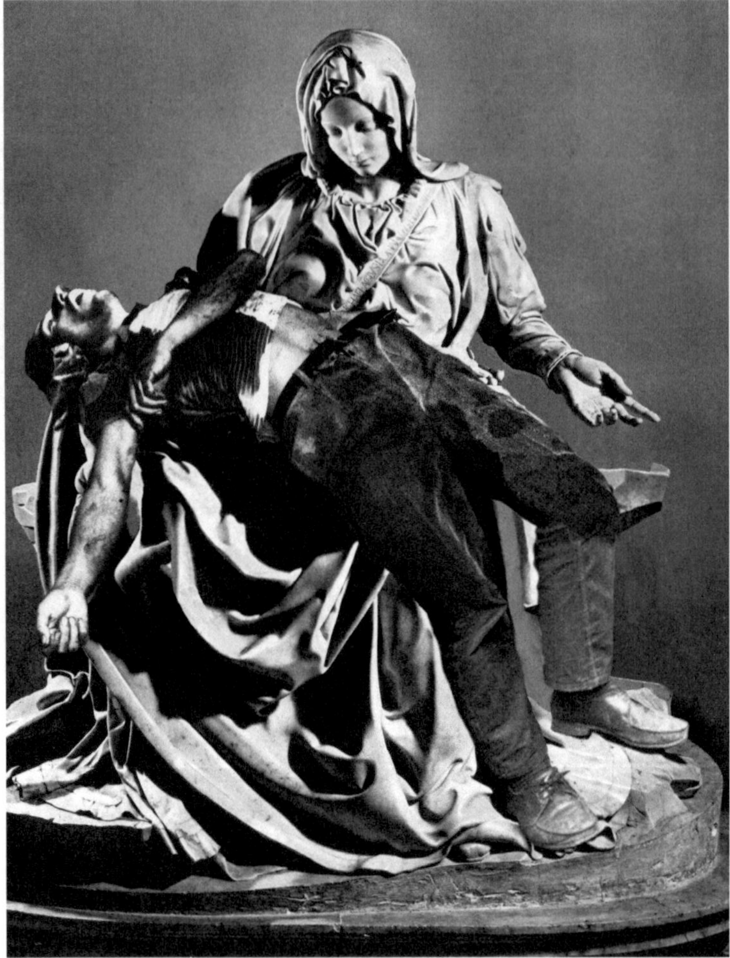

Figure 8.5   Gee Vaucher, *Pietà*, 2010, collage, 297mm × 200mm

It's a dead, massacred man, whether from war, whether from vindictive street
fights, who knows! The statement is for the world. That's the state of the
world. There's war everywhere. There's suffering everywhere, even if it's not a
war – there's a famine. It's going on and on and on and they're all
unnecessary … Caused by bad management, bad ideas, corruption, lies and
greed; and we are all part of the problem.[20]

This subversion of meaning in works within the established canon is also
evident in *The Great Dictator* (2009) (see Figure 8.6), which spoofs the famous
surrealist painting, *Le Viol/The Rape* (1935) by Rene Magritte, replacing the

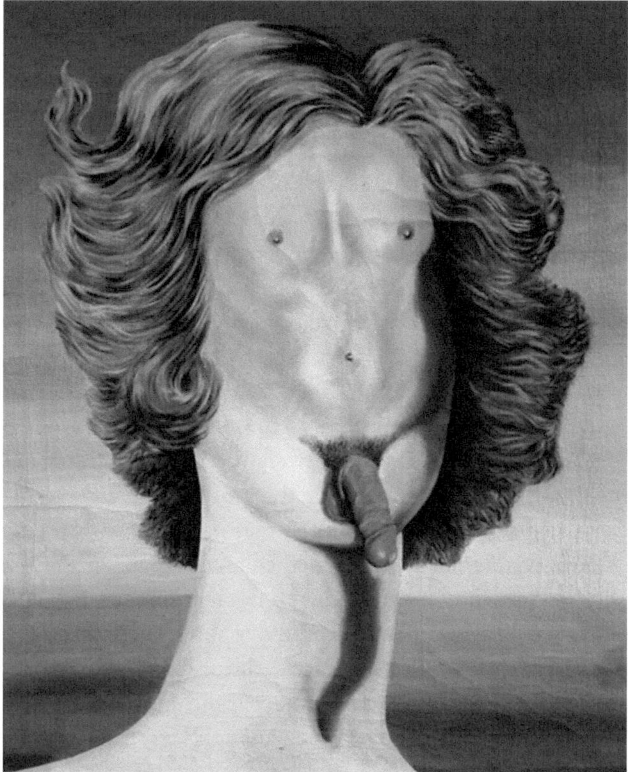

Figure 8.6   Gee Vaucher, *Dictator*, 2009, acrylic on canvas, 640mm × 535mm

female torso with a male one, replete with a penis in place of the vagina for the mouth. The original painting by Magritte was intended to provide a statement on the male sexual objectification of women. Vaucher renders Magritte's familiar work uncanny through her deconstruction of its intended meaning. Through her reversal of the process of objectification, Vaucher can be seen to ridicule the fantasy of male power alluded to in *The Rape*, instead presenting the male body as inert and male genitalia as inconsequential.

Vaucher is characteristically offhand about her intentions. She notes, 'I just thought it would be a laugh. Dick-tator! It was a fun piece. I thought of the word, and I looked at the Magritte painting and I thought hmmm, how about a dick-tator.'[21] Despite her dismissiveness, the painting could be interpreted as a comment on how women were represented in the male-dominated Surrealist art and literary movement. While Magritte's intention may have been to highlight the sexual objectification of women, it also added to the preponderance of work by male artists that has depicted, scrutinised and dissected the female body. If we take this essay by Norman Mailer (1923–2007) on Picasso as just one prominent example, 'For the last fifty years (if one is to take as his point of departure *Les Demoiselles D'Avignon*) Picasso has used his brush like a sword, disemboweling an eye to plaster it over the ear, lopping off a breast in order to turn it behind an arm, scoring the nostrils of his ladies until they took on the violent necessities of those twin holes of life and death, the vagina and the anus.'[22]

The casual way in which this violent visual dissection of a woman's body is described shows the ubiquity of such terminology throughout art historical discourse, prior to the women's movement in the 1970s. Mailer's essay on Picasso, first published in 1959, was praised by Jeff Nuttall in his book on the counterculture, *Bomb Culture* (1968), reflecting how widespread an acceptance of misogyny also was in this later libertarian milieu. Vaucher's play on gender in this respect is both humorous and subversive; perhaps alluding to her wider belief that women should acknowledge their 'masculine' side and vice versa.

Vaucher also produced a body of work that was less overtly political during this time.[23] However, while some seemed primarily to experiment with form and composition, much of it engaged with familiar themes. Her *Animal Rites* series, for instance, which seamlessly combines photos of human facial features with vintage, monochrome photographs featuring human–animal interaction, explores the tendency for humans to project anthropomorphic qualities onto animals. The insertions she makes for her *Animal Rites* series are so intricately melded that on first glance the viewer is not quite sure what they are looking at. The disparate elements of animal and human features are combined in a way that is both totally convincing and uncanny. Figure 8.7, for instance, features an unfolded hand holding a cracked egg from which a chick emerges. The bird's bedraggled fur blends seamlessly with the man's beard that it joins. It reveals a surrealist sense of humour, confounding expectations in a way that is playful, jarring and a little absurd.

While the series is playful, it touches upon the predatory and exploitative aspects of human–animal relationships. As such, it links to her wider preoccupation with relational abuses of power. Again, these seem to reflect the ideas of Laing concerning the constraints placed on the individual by familial and social conditioning.[24]

The *Animal Rites* series was released as a book in 2003, which opened with one of her rare self-portraits, here depicting the artist metamorphosing into an animal. As such, it can be seen to critique the hierarchical classification process engendered through speciesism. Vaucher's self-portrait (see front cover) dissolves these distinctions, seeing herself and all humans as part of the interconnectedness of all lifeforms.

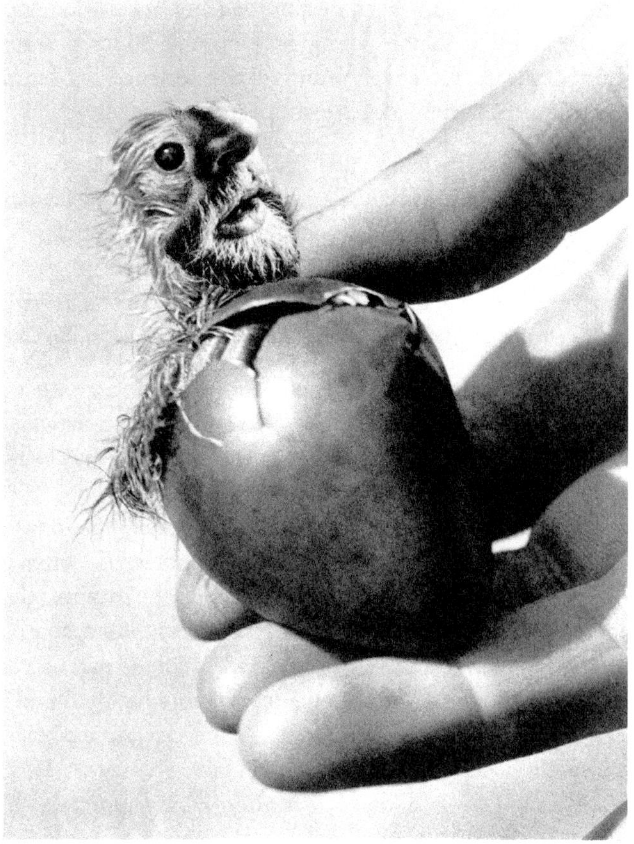

Figure 8.7   Gee Vaucher, Illustration for the *Animal Rites* series, 2003, collage

Vaucher's critique of power imbalance is also evident in her series of vast paintings, *Children Who Have Seen Too Much Too Soon* (2006–16). As the title indicates, these paintings feature children who have been prematurely aged by their experiences (see colour insert, Plates 18 and 19). However, rather than sentimentalising suffering, the portraits emphasise their strength in the face of hardship. As such, she avoids reducing the viewer response to pity, while showing empathy with those most affected by injustice.

It might be assumed that her inspiration for *Children …* arose from her concern at the situation in Palestine, or the crisis in Syria. She often donated works to Syrian refugee organisations and invited refugee families, who had just settled in Colchester, to create a pop-up cafe, serving Syrian food, at the Firstsite gallery during her exhibition (2016). She said this was appropriate, as much of her work reflected on 'loss and grief and matters pertinent to suffering and injustice.'[25] However, despite Vaucher acknowledging that she envisioned the children in the paintings as having 'suffered the effects of brutality from domestic violence to war and the destruction of innocence',[26] the inspiration for the series came from closer to home.

> I'd started to take the train into London instead of driving. I just kept seeing a lot of damaged children, or children that were straining at the bit and being shouted down all the time. After a few months of watching this closely, something started to bubble. Obviously I saw a lot of children from far-flung places and wondered what their story was? It was just watching every line and every face really and of course, what we as adults added to the soup.[27]

Unusually, her first step in creating the oil paintings was to produce a collage. She explains, 'I would collage it and then I would think, now what was that face that I saw? Has it captured that feeling of that child that I saw? Then I would work from that.'[28]

The paintings also comment on the increasingly stifling parenting techniques that have characterised society since the 1990s. She notes, 'The often ridiculous restrictions imposed by Health and Safety laws, plus the paranoia that parents instill in their children here in the UK are so claustrophobic, so inhibiting.'[29] In particular, she says she is saddened by her observations of parents consistently checking and demanding absurd obedience, when what the child might be doing wasn't even anti-social or dangerous.[30] The series was designed to study how such inhibitions manifested on a child's face. She says, 'Many children in the UK appear to have had their lust for life all but suppressed, and I have often thought that if I was born now, brought up with so many restrictions, I would probably have ended up in a mental institution.' She adds, 'Then of course there are those children who can hide nothing, and you can see that something very dramatic has happened in their lives; young faces that have already aged from unimaginable experiences.'[31]

Vaucher's film, *Angel* (2012), evolved from these large paintings of children. This time she decided to focus her observations on the face of her great-niece, Angel, just before her transition from a small local school of less than fifty children to a vast secondary school of over two thousand. Vaucher had already observed the changes in Angel's older sister when going through the same transition. She commented, 'It seemed that the innocence, a certain softness of the face, had disappeared, I suspect it was something to do with survival in the playground.' Over the course of making the film, she concluded that it was about the joy and fears of the child. She notes, 'It is a rare opportunity to stare and catch every slight change in face, when we were children we were not embarrassed to stare.'[32]

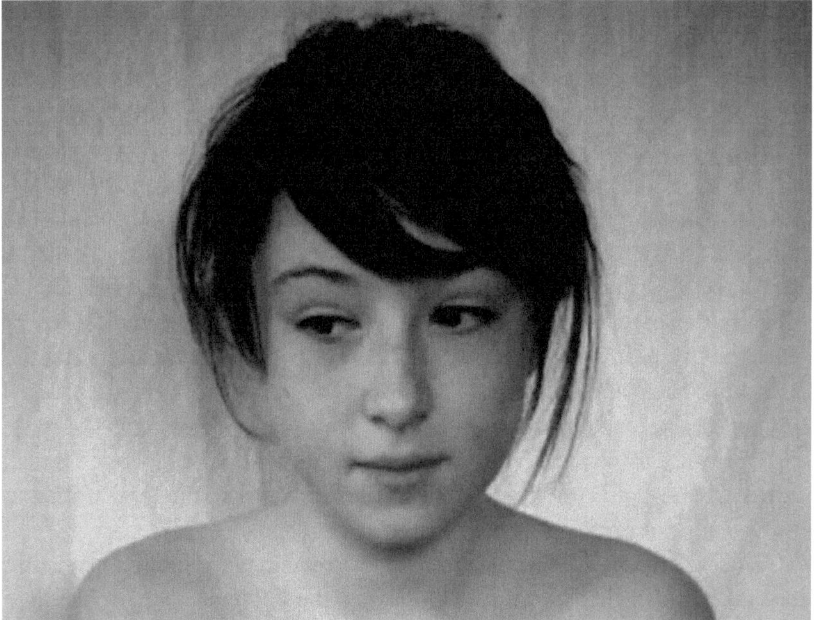

Figure 8.8   Gee Vaucher, Still from the film, *Angel*, 2012

The film is composed of a single head and shoulders shot, and documents the stillness and changes that register in Angel's face over its forty-five minute duration. Angel's apparent lack of self-consciousness is perhaps due in part to her close relationship with Vaucher, who was there at her birth. The silent, meditative quality of the film is interrupted at intervals by abrasive noise, reminiscent of industrial music. The experience of watching the film is highly subjective, with the viewer reading into Angel's face their own thoughts and experiences. I, for example, experienced the industrial sound interruptions as indicative of the move to a harsh, new, urban environment that marked a transitionary period in my childhood.[33] Vaucher says, 'It is quite confronting and can be a very emotional experience', citing the example of a man who approached her after a screening to tell her it was triggering for his childhood experience of abuse.[34]

By the 2010s, the art world reflected the changes afoot in the wider political-ideological sphere. The reckless conduct of multi-national banks, which played a significant contributory factor to the Global Financial Crash (2007–08), had added to a sense of disillusionment with political and corporate leadership and hierarchies. Along with the Iraq War, the government's willingness to leap to the defence of the banks had finally brought the country's love affair with New Labour to an end and highlighted the inherent contradiction in its attempts to marry a more ethical approach to government with its embrace of neo-liberalism. Ideologically driven austerity policies enacted by the Coalition (2010–15), and then Tory governments in the UK, further exacerbated this cynicism. In the wake of the enthusiasm generated by the international socio-political movement, Occupy (2008–), major arts events placed themes of collaborative as opposed to individualistic endeavour, political protest and contested public space, including squatting, at their centre. These concerns were, for instance, foregrounded at three major festivals in 2012: the 7th Berlin Biennial (Forget Fear), the Brighton Photo Biennial (Agents of Change: Photography and the Politics of Space) and the Venice Architecture Biennale (Common Ground). This period also marked a key moment in the historicisation of punk, and more specifically anarcho-punk.[35] The voices of several overlooked, yet influential, women in punk and controversial art groups also came to the fore, providing invaluable insight into these male-dominated milieus.[36]

Vaucher's work with Crass had already featured in two major group exhibitions on punk at The Barbican (London) in the 2000s: *Rock Style, Music + Fashion + Attitude* (2000–01), and *Panic Attack! Art in the Punk Years* (2007), curated by Mark Sladen and Ariella Yedgar. Her original work and stencils were then included in the high-profile exhibition *Someday all the Adults will Die: Punk Graphics 1971–1984* (with Johan Kugelberg and Jon Savage as curators), at the Hayward Gallery (2012). Kugelberg also curated an exhibition at the Boo-Hooray gallery in New York entitled *In All Our Decadence People Die: Exhibition of Fanzines, Presented to Crass Between 1976 and 1984*, which reflected the excitement engendered in the burgeoning anarcho-punk scene, and also featured Vaucher's work for *International Anthem* in original and printed form.

Two prominent and authoritative accounts of the origins, evolution and legacy of punk via its visual identity and language, *The Art of Punk* by Russ Bestley and Alex Ogg and *Punk: An Aesthetic* by Johan Kugelberg and Jon Savage (both published in 2012), gave prominence to Vaucher's work, stressing its importance to the development of anarcho-punk as a subgenre.[37] *Punk 45: The Singles Cover Art of Punk 1976–80* (Savage, 2013) included an interview with Vaucher and featured her image for Crass' 'Nagasaki Nightmare'/'Big A, Little A' 7" (1980).

This period also saw Crass involved in their own historicisation, with the release of their back catalogue on a seven-CD set termed the 'Crassical Collection' (2010–12). The released set included all the original artwork, but featured a new set of interlocking designs by Vaucher that provided a cool and restrained aesthetic, by contrast with her confrontational, often provocative, designs for Crass. In fact, the background and typography on the front and rear covers is reminiscent of tombstones.

Plans for the release brought the issues that had begun to surface at the Iraq War concert to a head. Some of the band members objected to Vaucher and Rimbaud's re-vamping of the catalogue, arguing for everything to be left as it had been in the original releases, while expressing strong disagreements about artwork, track listings, liner notes and the re-mastering itself.[38] While it did little to resolve the animosity, the re-releases were well received, and helped introduce Vaucher's designs to a new audience.

Vaucher's artwork beyond Crass also became more prominent during this period. Her work featured in twenty-eight group and twenty solo exhibitions in the 2000s, and twenty-three group and seventeen solo shows in the 2010s. The private venues she exhibited at were often ones with an ethos in keeping with her own – notably Boo-Hooray (NYC) and The Horse Hospital (London), as well as a range of community centres and squatted venues. She has developed a particularly strong connection with the Horse Hospital. Founded in 1992, it is a haven for artists on the edge or outside the mainstream, and gives them freedom to exhibit their work how and when they like. Vaucher exhibited there in 2001 and 2009 (solo and group shows respectively) and screened the *Angel* film there in 2013.[39] The venue was also at the forefront of the fight to save Dial House, hosting an auction to raise funds for the purchase in 2002. Recently, the venue has itself been under threat, giving Vaucher a chance to reciprocate. She notes. 'You know, a place like that needs to exist because it's not pretentious. It just does really kooky, strange stuff. A lot of it doesn't particularly interest me. But that's not the point. It shows stuff that other people would rather never show.'[40]

Vaucher's films were also widely screened at a range of international film festivals, independent cinemas and spaces.[41] Her film, *Gower Boy*, made for the jazz pianist Hugh Warren, provided a contemplative journey around his home turf of the Gower Peninsula in Wales. It featured at the Cheltenham Jazz Festival (2005) and was then screened again at Raindance Film Festival (2006), with the pianist playing live at both events. In 2007, Raindance graphic designer Dominic Thackray, who had remained friends with Vaucher and Rimbaud since first meeting them at the Crass film screening at the NFT (2002), invited Vaucher to design the poster for the festival.[42] She repeated this rare foray into commercial illustration work again in 2010 and also designed their 20th anniversary poster in 2012 (see Figure 8.9). This latter poster featured a fedora hat, floating independently in the sky, somewhat reminiscent of Magritte's colour palette and bowler hat motif.

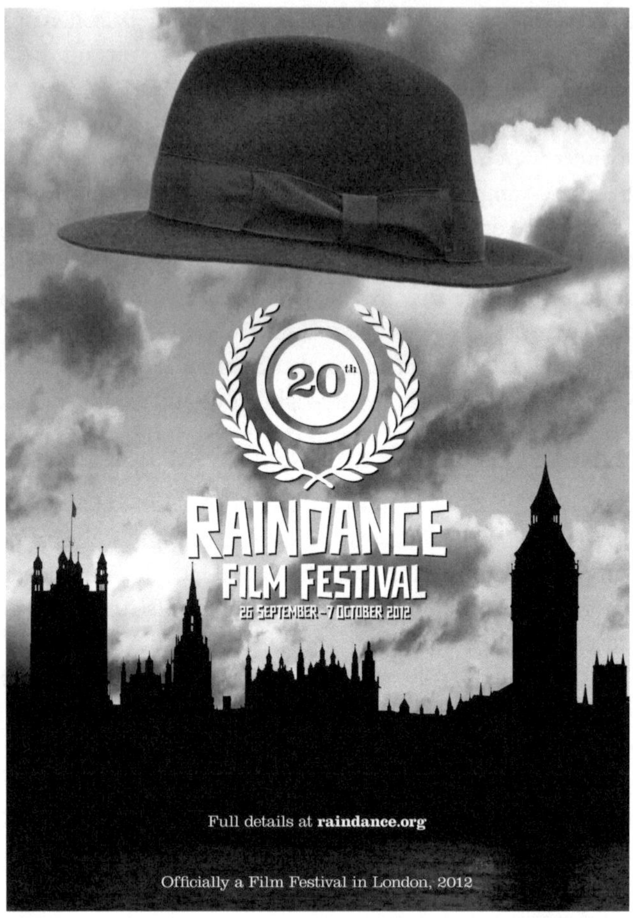

Figure 8.9   Gee Vaucher, Colour poster for the 20th Raindance film festival, 2012, collage

In addition to her work receiving long overdue attention through its inclusion in books and exhibitions, it reached new, millennial audiences through being featured in articles and online content for cultural magazines, including *Vice*, *The Quietus* and *The Wire*. The audiences for these outlets included the younger, politically engaged demographic associated with the Occupy movement, as well as what can loosely be described as 'hipsters'. Applied derogatorily by people in the cultural industries to anyone but themselves working in the field, the term came to symbolise the quest for 'authenticity' that characterised an era of increased estrangement, consolidated by the virtual world and relationships mediated by the interests of corporations. This sense of estrangement had been initiated in the 1980s, when privatisation, the switch from nationalised industries to the service economy and the destruction of trade unions had demolished other forms of social power and cohesion. In this context, the quest for authenticity, while being connected to a genuine desire to carve out alternative space and develop more ethical ways of living, also entails a degree of cultural appropriation. The renewed interest in outsider groups, radical art collectives and political movements and subcultures is not primarily informed by active participation in these movements, but because they provide cultural capital. As such, 'hipsters' can be seen as agents of capitalist appropriation, who reduce the value of any kind of genuine sentiment or cultural/political affinity to one of personal identity and marketability: the antithesis of authenticity.[43] By doing so, they reduce the subcultures and art movements they celebrate to an aesthetic, devoid of what Stuart Hall called their associated 'culture of resistance'.[44] In such a context, Vaucher's work was both the very thing these audiences were seeking, while simultaneously being the inverse of everything they represented.

The growing recognition of Vaucher's considerable influence on visual culture culminated in her first major (UK) retrospective, *Gee Vaucher: Introspective* at Firstsite (Colchester), 2016–17. Co-curated by Stevphen Shukaitis, University of Essex, and Firstsite's Marie-France Kittler, the exhibition saw her work covered by art magazines that had previously overlooked it. Although the *Guardian* and the *Daily Mirror* published promotional pieces about the exhibition, there was disappointingly little coverage in the mainstream press. This is in marked contrast to the widespread attention it received in the cultural press, reflecting the kind of audience that was engaging with her work at this time.[45] The show also coincided with an ambitious series of events staged to historicise and memorialise punk, *Punk London: 40 Years of Subversive Culture* (2016). These attracted a mixed response from punks and others involved in punk culture, who lauded the championing of punk, while expressing hostility towards it appropriating and presenting a narrow, clichéd and London-centric interpretation of the phenomenon.[46] Viv Albertine (The Slits) famously amended an exhibit at the *Punk 1976–78* exhibition (The British Library) featuring male-only bands, to foreground female performers; scrawling 'what about the women!!!' across it and adding The Slits, X-Ray Spex and Siouxsie and the Banshees to the list of bands.

Vaucher's major show succeeded in introducing new audiences to her work. For visitors familiar with the Crass material, it provided the opportunity to see up close the exquisite original paintings and collages that she had created for their music releases. It also greatly extended the parameters for the appreciation of the range and diversity of her work beyond Crass.

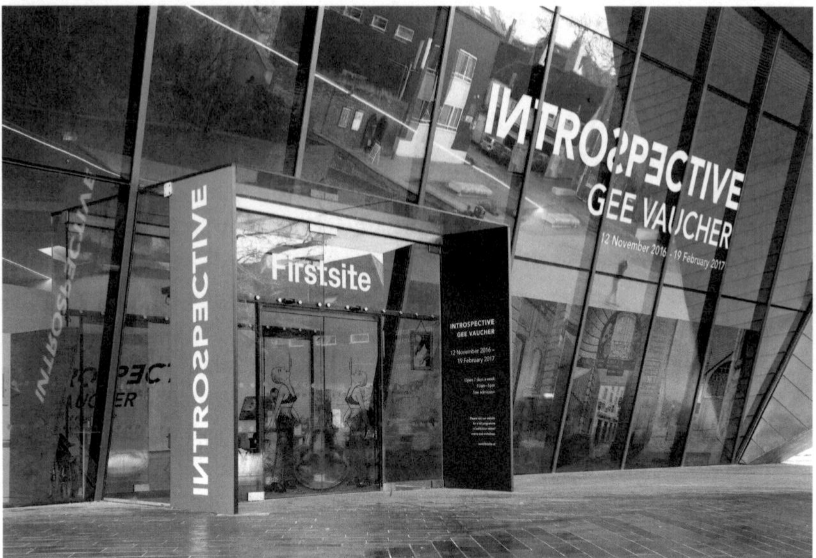

Figure 8.10   Gee Vaucher's Illustrations at Firstsite, 2016

By contrast with the narrow focus of Punk London, Vaucher's exhibition framed the 'punk' politics of her work with Crass within a wider ideological perspective that has permeated her oeuvre. At the same time, she also overcame her reticence and accepted an honorary doctorate from the University of Essex, saying it would have made her parents proud.[47] The exhibition's opening coincided with the shock election of Donald Trump as President in the United States. The *Daily Mirror* featured Vaucher's image (see Figure 8.11), *Oh America!* on its front cover, having been alerted to its widespread adoption as a meme on social media platforms. The publicity this generated meant the gallery incidentally received an added influx of visitors.

Oh America! arguably came to epitomise public sentiment towards the election of Donald Trump in the same way that Kennard–Phillips' *Photo Op* had encapsulated the disillusion of the general public with New Labour in the aftermath of the Iraq War. One telling difference, however, is while *Photo Op* had been created as a response to the current situation, *Oh America!* was an image from the 1980s that had been seized upon by social media. When *Photo Op* was created in 2007, Facebook had only been available for a few months, while Twitter was still a niche tech product without a clear purpose and memes were still largely spread by email forwards. By 2016, the online world had been transformed beyond recognition, and with this came the

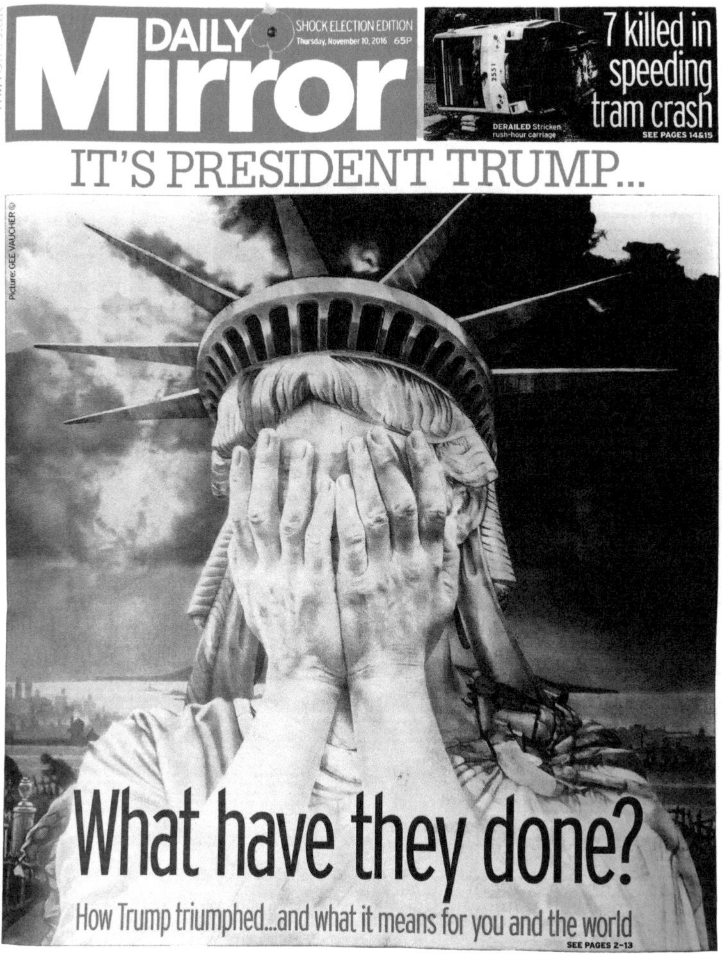

Figure 8.11   Gee Vaucher, *Oh America!* featured on cover of the *Daily Mirror*, Shock Election Issue, Thursday, 10 November 2016, gouache, 230mm × 230mm

potential for images to be re-purposed to signify something completely outside the original authorial intent.

Oh America! was created in 1989 as the front cover image for experimental hip-hop outfit Tackhead's *Friendly as a Hand Grenade* LP. The core members had previously been the rhythm section for Sugar Hill Records (NYC), providing the bass lines for iconic, early, politically inflected hip-hop tracks such as Grandmaster Flash's 'The Message' (1982), and Melle Mel's 'White Lines' (1983). By the late 1980s, UK producer Adrian Sherwood had persuaded them to re-locate to England, where they played a similar role on his pioneering

On-U Sound project. Tackhead was a collaboration between the band and Sherwood that brought heavy, industrialised sounds combined with a politicised message to hip-hop. Its staccato, collaged style, often using sampled 'found' vocals, has some associations to the visual style Vaucher used for Crass, especially in her visual backdrops for their live shows. Her contribution to the album, however, resists collage and is instead a painted depiction, although as with much of her work, it takes a recognisable image and alters it to communicate new meaning. Its release coincided with Reagan's vice-president, George Bush, being elected for a third term by a Republican candidate, but the image itself seems to be more a reflection on the failure of the American Dream. While her work with Crass had a clearly definable subcultural audience, away from their home territory of New York, Tackhead struggled to articulate any subcultural connection, and despite the power and innovation of the music, the project failed to live up to expectations. That said, the cover image provided by Vaucher served as a clear statement of intent and reflected the group's political leanings. Indeed, it influenced how the tracks – many of which were instrumental – were interpreted by the audience, who read into the heavy industrial beats a politicised commentary on contemporary America. By contrast, the meme came to function as a shorthand for despair, expressed humorously, in the wake of Trump's election victory. While retaining its power as an image, its functioning as a meme in this respect is fleeting and reductive. As such, while the image reached a far wider demographic than would have been the case with her earlier politically charged work, the complexity of the messaging was necessarily reduced.

Perhaps, however, the current more antagonistic and polarised time calls for more punchy and direct messaging. While there is an ongoing issue with real debate being reduced to catchy, oppositional statements, there is also the continual threat of anything that constitutes political or cultural resistance being undermined. Social media environments foster the presentation of a mediated version of self, with the image itself taking precedence over the production of meaning generated collectively by communities. Meaning is often tempered to appeal to as wide as audience as possible, which results in a relatively homogenised and anodyne culture overall. Such a flattening effect is particularly obvious in the continual appropriation of more recent political causes and movements, to serve as accolades for individuals and companies. Often companies are engaged in practices and outcomes that are the antithesis of the language of freedom, rights and equity they appropriate. The #Me Too and Black Lives Matter movements in particular are regularly hijacked by the worlds of fashion and advertising that do much to undermine an individual's agency and sense of worth. This practice is also notable in the greenwashing adopted by the fossil fuel industry, and pinkwashing engaged in by corporations and governments seeking to deflect unwanted attention from their unethical practices. The willingness of artists to engage with political issues has steadily increased since the turn of the century (in this latter period often also caught up with the politics of identity, be it race, ethnicity, sexuality or gender), while the efforts of artists to work collaboratively has grown exponentially. These egalitarian sentiments have, however, been undermined in two interconnected ways. Firstly, these changes have occurred in the context of the UK Government's 'war on woke', and the associated drastic cuts in funding for the arts. Secondly, the last twenty years have seen the increased dominance of the cultural industries by more privileged sections of society. The increasing withdrawal of government support can, sadly, only exacerbate this trend.[48]

Ironically, the Alt-right populism that helped to propel Trump to power and was evident among Eurosceptic politicians advocating Brexit in the UK, was cast by some as a 'punk'-like rebellion against societal elites, social consensus and norms; conveniently ignoring the fact that such figures were advocating authoritarian policies and were by definition 'the establishment'. This appropriation of public sentiment towards divisive ends was enabled through social dissatisfaction and disenfranchisement, including homelessness, precarious work practices and the cuts to social supports brought about by right-wing policies. Accordingly, the latter years of the 2010s have seen a resurgence of nationalist sentiment (in part a backlash to the refugee crisis) throughout Europe and the consolidation of masculinist leadership of governments in countries as diverse as Turkey, Brazil and Russia, as well as the USA (2016–20). Male chauvinism is a fundamental tenet of the far-right organisation, Proud Boys, in the USA, whose members were involved with the Unite the Right rally in Charlottesville, Virginia (2017), and the storming of the United States Capital (2021) in an attempt to overturn Trump's defeat in the election (2020). Ironically, Proud Boys was founded by an old friend of Vaucher's and Rimbaud's, Gavin McInnes,[49] who formerly co-founded the global publishing enterprise, *Vice*. While Crass always voiced scepticism towards left- as well as right-wing politics, and tolerated a variety of views across the political spectrum, the direction taken by McInnes proved to be something they did not want to be associated with, and Rimbaud released a public twitter statement to that effect in September 2020. Characteristically, however, Vaucher reflects, 'Nonetheless it is always better to sit down with who you might think is the enemy and find out what is driving their thinking.'[50]

To ponder on where Vaucher's work sits in the current climate, on the one hand there remains a strong social desire for authenticity, in part arising from a sense of estrangement, as well as interest in 'outsider', alternative and political forms of art practice within the art world and academia. On the other, there is the continual threat of appropriation of this sentiment, both from the cultural industries, and for political ends by the far right. At the time of writing, Vaucher was continuing to evade these overbearing tendencies. Amidst a global pandemic and lockdown, she has been more prolific than ever; perhaps facilitated to some degree by social distancing rules that have restricted visitors to Dial House. In the last year she contributed four pieces (two of them new) to a group show, *My Name is not Refugee,* at Firstsite (2020–21). She also contributed an installation to Droichead Arts Centre's Culture Night festivities (the Arts Centre had previously hosted her first solo show in Ireland in 2012). Nine artists were commissioned to respond to specific sites in the town, and Vaucher produced a window display in an abandoned shop that replaced the bland advertorial text you would expect to find with Situationist type sloganeering. The words were written by Rimbaud, and reflect their ongoing shared perspectives:

- Our Biological Needs are Co-opted, Commodified and then Sold Back to us as Synthetic Shams of the NATURAL Life that is Rightfully Ours.
- Liberation is Not a Political Game, But a Personal Imperative.
- The War is Within and You Have to Take Life Seriously, Otherwise it's no FUN.

While her work at this point deploys a wide range of mediums, and is exhibited at a diverse array of public and independent venues, she retains a deep scepticism about the art market. During the last few decades, the art world has become a vast global enterprise. Contemporary art started to command huge sums towards the end of the last century, as it became an asset for investment buyers akin to real estate, stocks, bonds and prestige wine. Rather than become victims of this process, artists often learnt as best they could to play the market.[51] Jeff Koons is perhaps the greatest exemplar of this naked embrace of commercial culture, both in his work's aesthetic and his business and advertising acumen. Vaucher's approach, however, represents a starkly contrasting method of staying ahead of the game.

Firstly, she deliberately sells her litho prints at rock-bottom prices – around £20 – and distributes them directly via the Exitstencil Press website and at events, such as the Anarchist Book Fair (London) where she regularly held a stall until its demise in 2017. She notes, 'I can't do them any cheaper, but it means that everyone can buy one and the Crass ones in particular sell well. That kind of underpins all the other work that I like to put out there because I think it deserves it, but doesn't sell so well. So it's kind of like a nice, circular project.'[52]

While she does on occasion issue limited edition prints, they are generally in large runs, thereby limiting their re-sale value on the open market. The precariousness of this strategy, however, is attested to by the fact that her *Flying High* prints, despite being issued in a run of 750, sell on Ebay for £500. Her real intervention here though is in her attitude to collectors, dealers and private galleries. She comments, 'As for the art market, well I'm not interested because I don't sell originals. As much as I could sell I don't choose to … I'm absolutely not interested in private collections.'[53] As the art market functions by speculation on the future value of original works, a process that the artist is often completely divorced from, her stance in this regard means that her work cannot become an investment commodity. All this means that it is hard to 'value' her work in art market terms, which serves to shift the focus onto its cultural as opposed to commercial value.

This has a knock-on effect in terms of interest from public institutions, which too often take their lead from the commercial world when applying value to art. While Vaucher claims to have no objection in principle to selling her work to public galleries, and has had an increasing number of offers since the exhibition at Firstsite, her attitude when approached by them suggests she's not particularly invested in the process. In the wake of the exhibition and Trump's election, for example, she was approached by the Head of the Arts Council about the purchase of the original painting for *Oh America!* She notes, 'I put a ridiculous, massive price on it, just for a joke really. I thought they wouldn't be interested and they weren't [laughs].'[54] This ambivalence is in some ways motivated by her scepticism about the fate of much of the art that ends up in public collections. 'I mean; I know the Arts Council is for the public, buys for the public and it gets shown. But also a lot of it doesn't. A lot of it gets stuck somewhere and doesn't get aired for years. So, I like the freedom of being able to air the work that I want to air at that particular show or institution. I like that. I like the freedom of that.' She adds, 'I don't like to have to ask someone. And as I'm not particularly interested in the money, that kind of works okay.'[55]

This raises interesting questions in terms of her legacy. Her burgeoning collection of work has to date been housed in various makeshift structures in and around Dial House. The *Children …* oil paintings, for instance (see Plates 18 and 19, colour insert), were stored in a cowshed, on the adjacent farm. Rimbaud believes they would be better served on display at a major gallery. Currently, her great-niece, Angel (who featured in Vaucher's film of the same name, 2012) is meticulously cataloguing her work. The fact she has chosen a family member rather than a professional archivist to undertake this onerous task is entirely characteristic. Rimbaud has commented that Banksy put a lot of effort into supporting her work in the past, but she shied away from embracing it fully out of fear of losing her independence. Likewise, at her first major solo show in New York (2006),[56] the gallerist Gavin Brown, who was by then famed for guiding artists from underground to mainstream recognition, could not understand why she 'wouldn't accede one drop' to him when he was trying to promote her.[57]

This brings us to the issue of what drives this artist's autonomy. Rimbaud believes her class and gender play into her reticence and modesty. While he admires these qualities, he also expresses concern that they have held her back from pushing for the recognition she deserves. While there may be some truth to this, these characteristics also point to her great strength. Her lack of self-promotion can be seen as an active choice rather than the result of internalising the expectations she was born into.

Vaucher's reflections on the world aren't ameliorated by the inevitable compromises of marketing herself and her work towards satisfying its requirements. This applies to her nonengagement with the art world, but also to her sidestepping of the arts funding infrastructure, unlike the mainstay of left-leaning, radical artists and collectives in the 1970s and 1980s. Following the true spirit of the avant-garde, this has allowed her to consistently engage with the politics of the era, without being compromised by any of its expectations. In the 1970s and 1980s, she responded to the advent of punk by bringing ideas from the counterculture into this more oppositional milieu. In the 1990s, her work reflected the less didactic form of messaging that typified the era, while still managing to have something to say. Similarly, in the twenty-first century, her work moved with the times, once again embracing more collaborative, political and public art. Through all this, she maintained the ideals she had taken from the counterculture, something that's reflected in her approach to the *Sound of Stones in the Glasshouse* project (see Figure 8.1). While the concept of growing a lawn in Brett's structure over the course of the project, and engaging the audience in the process, was in sync with the move towards active participation in gallery settings in the 2000s, it also reflects the spontaneous, participatory gestures of the radical art collectives such as EXIT and Stanford Rivers Quartet she'd been engaged with in the 1970s.

The living metaphor of the seeds for growth inherent to the *Sound of Stones …* project is reflected in the immense importance of the garden at Dial House. In this context, Vaucher's approach can be seen to involve 'cross fertilizing the connections between different artistic countercultures and practices, working between them.'[58] This in turn mirrors Murray Bookchin's anarchist idea of 'social ecology': that diversity in ecology is a prerequisite for a unified, healthy whole – in other words, individual autonomy is the chief requirement for the creation of a better society. The countercultural position of belief in changing the world has met seemingly insurmountable challenges since the 1960s, but in the face of the dissolution of that dream, Vaucher has somehow maintained a belief that you don't give up. She has lived through an era where rampant individualism has brought us to the brink of both social and environmental collapse, and as such her work and life choices stand as an example of how true autonomy means personal accountability, and an embrace of the fundamental principle of environmentalism – that you try to leave more behind than you took. To strive, despite the odds, to leave the world a better place than you found it.

Notes

1 See J. Stallabrass, *High Art Lite: The Rise and Fall of Young British Art* (London: Verso, 2006), pp. 292–300. Claire Bishop notes that a turn towards the social, as the context for the production of art, grew exponentially, also acquiring an international focus, throughout the 2000s. See C. Bishop, *Artificial Hells: Participatory Art and the Politics of Spectatorship* (London: Verso, 2012), p. 2.

2 Vaucher in interview with Groß, 2002.

3 M. Hardt and A. Negri, *Empire* (London: Harvard University Press, 2001). Also see E. Laclau and C. Mouffe, *Hegemony and Socialist Strategy: Towards a Radical Democratic Politics* (London and New York: Verso, 2001 [1985]).

4 Vaucher in interview with Groß, 2002.

5 M. Bookchin, 'Ecology and Revolutionary Thought', in M. Bookchin, *Post Scarcity Anarchism* (Edinburgh/Oakland/West Virginia: AK Press, 2004 [1971]), pp. 19–41.

6 Vaucher in email correspondence, July 2021.

7 Thackray in conversation with Binns, June 2021.

8 Thackray in conversation with Binns, June 2021. See Thackray's account of meeting Vaucher and Rimbaud at the NFT Never Mind the Jubilee Season (2002) in R. Ryde, L. Sofianos and C. Waterhouse, *The Truth of Revolution, Brother: The Philosophies of Punk* (London: Situation Press, 2015), pp. 62–67.

9 Rimbaud in interview with Binns, 2021.

10 Vaucher in interview with Binns, 2021.

11 Banksy via email correspondence, July 2021.

12 G. Debord, *The Society of the Spectacle* (New York: Zone Books, 1994).

13 Banksy, *Wall and Piece* (London: Random House Group Ltd, 2005), p. 19.

14 Vauher in email correspondence, July 2021.

15 S. Armstrong, *Street Art* (London: Thames & Hudson, 2019), p. 67. This sentiment is also voiced by Palestinian groups and Noam Chomsky among others.

16 Vaucher in email correspondence, July 2021.

17 See P. Tatchell, 'The Stop the War Coalition is more interested in fighting the West than fighting for Syrians', *Independent* (10 September 2016). Available at www.independent.co.uk/voices/the-stop-the-war-coalition-the-west-than-fighting-for-syrians-russia-assad-a7461316.html (accessed 15 June 2021).

18 Vaucher in conversation with Binns, July 2018.

19 See C. K. Madsen (ed.), *Art Strikes Back-from Jorn to Banksy* (Silkeborg, Denmark: Museum Jorn, 2019), which accompanied an exhibition of the same name. It features the work of a wide selection of artists, including Gee Vaucher, who have used détournement as a design technique and cultural and rhetorical strategy, drawing connections with the method of childlike painterly 'modifications' applied to old paintings by the Situationist Asper Jorn.

20 Vaucher in interview with Binns, June 2021.

21 Vaucher in interview with Binns, June 2021.

22 N. Mailer, 'Picasso' in *Advertisements for Myself* (first published in 1959), quoted in J. Nuttall, *Bomb Culture* (London: Paladin), p. 88.

23 See for instance her *Inside/Outside* series (2010), which similarly to her earlier anatomical sketches in pastels from 1994, was concerned with breaking down the body compositionally, and her series, *FaceOff* (2009–11), which featured subjects with their faces concealed through collaging.

24 R. Binns, 'Animal Rites: A Pictorial Study of Relationships (Gee Vaucher, Existential Press)', *SOURCE Photographic Review* (Winter, 2016), pp. 30–32. Similar concerns also underpin her plastic sculptures; *Chained* (2004), featuring hybrid dogs and baby dolls, and plaster busts that feature a pantheon of men, including Bach and Beethoven, deemed genius throughout history, with human combined with animal features.

25 Vaucher in email correspondence, July 2021.

26 J. Macphee and E. Reuland, *Realising the Impossible: Art Against Authority* (Edinburgh/ Oakland, CA: AK Press, 2007), p. 75.

27 Vaucher in interview with Binns, 2018.

28 Vaucher in interview with Binns, 2018.

29 Vaucher in interview with Groß, 2015, quoted in R. Binns, 'Freedom, Desire and the Questioning of "isms" in Gee Vaucher's Early Designs (1975–79)', in S. Shukaitis (ed.), *Gee Vaucher: Introspective* (Colchester: Firstsite, published in collaboration with Minor Compositions, 2016), p. 52.

30 Vaucher in email correspondence, July 2021.

31 Vaucher in interview with Groß, 2015, quoted in Binns, 'Freedom, Desire …' p. 53.

32 Vaucher in email correspondence, July 2021.

33 Screening of Gee Vaucher's film, *Angel* (2012) at the *Nowhere Gallery*, Bethnal Green (London), 21 November 2016.

34 Vaucher in interview with Groß, 2015, quoted in Binns, 'Freedom, Desire …', p. 54.

35 George McKay's book, *Senseless Acts of Beauty: Cultures of Resistance Since the 1960s* (London/New York: Verso, 1996) was the forerunner in this respect. Ian Glasper's, *The Day the Country Died: A History of Anarcho Punk, 1980–1984* (London: Cherry Red

Books, 2006) provided an in-depth account of the anarcho-punk scene throughout the UK during the early 1980s. *The Aesthetics of Our Anger: Anarcho Punk, Politics and Music* (Colchester/New York: Minor Compositions, 2016) edited by Mike Dines and Matthew Worley, brought together texts by a variety of contributors, often drawn from punk and/or anarcho-punk scenes. See also *Crass Reflections* by Alistair Gordon (2016) and Rich Cross' extensive writings, listed at https:// thehippiesnowwearblack.org.uk/writings/ (accessed 20 January 2021).

36　Autobiographies written by female protagonists, artists and/or musicians in punk/ controversial scenes of the 1970s and 1980s, published in recent years, include *Clothes, Clothes, Clothes. Music, Music, Music. Boys, Boys, Boys* (2015), by Viv Albertine, of all-female punk band The Slits; *Reckless* (2016) by Chrissie Hynde of New Wave band The Pretenders; and *Art, Sex, Music* (2017) by Cosey Fanni Tutti of avant-garde group Throbbing Gristle.

37　Vaucher also wrote the preface to *Punk: An Aesthetic*.

38　CRASS JOURNAL: A record of letters, articles, postings and emails, February 2009–September 2010 concerning Penny, Gee and Allison's 'Crassical Collection'. Available at (www.crassicalcollection.com/crass.pdf (accessed 17 February 2021).

39　See R. Sabin, 'Gee Vaucher at the Horse Hospital Gallery, London, July 2001', *Visual Communication* (London, Thousand Oaks, CA and New Delhi: Sage Publications 2002), pp. 223–227.

40　Vaucher in interview with Binns, June 2021.

41　Vaucher's films were screened at Lost Films at Philadelphia Film Festival (2004), Berlin Underground Film Festival and Santa Monica (2008) and the National Film Theatre, London (2010). An anthology, Semi Detached: The Films of Gee Vaucher 1978–1984 also featured at Northern Lights Film Festival (2005).

42　Thackray in conversation with Binns, June 2021.

43　See R. Horning, 'The Death of the Hipster', *PopMatters* (13 April 2009). Available at www.popmatters.com/the-death-of-the-hipster-panel-2496026662.html (accessed 20 April 2021).

44　See S. Hall and T. Jefferson (eds), *Resistance Through Rituals: Youth Subcultures in Post War Britain* (Cultural Studies Birmingham: Routledge, 1993).

45　See the Select Bibliography in this volume.

46　See F. Stewart, '"No more heroes anymore": Marginalized identities in punk memorialization and curation', *Punk & Post-Punk*, 8:2 (2019), pp. 209–266.

47　Vaucher in conversation with Binns, November 2016.

48　In N. Olah, *Steal as Much as You Can: How to Win the Culture Wars in an Age of Austerity* (London: Repeater, 2019). Olah argues that there has been a vast reduction of working-class voices in the cultural industries since 2000. With regards to drastic cuts to funding simultaneously to the UK Government's anti-'woke' agenda, in relation to Turner Prize nominees (2021), see J. Jacques, 'What the 2021 Turner Prize Nominees Tell Us About the Politics of Art', *Frieze* (12 May 2021). Available at www.frieze.com/article/what-2021-turner-prize-nominees-tell-us-about-politics-art (accessed 1 June 2021).

49 Gavin McInnes was featured as an influential figure within punk in the book, L. Sofianos, R. Ryde and C. Waterhouse (eds), *The Truth of Revolution, Brother: An Exploration of Punk Philosophy* (London: Situation Press, 2014).

50 Vaucher in email correspondence, July 2021.

51 See N. Kahn (director), *The Price of Everything* (USA: HBO, 2018).

52 Vaucher in interview with Binns, June 2021.

53 Vaucher in interview with Binns, June 2021.

54 Vaucher in interview with Binns, June 2021.

55 Vaucher in interview with Binns, June 2021.

56 As with her Firstsite Show, the exhibition at Gavin Brown Gallery was entitled *Introspective*.

57 Rimbaud in conversation (skype), July 2021. Also see P. Rimbaud, 'A Very Private Person', in S. Shukaitis (ed.), *Gee Vaucher: Introspective* (Colchester: Firstsite, published in collaboration with Minor Compositions, 2016), pp. 30–44.

58 S. Shukaitis 'The Door to the Garden: Gee Vaucher and the Cultivation of Artistic Counterculture' in S. Shukaitis (ed.), *Gee Vaucher: Introspective* (Colchester: Firstsite, published in collaboration with Minor Compositions, 2016), p. 14.

Select bibliography

Books

Ades D., E. Butler and D. Hermann, *Hannah Höch* (London: Whitechapel Gallery and Prestel, 2014)

Beckett A. *When the Lights Went Out: Britain in the 1970s* (London: Faber and Faber, 2009)

Berger G. *The Story of Crass* (Oakland: PM Press, 2009)

Bestley R. and A. Ogg, *The Art of Punk* (London: Omnibus Press, 2012)

Bishop C. *Artificial Hells: Participatory Art and the Politics of Spectatorship* (London: Verso, 2012)

Black Rose Anarcho-Feminists, Chicago Anarcho-feminists, V. de Cleyre, C. Ehrlich, L. Farrow, P. Kornegger, M. Leighton. *Quiet Rumours, An Anarcha-Feminist Anthology* (London: Dark Star, 1980)

Bookchin M. *Post Scarcity Anarchism* (Edinburgh/Oakland: AK Press, 2004)

Bovier L. (ed.). *Linder: Works, 1976–2006* (Zurich: JRP/Ringier, 2006)

Buszek M. E. *Pin-Up Grrrls: Feminism, Sexuality, Popular Culture* (Durham and London: Duke University Press, 2006)

Dale P. *Anyone Can Do It: Empowerment, Tradition and the Punk Underground* (eBook) (Farnham: Ashgate Publishing Ltd, 2012)

Debord G. *The Society of the Spectacle* (New York: Zone Books, 1994 [originally published in French by Buchet-Chastel, in 1967 and in English by Black and Red, Detroit, 1970])

Dines M. and M. Worley, *The Aesthetic of Our Anger. Anarcho-Punk, Politics and Music* (Colchester/New York: Minor Compositions, 2016)

Evans D. *Photomontage: A Political Weapon* (London: G. Fraser, 1986)

Farren M. *Give the Anarchist a Cigarette* (London: Pimlico, 2001)

Fountain N. *Underground: The London Alternative Press, 1966–74* (London/New York: Routledge, 1988)

Glasper I. *The Day the Country Died: A History of Anarcho Punk, 1980–1984* (SF/LA/ West Virginia: PM Press, 2014)

Goldman E. *Anarchism and Other Essays* (Auckland: Floating Press, 2008 [originally published in New York: Mother Earth Publishing Association, 1910])

Gordon A. *Crass Reflections* (Portsmouth: Itchy Monkey Press, 2016)

Gorman P., D. Thorpe and F. Vermorel, *Eyes for Blowing Up Bridges: Joining the Dots from the Situationist International to Malcolm McLaren* (Southampton: John Hansard Gallery, 2015)

Gray C. *Leaving the 20th Century, The Incomplete Work of the Situationist International* (London: Free Fall Publications, 1974)

Hardt M. and A. Negri, *Empire* (London: Harvard University Press, 2001)

Ignorant S. *The Rest is Propaganda* (Norfolk: Dimlo Productions, 2020 [3rd edn])

Kennard P. *Images for the End of the Century: Photomontage Equations* (London: Journeyman Press, 1990)

Kaplan G. *Power to the People: The Graphic Design of the Radical Press and the Rise of the Counter-culture, 1964–1974* (Chicago: University of Chicago Press, 2013)

King D. and E. Volland, *John Heartfield: Laughter is a Devastating Weapon* (London: Tate Gallery Publications, 2015)

Kugelberg J. and J. Savage, *Punk: An Aesthetic* (New York: Rizzoli, 2012)

Laclau E. and C. Mouffe, *Hegemony and Socialist Strategy: Towards a Radical Democratic Politics* (London and New York: Verso, 2001 [1985])

Laing R. D. *The Politics of the Family and Other Essays* (New York: Vintage Books, 1972)

Laing R. D. *Knots* (Middlesex: Penguin Books, 1973)

Madsen C. K. (ed.), G. Grindon, A. Heil, M. Sanders and J. Thage, *Art Strikes Back-from Jorn to Banksy* (Silkeborg, Denmark: Museum Jorn, 2019)

Marwick A. *The 1960s: Cultural Transformation in Britain* (Oxford: Oxford University Press, 1998)

McKay G. *Senseless Acts of Beauty: Cultures of Resistance Since the 1960s* (London/New York: Verso, 1996)

Musgrove F. *Ecstasy and Holiness: Counterculture and the Open Society* (Norfolk: Cox and Wyman Ltd, 1974)

Nuttall J. *Bomb Culture* (London: Paladin, 1972)

Plant S. *The Most Radical Gesture: The Situationist International in a Postmodern Age* (London: Routledge, 1992)

Reid J. and J. Savage, *Up They Rise: The Incomplete Works of Jamie Reid* (London: Faber and Faber, 1987)

Rimbaud P. *Shibboleth: My Revolting Life* (Edinburgh: AK Press, 1998)

Rimbaud P. *The Last of the Hippies: An Hysterical Romance* (Oakland: PM Press, 2015)

Rowbotham S., Segal L. and H. Wainwright, *Beyond the Fragments: Feminism and the Making of Socialism* (Pontypool, Wales: The Merlin Press Ltd, 2013. [Originally published by The Newcastle Socialist Centre and the Islington Community Press in 1979])

Sabin R. *Punk Rock: So What?: The Cultural Legacy of Punk* (London and New York: Routledge, 1999)

Savage J. *England's Dreaming: Anarchy, Sex Pistols, Punk Rock, and Beyond* (New York: St. Martin's Griffin, 2002)

Shukaitis S. (ed.) *Gee Vaucher: Introspective* (Colchester: Firstsite, published in collaboration with Minor Compositions, 2016)

The Subcultures Network (ed.) *Ripped, Torn and Cut: Pop, Politics and Punk Fanzines from 1976* (Manchester: Manchester University Press: 2018)

Taylor B. *Collage: The Making of Modern Art* (London: Thames and Hudson, 2004)

Tomlinson J. *The Politics of Decline: Understanding Post War Britain* (Oxon: Routledge, 2000)

Vaneigem R. *The Revolution of Everyday Life* (Oakland: PM Press, 2012 [Originally published in French, by Gallimard 1967 and in English by Practical Paradise Publications in 1972])

Vaucher G. *Animal Rites: A Pictorial Study of Relationships* (Essex: Exitstencil Press, 2003)

Vaucher G. *Much Ado About Something: A Play of Metaphors* (Essex: Exitstencil Press, 2011)

Vaucher G. *A Week of Knots: Sunday –The Family* (Essex: Exitstencil Press, 2013)

Vaucher G. *Crass Art and Other Pre Post-modernist Monsters* (Colchester: Firstsite, published in collaboration with Minor Compositions, 2nd edn, 2014)

Vaucher G. *A Week of Knots: Tuesday – Father* (Essex: Exitstencil Press, 2016)

Vaucher G. *International Anthem: Nihilist Newspaper for the Living (issues 1–5)* (Essex: Exitstencil Press, 2017)

Walker J. A. *Cross-overs: Art into Pop/Pop into Art* (New York: Methuen, 1987)

Walker J. A. *Left Shift: Radical Art in 1970s Britain* (London: Taurus, 2002)

Ward C. *Anarchy in Action* (London: George Allen & Unwin Ltd, 1973)

Worley M. *No Future: Punk, Politics and British Youth Culture, 1976–1984* (Cambridge: Cambridge University Press, 2017)

Zervigón A. M. *John Heartfield and the Agitated Image: Photography, Persuasion, and the Rise of Avant-Garde Photomontage* (London/Chicago: University of Chicago Press, 2013)

Articles and Reviews

Bestley, R. 'From "London's Burning" to "Sten Guns in Sunderland"', *Punk & Post-Punk*, 1:1 (2012)

Bestley, R. '"I wonder who chose the colour scheme, it's very nice…": Mike Coles, Malicious Damage and Forty Years in the Wilderness', *Punk & Post-Punk*, 5:3 (2016)

Bestley, R. 'Design it Yourself? Punk's Division of Labour', *Punk & Post-Punk*, 7:1 (2018)

Binns, R. 'Gee Vaucher: Introspective, Firstsite, Colchester, 12 November 2016 to 19 February 2017', *Punk & Post-Punk*, 5:3 (2016)

Binns, R. 'Between the Human and the Animal: Gee Vaucher at Firstsite', *The Quietus* (15 January 2017)

Binns, R. '"It's your world too, you can do what you want": The Role of Subcultural Activism in Stop the City Protests (1983–1984) and its Implications for Political Protest in Britain', *Contemporary British History* (forthcoming, 2022)

Bishop, C. 'Antagonism and Relational Aesthetics', *October*, 110 (Autumn, 2004)

Bowman, M. 'Review of Gee Vaucher: Introspective', *Art Monthly*, Issue 402 (December–January 2016/17)

Burgess, P. 'The Future is Junk', *Varoom* 12 (March 2010)

Burgess, P. 'The Feeding of the 5000', *Varoom* 19 (September 2012)

Cogan, B. 'Do They Owe Us a Living? Of Course They Do! Crass, Throbbing Gristle and Anarchy and Radicalism in Early English Punk Rock', *Journal for the Study of Radicalism*, 1:2 (2008)

Cross, R. 'The Hippies Now Wear Black: Crass and the Anarcho-Punk Movement, 1977–1984', *Socialist History*, Issue 26: Youth Cultures and Politics (2004)

Cross, R. 'There is no Authority but Yourself. The Individual and the Collective in British Anarcho-Punk', *Music & Politics*, IV:2 (Summer, 2010)

Cross, R. 'Take the Toys From the Boys: Gender, Generation and Anarchist Intent in the Work of Poison Girls', *Punk & Post-Punk*, 3:2 (October, 2014)

Demos, T. J. 'Moving Images of Globalization', *Grey Room*, 37 (Autumn, 2009)

Donaghey, J. 'Bakunin Brand Vodka: An Exploration into Anarchist-Punk and Punk-Anarchism', *Anarchist Developments in Cultural Studies*, 1 (2013)

Gadgil, S. 'Introspective – Gee Vaucher from Crass to Trump', *Creative Review* (11 November 2016)

Hay, C. 'Narrating Crisis: The Discursive Construction of the "Winter of Discontent"', *Sociology*, Issue 30 (May, 1996)

Hay, C. 'Chronicles of a Death Foretold: The Winter of Discontent and Construction of the Crisis of British Keynesianism', *Parliamentary Affairs*, 63:3 (2010)

Jackson, J. 'From Punk to Trump – A Compelling Introspective', *Socialist Worker*, Issue No 2536 (10 January 2017)

Jones, P. 'Anxious Images: Linder's Fem-Punk Photomontages', *Women: A Cultural Review*, 13:2 (2002)

Mitchell, J. 'Women: The Longest Revolution', *New Left Review*, No 40 (1966)

Pauli, B. J. 'Pacifism, Nonviolence, and the Reinvention of Anarchist Tactics in the Twentieth Century', *Journal for the Study of Radicalism*, 9:1 (2015)

Sabin, R. 'Gee Vaucher at the Horse Hospital Gallery, London, July 2001', *Visual Communication*, Sage Publications (2002)

Stewart, F. '"No more heroes anymore": Marginalized Identities in Punk Memorialization and Curation', *Punk & Post-Punk*, 8:2 (2019)

Taylor, J. D. 'The Party's Over? The Angry Brigade, the Counterculture and the British New Left, 1967–72', *The Historical Journal*, 58:3 (2015)

Thompson, S. 'Crass Commodities', *Popular Music and Society*, 27:3 (2004)

Triggs, T. 'Bullshit Detector: The Radical Visions of Ex Crass Member, Gee Vaucher', *Graphics International*, Issue 76 (2000)

Trowell, I. (2020), 'Counter-Realities and Conflicted Place: Gee Vaucher's The Feeding of the Five Thousand in the Punk Art Tradition', *Punk & Post-Punk* (2020)

Worley, M. 'One Nation Under the Bomb: The Cold War and British Punk to 1984', *Journal for the Study of Radicalism*, 5:2 (Autumn, 2011)

Worley, M. 'Shot by Both Sides: Punk, Politics and the End of "Consensus"', *Contemporary British History* 26:3 (2012)

Worley, M. 'Punk, Politics and British (fan) zines, 1976–84: While the World was Dying, Did You Wonder Why?', *History Workshop Journal*, Issue 79 (2015)

Theses

Bestley, R. 'Hitsville UK: Punk Rock and Graphic Design in the Faraway Towns, 1976–84' (PhD thesis), University of the Arts, London, 2007

Binns, R. 'Beyond Symbolic Representation: Alternate Identity in Gee Vaucher's Visual Representations and the Communal Functioning of Crass' (MA Dissertation), University College London, 2013

Binns, R. 'There is No Authority but Yourself: Political Autonomy, Collective Art Practice, Crass and Anarcho-Punk Visual Conventions in the work of Gee Vaucher' (PhD Thesis), University of the Arts, London, 2019

Dale, P. 'Anyone Can Do It: Traditions of Punk and the Politics of Empowerment' (PhD Thesis), University of Newcastle upon Tyne, 2011

Dines, M. 'An Investigation into the Emergence of the Anarcho-Punk Scene of the 1980s' (PhD thesis), University of Salford, 2004

Donaghey, J. 'Punk and Anarchism: UK, Poland, Indonesia' (PhD thesis), Loughborough University, 2016

Gordon, A. 'The Authentic Punk: An Ethnography of DIY Music Ethics' (PhD thesis), Loughborough University, 2005

Raposo, A. '30 Years of Agitprop: The Representation of "Extreme" Politics in Punk and Postpunk Music Graphics in the United Kingdom from 1978 to 2008' (PhD Thesis), University of the Arts, London, 2012

Fanzines

Acts of Defiance
Adventures in Reality
Allied Propaganda
Anathema
Antigen
Artificial Life
Blast
Blind Faith
Brass Lip
Chainsaw
Children of the Revolution
Cobalt Hate
Don't Dictate
Ears of a Dead Man
Enigma
Fack

Gee Vaucher

Infection
In the City
Jolt
Incendiary
Kill Your Pet Puppy
Megalomania
New Crimes
Oh Four One
Obituary
Panache
Pigs for Slaughter
Remember Who We Are
Ripped and Torn
Rising Free
Roar
Scum
Sideburns
Sniffin' Glue
Temporary Hoarding
Tigers on t'Moor
Time Bomb
Toxic Graffiti
Vague
Wake Up
Zero

Underground Press Publications
Black Dwarf
Frendz
Friends
International Anthem
International Times
Oz

Index